F V

WITHDRAWN

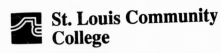

NEW HANDBOOK OF
TROUBLESHOOTING TECHNIQUES
FOR MICROPROCESSORS
AND MICROCOMPUTERS

Other books by the Author:

New Ways to Use Test Meters: A Modern Guide to Electronic Servicing
Troubleshooting Electronic Equipment Without Service Data
New Digital Troubleshooting Techniques: A Complete, Illustrated Guide

New Handbook of Troubleshooting Techniques

for Microprocessors and Microcomputers

Robert G. Middleton

PRENTICE-HALL, INC.

Business & Professional Division

Englewood Cliffs,

New Jersey

Prentice-Hall International, Inc., *London*
Prentice-Hall of Australia, Pty., Ltd., *Sydney*
Prentice-Hall of Canada, Inc., *Toronto*
Prentice-Hall of India Private Ltd., *New Delhi*
Prentice-Hall of Japan, Inc., *Tokyo*
Prentice-Hall of Southeast Asia, Pte., Ltd., *Singapore*
Whitehall Books, Ltd., *Wellington, New Zealand*
Editora Prentice-Hall do Brazil Ltda., *Rio de Janeiro*

© 1984, *by*

PRENTICE-HALL, INC.
Englewood Cliffs, N.J.

First Printing . . . October 1984

Editor: George E. Parker

Library of Congress Cataloging in Publication Data

Middleton, Robert Gordon
  New handbook of troubleshooting techniques for microprocessors and microcomputers.

  Includes index.
  1. Microcomputers—Maintenance and repair. 2. Microprocessors—Maintenance and repair. I. Title.
TK7887.M54   1984   621.3819'58   84-9916

ISBN 0-13-613464-5

Printed in the United States of America

A Word from the Author

Microprocessors and microcomputers tend to seem rather arcane to those whose previous experience has been in linear (analog) and introductory digital technology. Evolution of large-scale and very-large-scale integration has compounded the outward mystery of microprocessors. This formidable aura rapidly disappears, however, when we observe that an elementary microcomputer is not difficult to understand, and that we can proceed in easy steps to comparatively sophisticated microprocessors and microcomputers.

This is the approach that is used in this book. It starts with a description of an "embryo" microprocessor, and shows how this simple device can add and subtract numbers. Since any microprocessor necessarily operates on binary numbers, the author introduces you to this topic at the outset. The text continues with a demonstration of multiplication and division by shift-left and shift-right action in an embryo microprocessor.

Next, we examine microprocessor building blocks—the basic gates. Fundamentals of gate troubleshooting are noted. From this point, you proceed step-by-step through the digital circuitry employed in microprocessor design. You become familiar with latches and flip-flops, along with reinforced learning provided by experimental projects and demonstrations. You then progress to more elaborate microprocessor subsections in the descriptions of counters, shift registers, and accumulators. Practical troubleshooting techniques are included along with explanations of circuit action.

With this basic foundation established, you are in good position to cope with the arithmetic subsection in a microprocessor. Thus, half adders and full adders are explained, and are supplemented by experimental projects. The fundamental 2's-complement adder/subtracter is detailed, and it is shown how this device processes both positive numbers and negative numbers with simple circuitry.

Building upon your knowledge of shift-register operation, a "painless" introduction to multiplication, division, and binary fractional processing is provided. Inasmuch as encoders and decoders are among the key subsections in microprocessor systems, their circuit action is described and supplemented by interesting experimental projects. ASCII, BCD, XS3, and other widely used codes are discussed, along with explanation of code-converter action. Standard troubleshooting techniques are illustrated, and case histories are presented to familiarize the reader with the "real world."

Multiplexers and demultiplexers are also key subsections in microprocessor systems, and examples of their circuitry are analyzed along with related data-selector and data-distributor applications. Clock skew troubleshooting notes are included, and oscilloscope tests are explained. The importance of static stimulus tests in preliminary troubleshooting procedures is illustrated.

Essential microprocessor comparator and parity generator/checker functions are explained, with notes on hardware operation in system environments. For example, a "firewalking" operating environment is noted wherein the display devices are greatly overdriven, but for such brief intervals that they are not damaged—although if the troubleshooter "stops the clock," the display devices would be subject to damage.

Experimental projects are included for reinforced learning. The reader proceeds with a practical overview of memory organization and operation. Widely used types of TTL, CMOS, and dynamic MOS memories are explained, and the various specialized troubleshooting requirements are noted. Terms that often confuse the beginner, such as "program memory," are clarified. Practical considerations in handling and replacement of MOS memory devices are included.

With this established perspective, you are in good position to cope with the elements of microprocessor architecture. This discussion starts with a "chopped down" version of a microcomputer that includes the minimum hardware requirements for stored-program addition of a pair of binary numbers. It is supplemented by an experimental microcomputer project which clearly illustrates "bare-bones" architecture. Notes are included on bugging and debugging the elementary system.

Next, you are introduced to buffer registers and to register-transfer action in bus-oriented microcomputers. It is shown how the program counter is the "heart" of microprocessing, and how it directs RAM or ROM address-decoding and unloading action. An elementary diagnostic program for microcomputer troubleshooting is introduced, plus notes on the fundamentals of programming.

Instruction sets are described with detailed explanations of the fetch cycle, address phase, increment phase, and execution cycle. Basic LDA, ADD, SUB, and OUT routines are analyzed, with notes on instruction decoder and control matrix operation. At this point, you are briefly introduced to the logic analyzer, with examples of its importance in analysis of data-processing operations. Both hardware faults and program "bugs" are exemplified.

Progressively elaborated microprocessor architectures are described, with detailed examples of jump instructions and subroutine counter operations. Commercial arithmetic-logic units are illustrated. Index and output register operation is followed, along with explanation of compiler and assembler operation. At this point, you will have a good understanding of machine language and high-level language. Note in passing that a programmer does not need to know how a microcomputer works. On the other hand, the troubleshooter must know how programs are written, and how they are processed by a microcomputer.

"New Microcomputer Test Equipment You Can Build" is a helpful "plus" in this text—it shows the reader how to construct simple and useful microcomputer testers, and how to apply them. For example, a charge-storage logic-level beeper is described which is both economical and highly utilitarian. Troubleshooters with commercial microcomputer test equipment available will nevertheless be interested in some of the novel approaches that are explained, such as construction and use of a differential temperature probe.

Accordingly, this book will serve as an excellent training manual for anyone who wishes to understand how microprocessors and microcomputers work, and how to troubleshoot them. Because the text starts at the beginning and assumes no prior knowledge of the art, it is easily comprehensible by prep-school students and hobbyists. However, the reader should have a background of introductory physics; familiarity with the new math will also be helpful.

The most important new-math topic, from the troubleshooter's viewpoint, is base-2 arithmetic. Other important topics include the hexadecimal system (base-16 arithmetic), and the octal system (base-8 arithmetic). Discussion of data is also of importance.

Professional microcomputer troubleshooters know that knowledge is power, and that time is money. Their goal is an effective mastery of microprocessor and microcomputer operation, with knowledge of troubleshooting techniques and recognition of malfunction symptoms in defective equipment. Your success in the field of computer technology is limited only by the horizons of your technical know-how. This readily understandable text, with its profuse illustrations, troubleshooting explanations, and case histories, provides key stepping-stones to your goal.

Robert G. Middleton

CONTENTS

Microprocessor and Microcomputer Fundamentals

Overview * Embryo Microprocessor * Up-Counter Action * Counter Troubleshooting * Down-Counter Action * Decimal Readout * Rules for Binary Addition * Rules for Binary Subtraction * Introduction to Binary Fractions * Dedicated Versus General-Purpose Microprocessing

Overview

Microprocessors and microcomputers are not the mysterious devices and machines that elude understanding and defy troubleshooting, as popular news writers might lead their readers to suppose. Quite to the contrary, as explained in the following chapters, microprocessors and microcomputers are as easy to understand as they are interesting, and they are no more difficult to troubleshoot than is a color-TV receiver, for example.

A microprocessor is exemplified in Fig. 1-1. It is a large-scale integrated circuit (LSI) which adds, subtracts, multiplies, divides, and performs logical operations such as: *If A is less than B, then transfer program control to line 29.* All arithmetical and logical operations are accomplished by means of microscopic electronic switching circuits— whence the "micro" terminology.

A microcomputer is illustrated in Fig. 1-2. Its "heart" is a microprocessor which is controlled by a stored program. This stored program is determined by the keyboard operator (programmer), and is stored in an electronic memory. The microcomputer has no intelligence (in the human sense of the term), and it can process data only as commanded by the programmer.

13

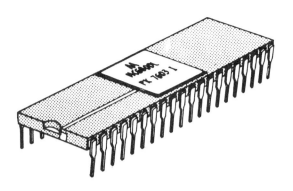

Fig. 1-1. A typical microprocessor IC package.

Radio Shack TRS-80 Microcomputer System

Fig. 1-2. The "heart" of a microcomputer is a microprocessor (*Courtesy, Radio Shack, a Division of Tandy Corp*).

Fig. 1-3. A digital voltmeter that employs a microprocessor (*Courtesy, Sencore*).

Microprocessors are also used in electronic instruments such as the digital voltmeter (DVM) shown in Fig. 1-3. The microprocessor automatically makes logical decisions such as: *If the input voltage is greater than 1 volt, but is less than 10 volts, then display the decimal point to the right of the first numeral in the readout.* Microprocessors are used in intelligent oscilloscopes ("smart scopes") to automatically calculate and display waveform parameters such as rise time, peak voltage, frequency, and so on.

We will also encounter microprocessors in microwave ovens, video games, automotive electrical/electronic systems, traffic controllers, digital calculators, and in scores of medical and industrial applications. All microprocessors operate in combination with memory, control, interfacing, and peripheral devices as explained in the following chapters.*

Embryo Microprocessor

For a basic understanding of how a microprocessor adds numbers, observe the "embryo microprocessor" depicted in Fig. 1-4. This is an example of a digital up-counter. It consists of a chain of electronic switches (12 switches, in this example). At the start, all of the switches are off, or their outputs are logic-low. When the first pulse is inputted, the first switch goes logic-high; the remainder of the switches remain logic-low.

---

*If you want to know more about IC's used in microprocessor systems, refer to pages 111-344 in *Encyclopedia of Integrated Circuits,* by Walter H. Buchsbaum, Sc.D.

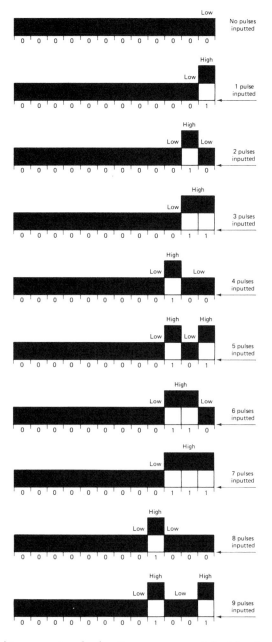

Note: A binary counter also functions as a sequential adder. For example, if two pulses are inputted, the readout will be 10; then, if three more pulses are inputted, the readout will be 101 (10 + 11 = 101). This sum is retained as long as no further pulses are inputted. In other words, the counter also functions as a memory.

Fig. 1-4. Binary counter operation.

Next, when the second pulse is inputted, the first switch goes logic-low, and the second switch goes logic-high. Then, when the third pulse is inputted, the first switch goes logic-high, and the second switch remains logic-high. In other words, the digital up-counter is adding the inputted pulses and indicating their sum in binary number notation (see Fig. 1-5).

The electronic switch devices in the up-counter are arranged to develop the sequential high/low states depicted in Fig. 1-5 as explained in greater detail subsequently. Observe that each switch device drives the following switch device, from right to left. The counter circuitry is configured so that only on-to-off (high-to-low) transitions generate a drive pulse to the following switch device. Thus, an off-to-on (low-to-high) transition of a switch device generates no drive pulse to its following switch device.

This type of circuit action is called "toggling," and it is of basic importance in microprocessor operation. In the present example, toggle action provides development of binary-number readout and storage of a given number of input pulses. In other words, the up-counter is also a

Decimal	Binary
0	0000
1	0001
2	0010
3	0011
4	0100
5	0101
6	0110
7	0111
8	1000
9	1001
10	1010
11	1011
12	1100
13	1101
14	1110
15	1111
16	0001 0000
17	0001 0001
30	0001 1110
31	0001 1111

Note: A microprocessor employs binary numbers because reliability is paramount. Electronic circuit action has maximum reliability when each transistor is either cut off or driven into saturation. In other words, the transistors operate in the switching mode—a stage in the electronic switch chain is either on, or it is off; it is either logic-high, or it is logic-low. The logic-high state is denoted 1; the logic-low state is denoted 0.

Fig. 1-5. Corresponding decimal and binary numbers.

form of digital memory. When it is used for short-term storage, the arrangement is commonly called a register.

Up-Counter Action

A mechanical switching analogy of up-counter action is shown in Fig. 1-6. When a toggle-output arrow contacts the conductive arc on a pulley, the switch is closed and the toggle output is logic-high (1). On the other hand, while the insulated portion of a pulley is passing the toggle-output arrow, the switch is open and the toggle output is logic-low (0). Each pulley is belt-driven from the preceding pulley, in this example.

An input pulse is represented by one complete rotation of pulley U1. It is evident that two complete rotations of U1 are required to produce one output "pulse" from U2. Similarly, four complete rotations of U1 are required to produce one output "pulse" from U3. Thus, after four complete rotations of U1, the output states of the up-counter can be represented by the binary number 100.

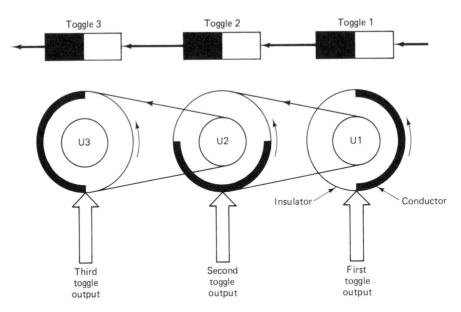

Note: Pulley U2 rotates half as rapidly as pulley U1, and pulley U3 rotates half as rapidly as pulley U2. Pulley U3 rotates one-quarter as rapidly as pulley U1. Thus, switch U2 remains on or off twice as long as switch U1, and switch U3 remains on or off twice as long as switch U2. Switch U3 remains on or off four times as long as switch U1.

Fig. 1-6. Mechanical switching analogy of up-counter action.

Counter action is shown to good advantage by means of timing diagrams, or oscilloscope displays, of the toggle output states as exemplified in Fig. 1-7. A complete pulse consists of a logic-high state followed by a logic-low state. The successive toggle outputs have binary values of 1, 2, 4, 8, 16, and so on. Note that timing diagrams and oscilloscope patterns always show data development from left to right.

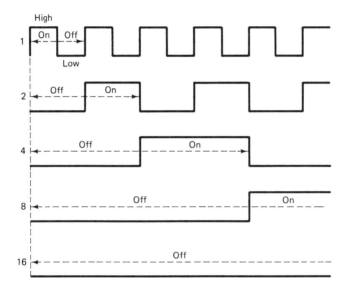

Note: Observe that the "2" toggle output remains logic-high twice as long as the "1" toggle output. The "4" toggle output remains logic-high twice as long as the "2" toggle output. The "8" toggle output remains logic-high twice as long as the "4" toggle output, and so on.

Fig. 1-7. Timing diagram (oscilloscope display) of counter output states.

Counter Troubleshooting

Counter action can be checked by inputting a chosen number of pulses, and verifying output logic states as shown in Fig. 1-8. A logic pulser functions to inject one or more standard digital pulses. A logic probe provides indication (usually visual) of the logic state at the test point (whether the test point is logic-high or logic-low).

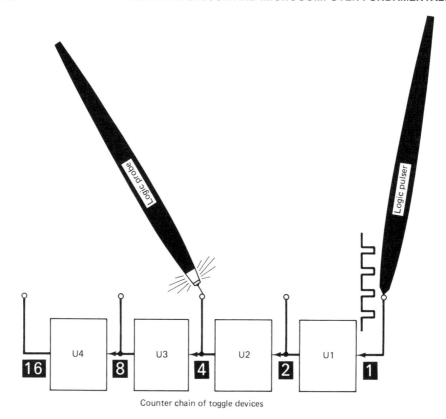

Fig. 1-8. A logic pulser may be used to inject a given number of pulses, and a logic probe utilized to indicate an output pulse.

Down-Counter Action

Microprocessors also employ down-counters, as depicted in Fig. 1-9. In this example, the starting readout (preset) is 9 (1001). When the first pulse is inputted, the readout decreases to 8 (1000). Similarly, when the second pulse is inputted, the readout decreases to 7 (111). In other words, each pulse that is inputted to the down-counter subtracts one from the readout.

Commercial counters are often arranged to either count up, or to count down, according to the state of a control line. Thus, if the control line is driven logic-high, the counter will count up. On the other hand, if the control line is driven logic-low, the counter will count down. In turn, the counter will add input pulses, or it will subtract input pulses from the readout, as instructed.

In the example of Fig. 1-4, the counter is adding—a total of nine input pulses are applied, and the readout is 1001. Next, in Fig. 1-9,

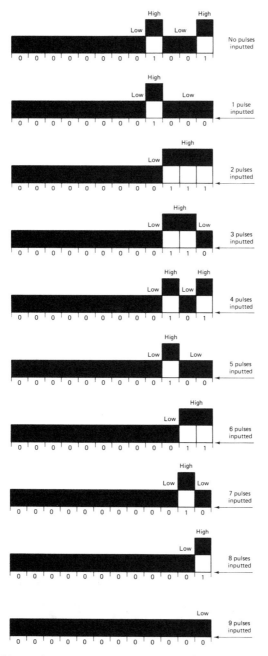

Note: A binary down-counter operates as a subtracter. In other words, the readout decreases by one each time that a pulse is inputted. The starting readout (preset) may be any value. In any case, the readout will decrease by one for each pulse that is inputted.

Fig. 1-9. Binary down-counter operation.

the counter is subtracting—a total of nine input pulses are applied, and the readout is 0000. Note in passing that the readout 000000001001 is the same as 1001; the first eight zeros are called nonsignificant zeros.

Decimal Readout

Microcomputers and calculators generally provide decimal readout, instead of binary readout. With reference to Fig. 1-10, the logic states of an up-counter are processed through a binary-to-decimal decoder. In turn, the decoder drives a decimal display device, and the 1001 counter readout is converted into a 9 readout. Decoder operation is subsequently explained.

Observe that the decimal display in Fig. 1-10 is provided by a seven-segment display device. In this example, six of the seven segments are energized. The segments are energized by a seven-segment driver (not shown). Note also that nonsignificant zeros are automatically blanked out on the decimal display device. Blanking provides traditional format in the numerical display.

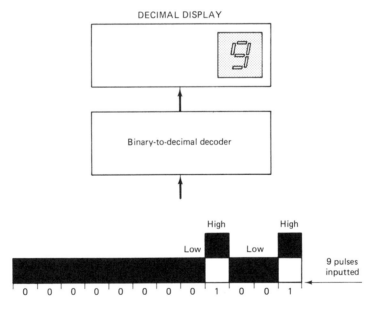

Note: Incorrect readout can be caused by defects in semiconductor devices, by false pulses (glitches) in the data stream, by faults in circuits external to the devices, and by abnormally high operating temperature.

Fig. 1-10. A binary-to-decimal decoder converts the binary counter readout to its corresponding decimal readout.

Rules for Binary Addition

It is helpful to note the rules for binary addition, as follows:

$$0 + 0 = 0$$
$$1 + 0 = 1$$
$$0 + 1 = 1$$
$$1 + 1 = 0 \text{ and } 1 \text{ to carry}$$

Basic examples of binary addition are shown in Fig. 1-11. Note that any addition problem may be solved in terms of the above steps. For example:

$$1 + 1 + 1 = 10 + 1 = 11$$
$$1 + 1 + 1 + 1 = 10 + 10 = 100$$
$$11 + 11 = 10 + 100 = 110$$
$$111 + 11 = 10 + 100 + 100 = 1010$$

$\begin{matrix}1\\0\\\hline 1\end{matrix}$	$\begin{matrix}1\\1\\\hline 10\end{matrix}$	$\begin{matrix}10\\1\\\hline 11\end{matrix}$	$\begin{matrix}101\\11\\\hline 1000\end{matrix}$	$\begin{matrix}1010\\101\\10\\\hline 10001\end{matrix}$	*Binary*
$1 + 0 = 0$	$1 + 1 = 2$	$2 + 1 = 3$	$5 + 3 = 8$	$10 + 5 + 2 = 17$	*Decimal*

Note: Observe that place values are employed in binary addition, in the same basic manner as in decimal addition. That is, the first place on the right of a binary number will have a value of either 0 or 1. However, the next place to the left will have a value of either 0 or 2. Again, the next place to the left will have a value of either 0 or 4. It is possible that all of the first places on the right may be 0—in such a case, this is called an "empty column." Similarly, it is possible that all of the values in the next column to the left may be 0—as before, this will then be called an "empty column."

Fig. 1-11. Some basic examples of binary addition.

To convert decimal numbers into binary numbers with pencil and paper, the divide-by-two method may be used, as exemplified in Fig. 1-12.

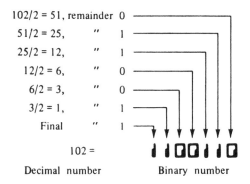

102/2 = 51, remainder 0
51/2 = 25,   "   1
25/2 = 12,   "   1
12/2 = 6,   "   0
6/2 = 3,   "   0
3/2 = 1,   "   1
Final   "   1

102 =

Decimal number   Binary number

Note: As would be anticipated, a microcomputer can easily be programmed to convert any decimal number into a binary number, or to convert any binary number into a decimal number.

Fig. 1-12. Example of pencil-and-paper conversion of a decimal number into its corresponding binary number.

Rules for Binary Subtraction

It is also helpful to note the rules for binary subtraction, as follows:

$$0 - 0 = 0$$
$$1 - 1 = 0$$
$$1 - 0 = 1$$
$$0 - 1 = 1 \text{ and } 1 \text{ to borrow}$$

We will find that microprocessors may employ subtracter hardware. However, the general practice is to perform subtraction by means of the two's-complement method with an adder, as will be explained subsequently. This is the preferred method of subtraction because it minimizes the amount of hardware that is required to perform both addition and subtraction.

We will also find that adders are used to perform multiplication and division in microprocessor systems. In other words, multiplication is basically a process of repeated addition, and division is basically a process of repeated subtraction. Thus, although it is possible to design separate multiplication hardware and division hardware, this is seldom done in order to minimize hardware requirements.

Note in passing that a binary number can also be multiplied by shifting. If the number is shifted one place to the left, it is multiplied by 2; if the number is shifted two places to the left, it is multiplied by 4, and so on. For example:

0011 = 3   (Note that only multiplication by 2, 4, 8, and so
0110 = 6   on can be accomplished by merely shifting the
1100 = 12   digits. Generalized multiplication procedures are
           detailed subsequently.)

If we reverse the foregoing sequence of operations, we recognize that a binary number can be divided by shifting. Thus, if the number is shifted one place to the right, it is divided by 2; if the number is shifted two places to the right, it is divided by 4; and so on. Shifting is accomplished in microprocessors by means of shift registers, as explained in a following chapter.

Introduction to Binary Fractions

Microprocessors operate with fractions as well as whole numbers. As an introduction to the processing of fractions, consider the following example of right-shifting:

1100 = 12
0110 = 6
0011 = 3
0001.1 = 1½
0000.11 = 3/4
0000.011 = 3/8

Thus, 3 divided by 2 = 1.5, 1.5 divided by 2 = 0.75, and 0.75 divided by 2 = 0.375. When we write the binary number 0001.1, the point is called a binary point; whereas, when we write the decimal number 1.5, the point is called a decimal point.

Observe in the foregoing example that the place values to the left of the binary point have "weights" of 1, 2, 4, 8, and so on; whereas, the place values to the right of the binary point have "weights" of 1/2, 1/4, 1/8, 1/16, and so on. In other words, the weights to the right of the binary point are the reciprocals of the weights to the left of the binary point (omitting the "1" place).

Observe also that just as the place values to the left of the binary point are additive, so are the place values to the right of the binary point additive. Thus, 111 = 100 + 10 + 1, or 7 = 4 + 2 + 1; 0.111 = 0.1 + 0.01 + 0.001, or, 7/8 = 1/2 + 1/4 + 1/8. Stated otherwise, 0.875 = 0.5 + 0.25 + 0.125. The foregoing relations simplify the task of working with binary fractions.

Dedicated Versus General-Purpose Microprocessing

Dedicated microprocessing denotes the designing or programming of a microprocessor for a particular application, or for a particular group of applications. As an illustration, video games, calculators, traffic controllers, and electrical appliances employ dedicated micro-processing systems. Another familiar example is the microprocessor calculating and control system used in automotive electrical and electronic functions.

General-purpose microprocessing is employed in digital computers that are designed to meet a very large class of applications. This general-purpose capability is provided by microprocessor operation from a stored program written in terms of general commands such as NEW, RUN, LIST, CONT, and general statements such as PRINT, INPUT, READ, DATA, RESTORE, LET, GO TO, IF-THEN, FOR-NEXT, STEP, STOP, END, GOSUB, RETURN, ON, with print modifiers such as AT, TAB, and supplemented by graphic statements such as SET, RESET, POINT, and CLS.

A general-purpose microcomputer has various built-in functions such as MEM, INT(X), ABS(X), RND ($\emptyset$), and RND(N). It also provides math operators such as $+$, $-$, $*$, $/$, and $=$; supplemented by relational operators such as $<$, $>$, $=$, $<=$, $>=$, and $<>$; logical operators such as $*$ and $+$; and variables such as A through Z, A\$ and B\$, and A(X)†. These general statements, general commands, print modifiers, graphic statements, built-in functions, math operators, relational operators, logical operators, and variables are detailed subsequently.

With reference to Fig. 1-2, a typical microcomputer comprises a keyboard, video display, cassette recorder, and power supply. The microprocessor is inside of the keyboard assembly. The keyboard per se, video display, and cassette recorder are called peripherals. A popular term for the keyboard and video display is "TV typewriter." Cables linking the peripherals are called interconnects. Note that the cassette recorder in this example is used to store programs; it is an external memory device.

Inside the keyboard assembly are several integrated circuits other than the microprocessor above noted. The microprocessor can be characterized as the "heart" of the microcomputer; it is also called the central processing unit (CPU). A CPU consists of an arithmetic-logic unit (ALU) and a control-logic unit, as detailed subsequently.

In addition to the microprocessor, the keyboard assembly in this example also contains three memories. A video divider chain, a video processing unit, a tape interface, master clock oscillator, multiplexer, keyboard/video-select unit, and a ROM/RAM select unit. (ROM and RAM are abbreviations for particular types of memories.) Although these terms may seem strange, we will soon become quite familiar and at ease with them.

---

†Note that $*$ is the symbol for multiplication; $/$ is the symbol for division.

2

Gates and
Basic Digital-Logic
Devices

Microprocessor Building Blocks * AND, OR, NOR, XOR, and XNOR Gates * Gate Arrangements as Equivalent Buffers or Inverters * A AND-NOT B, and A OR-NOT B Gates * Gates with All Inputs Inverted * Equivalent Gates * AND-OR Gates * AND-OR-INVERT Gates * NAND Implementation * Experimental Project

Microprocessor Building Blocks*

Logic gates are the basic microprocessor building blocks. A logic gate is an electronic component that performs a logical operation. It is a switching device that has two or more inputs and one output. Its output remains unenergized until specified input conditions are met. The four basic digital-logic gates are termed AND, OR, NAND, and NOR types.

Each type of gate has a distinctive symbol, and its function is defined by a truth table, as shown in Fig. 2-1. These are two-input gates; the inputs are denoted by A and B; gate output is denoted by Q. An input or an output is either logic-high or logic-low. Logic-high ordinarily corresponds to a level of 2.4 volts or more; logic-low corresponds to a near-ground potential of approximately 0 volts.

---

*See Chart 2-1.

MICROWAVE OVEN:

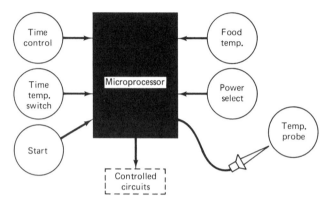

TELEVISION RECEIVER:

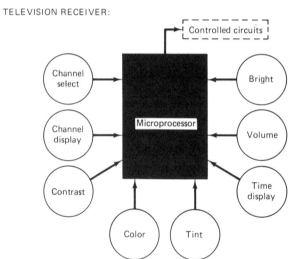

Chart 2-1

Examples of Microprocessor Application

VIDEO GAME:

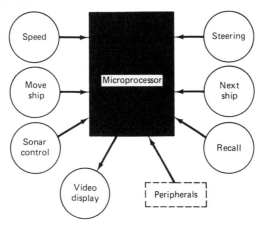

MICROCOMPUTER:

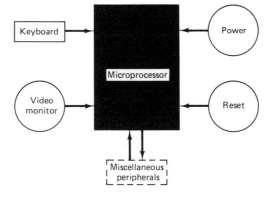

Chart 2-1 (*continued*)

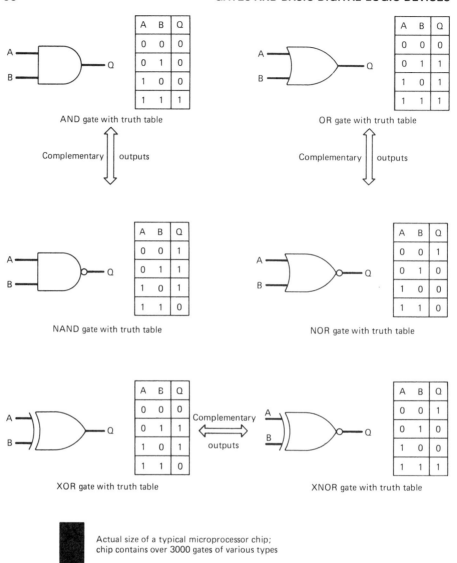

Fig. 2-1. Comparison of truth tables for basic gates.

AND, OR, NAND, NOR, XOR, and XNOR Gates

As seen in Fig. 2-1, the output from an AND gate is logic-high if both of its inputs are simultaneously logic-high—otherwise, the AND-gate output is logic-low. The logic-high state is commonly denoted by 1, and the logic-low state is commonly denoted by 0. The 1 state is often called "high," and the 0 state is often called "low." The "high"

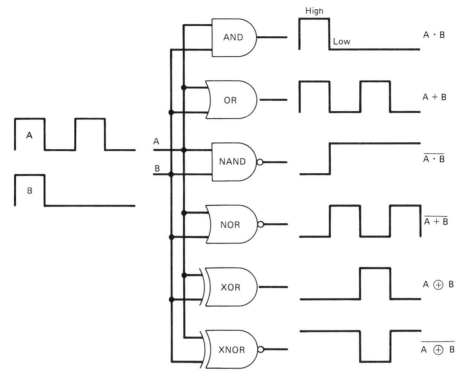

Note: A·B is read "A AND B." This logic expression is also written AB, and is read "A AND B." A + B is read "A OR B." A small circle following a symbol denotes inversion (complementation). $\overline{A \cdot B}$ is read "A AND B NOT." $\overline{A + B}$ is read "A OR B NOT." A ⊕ B is read "A EXCLUSIVE-OR B." $\overline{A \oplus B}$ is read "A EXCLUSIVE-OR B NOT."

Fig. 2-2. Pulse responses of basic gates.

state is sometimes called "true," and the "low" state is sometimes called "false." Note that the 1 level is the complement of the 0 level; similarly, the 0 level is the complement of the 1 level.

We observe that a NAND gate has an output which is the complement of the AND-gate output. Similarly, a NOR gate has an output which is the complement of the OR-gate output. This is just another way of saying that a NAND gate consists of an AND gate followed by an inverter; a NOR gate consists of an OR gate followed by an inverter. An inverter is a device which complements its input. An inverter is an operator—it is not a gate, inasmuch as the inverter has only one input.

Note in Fig. 2-1 that EXCLUSIVE-OR (XOR) and EXCLUSIVE-NOR (XNOR) gates are listed with the basic types of gates. By way of comparison, an OR gate is also called an INCLUSIVE-OR gate, and a NOR gate is also called an INCLUSIVE-NOR gate. The XOR gate has a logic-high output if its inputs are simultaneously at opposite logic levels; if its inputs are at the same logic level, the XOR gate has a logic-low output. An XNOR gate has an output which is the complement of the XOR gate output.

Pulse responses of basic gates are depicted in Fig. 2-2. Observe how the AND-gate and the NAND-gate output waveforms are the complements of each other. Similarly, the OR-gate and NOR-gate output waveforms are the complements of each other. The XOR-gate and XNOR-gate output waveforms are the complements of each other.

Gate Arrangements as Equivalent Buffers or Inverters

A buffer is comparable to a noninverting amplifier. It is connected between logic devices to prevent interaction between them, or to restore an attenuated logic level to a normal value. A buffer may also be used to provide a higher output-current capability than its associated gate. An inverter is comparable to an inverting amplifier. Its basic function is to complement the input logic state.

As previously noted, this type of device is not a gate because it has only one input. Nevertheless, gates with two or more inputs may be (and often are) pressed into service as buffers or inverters, as seen in Fig. 2-3. The truth tables for these gates show that paralleled inputs will function as the single input for buffer or inverter action.

Of course, it would be pointless to parallel the inputs of an XOR gate, or of an XNOR gate, because the gate output would be unresponsive to an input logic-state change. Note, however, that if one input of an XOR gate is grounded, the gate functions as a buffer. Conversely, if one input of an XOR gate is held logic-high, the gate functions as an inverter (logic-high in this example is the power supply, or V_{CC} voltage). We will find that there is an important microprocessor circuit subsection in which one input to an XOR gate may be switched either logic-high or logic-low in order to obtain inverter action or buffer action, as required.

A AND-NOT B, and A OR-NOT B Gates

Microprocessors also employ gates with various negated inputs, such as those depicted in Fig. 2-4. Observe that an AND gate with a negated input is distinctively different from an AND gate or a NAND

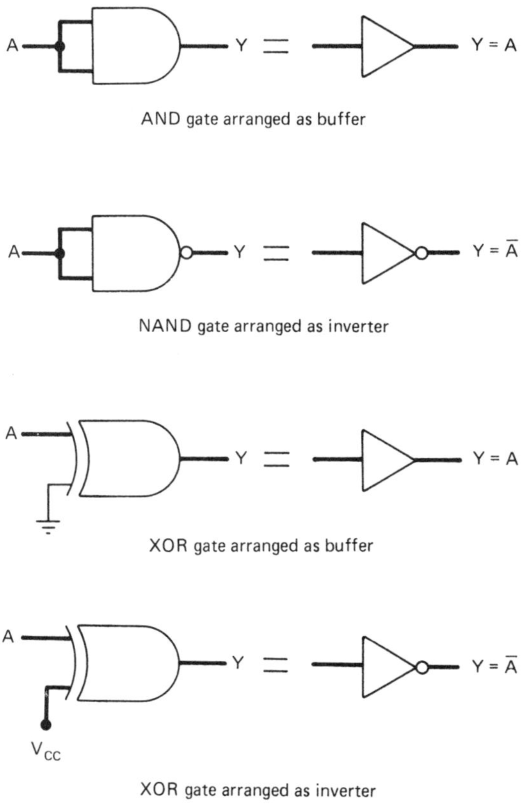

AND gate arranged as buffer

NAND gate arranged as inverter

XOR gate arranged as buffer

XOR gate arranged as inverter

Note: Gate malfunctions are usually catastrophic. For example, a gate may become unresponsive to input pulses (gate output becomes "stuck high" or "stuck low.") In case a short-circuit occurs inside of an IC package, its temperature may rise excessively.

Fig. 2-3. Gate arrangements as equivalent buffers or inverters.

gate, not only with respect to truth tables, but also with respect to order of inputs. Thus, the A and B inputs of an AND gate can be interchanged, and its truth table remains unchanged. On the other hand, if the A and B inputs of an A AND-NOT B gate are interchanged, its truth table becomes modified.

Note also in Fig. 2-4 that if the output from an A AND-NOT B gate were followed by an inverter, its truth table would become the same as for the B OR-NOT A gate. In other words, a NAND gate with an inverted input is the same as an OR gate with its opposite input inverted. Similarly, if the output from a B AND-NOT A gate is inverted, its truth table becomes the same as for the A OR-NOT B gate.

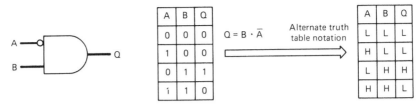

B AND-NOT A gate with truth table

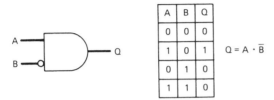

A AND-NOT B gate with truth table

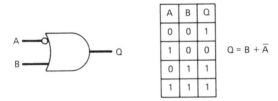

B OR-NOT A gate with truth table

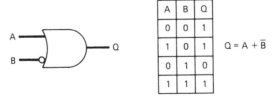

A OR-NOT B gate with truth table

(a)

Note: Some manufacturers employ 0,1 notation in truth tables. Others utilize L,H notation. The same logic equation is represented in either case. Note also that inputs may be denoted by C,D instead of A,B, for example. Similarly, an output may be denoted by Y, instead of Q.

Fig. 2-4(a). Comparison of truth tables for gates with a negated input.

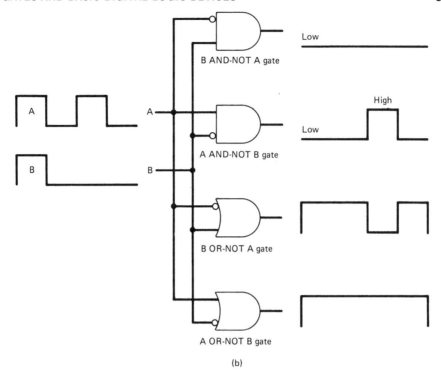

(b)

Note: The B AND-NOT A gate cannot output a logic-high pulse unless it
simultaneously inputs a logic-low A pulse and a logic-high B pulse.
Since this combination of pulses is not inputted in this example, the
output of the B AND-NOT A gate remains logic-low.

Fig. 2-4(b). Pulse response of basic gates with a negated input.

Gates with All Inputs Inverted

Gates may also be operated with all inputs inverted, as shown
in Fig. 2-5. Note particularly that when an AND gate has its inputs
inverted (negated), its response is different from that of a NAND gate.
The negated-AND gate has a logic equation $\overline{A} \cdot \overline{B}$, which is read: "Not
A AND-NOT B." On the other hand, the NAND gate has a logic
equation $\overline{A \cdot B}$, which is read: "A AND B NOT."

Note particularly that when all the inputs of a NAND gate are
negated, it responds the same as an OR gate. Again, when all of the
inputs of an OR gate are negated, it responds the same as an AND
gate. These relations lead us to the general principle: If all of the level
indicators of an AND gate are complemented, the AND symbol is

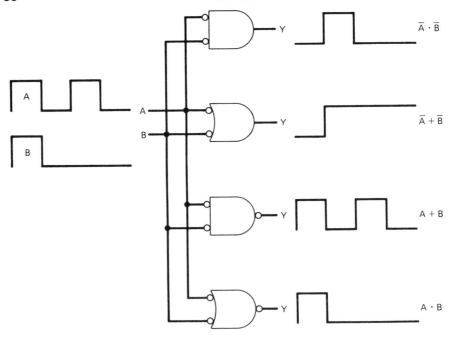

Note: When the inputs to a NAND gate are negated, its logic equation becomes $\overline{\overline{A} \cdot \overline{B}}$ and this equation is read: "NOT A AND NOT B NOT." Then, we may remove the double-inversion bars by replacing the AND symbol with an OR symbol. Thus, $\overline{\overline{A} \cdot \overline{B}} = A + B$. Similarly, the logic equation for a NOR gate with its inputs inverted becomes the same as the logic equation for an AND gate.

Fig. 2-5. Pulse responses of basic negated gates.

correspondingly replaced by an **OR** symbol. Similarly, if all of the level indicators of an **OR** gate are complemented, the **OR** symbol is correspondingly replaced by an **AND** symbol.

Inspection of their truth tables shows that an **XOR** gate functions the same if its inputs are negated, and that an **XNOR** gate functions the same if its inputs are negated. A buffer with its input inverted functions as an inverter. An inverter with its input inverted functions as a buffer. Although it might seem inconsequential whether an inverter is symbolized as in Fig. 2-6(a) or (b), we will find that there is a "contextual" distinction in microprocessor circuitry. In other words, an inverter does not stand alone, but functions in association with input and output devices. The circuitry becomes easier to understand if the inverter's negated terminal is consistent with intended circuit function, as detailed subsequently.

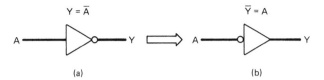

(a)   (b)

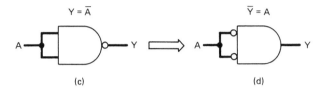

(c)   (d)

Note: A NAND gate is occasionally used as an inverter because commercial IC packages contain several (typically four) NAND gates. In turn, if a logic circuit calls for three NAND gates, the designer will have one gate "left over" in the IC package. Then, if an inverter is needed, it is more economical to operate the "leftover" gate as an inverter, instead of installing a separate inverter IC package.

Note: Insofar as the end result in signal processing is concerned, $Y = \overline{A}$ is the same as $\overline{Y} = A$. Thus, a logic-high output corresponds to a logic-low input, and a logic-low output corresponds to a logic-high input. However, if the circuit action of interest involves a logic-high output, we prefer to write $Y = \overline{A}$. On the other hand, if the circuit action of interest involves a logic-low output, we prefer to write $\overline{Y} = A$.

Fig. 2-6. Inverter arrangements. (a) Buffer followed by inverter; (b) inverter followed by buffer; (c) NAND gate with inputs tied together; (d) AND gate with negated inputs tied together.

Equivalent Gates

It was previously noted that if all of the level indicators of an AND gate are complemented, that AND symbol is correspondingly replaced by an OR symbol. Thus, with reference to Fig. 2-7, if we remove the "bubbles" from the AND-gate inputs and insert a "bubble" in the output, the gate function remains the same if the AND symbol is replaced by an OR symbol. This is just another way of saying that an AND gate with negated inputs functions as a NOR gate.

In accordance with this basic principle, a NAND gate with negated inputs functions as an OR gate; an OR gate with negated inputs functions as a NAND gate; a NOR gate with negated inputs functions

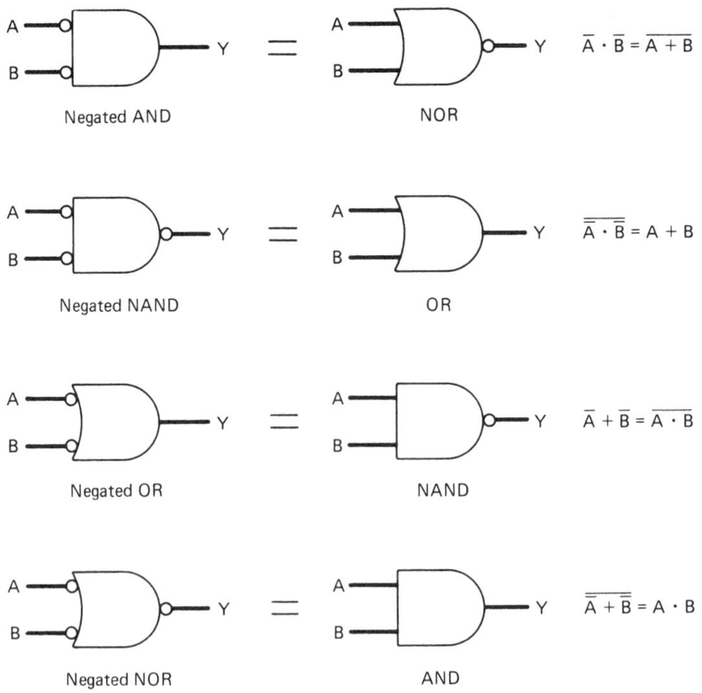

$$\overline{A} \cdot \overline{B} = \overline{A + B}$$

Negated AND — NOR

$$\overline{\overline{A} \cdot \overline{B}} = A + B$$

Negated NAND — OR

$$\overline{A} + \overline{B} = \overline{A \cdot B}$$

Negated OR — NAND

$$\overline{\overline{A} + \overline{B}} = A \cdot B$$

Negated NOR — AND

Note: Double negation restores the original value. Thus, $\overline{\overline{A}} = A$, $\overline{\overline{1}} = 1$, and $\overline{\overline{0}} = 0$. Observe that $\overline{1} = 0$, and $\overline{0} = 1$. (A negated logic-high is a logic-low, and a negated logic-low is a logic-high state.) Observe also that $\overline{\overline{A + B}} = A + B$, but that $\overline{\overline{A} + \overline{B}} = A \cdot B$.

Fig. 2-7. Equivalent gates.

as an AND gate. These relations are generally summarized by DeMorgan's Theorem, which states:

$$\overline{A} \cdot \overline{B} \cdot \overline{C} = \overline{A + B + C} \qquad \overline{A} + \overline{B} + \overline{C} = \overline{A \cdot B \cdot C}$$

Three-input gates are exemplified in these DeMorgan equations. We will find that AND, OR, NAND, and NOR gates may have any number of inputs. On the other hand, XOR and XNOR gates are limited to two inputs.

Microprocessors employ AND gates with various negated inputs as digital word recognizers. For example, the AND gate depicted in Fig. 2-8 has its A, B, and C inputs negated; its D input is not negated. In turn, its Y output will go logic-high only if ABCD = 0001. Any other combination of input states will result in Y = 0. Observe that a NOR gate with its D input negated will serve the same purpose as the AND gate with its A, B, and C inputs negated.

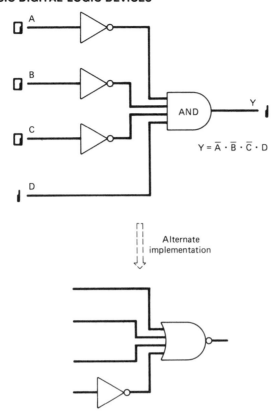

$$Y = \overline{A} \cdot \overline{B} \cdot \overline{C} \cdot D$$

Alternate
implementation

Note: This is an example of combinatorial or combinational logic. This
category of logic is distinguished by the circumstance that the output
state depends only on the present combination of input states (not
upon any previous input states that may have been applied).

Fig. 2-8. Detailed input circuitry for an AND gate that
responds with a logic-high output from a 0001 input.

AND-OR Gates

Microprocessors also utilize AND-OR gates, as exemplified in Fig.
2-9(a). The output will go logic-high if A and B are simultaneously
driven logic-high, or if C and D are simultaneously driven logic-high.
Of course, Y goes logic-high if all four inputs are simultaneously driven
logic-high. This AND-OR gate is an example of combinatorial logic,
wherein basic gates are interconnected to obtain a specified function.

Next, observe the arrangement shown in Fig. 2-9(b). Here, the
outputs of a pair of AND gates are paralleled. It is a logic circuit
that is seldom used. Note particularly that this configuration does not

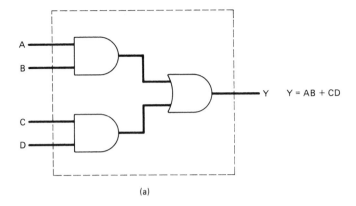

(a)

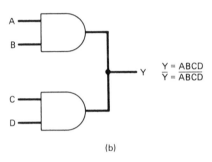

$$Y = ABCD$$
$$\overline{Y} = \overline{ABCD}$$

(b)

Note: The output goes logic-high if all of the inputs are logic-high. The
output goes logic-low if all of the inputs are logic-low. If any one
input is logic-low, the output is constrained logic-low.

Fig. 2-9. Example of an AND-OR gate. (a) Implementation;
(b) example of an unworkable arrangement.

provide AND-OR action. Instead, the gates can go logic-high together,
or they can go logic-low together—but Y remains logic-low if one
gate is logic-low and the other gate is driven logic-high. The reason
for this circuit action is briefly explained as follows:

In transistor-transistor logic (TTL) circuitry, basic gates
employ totem-pole output configurations, as detailed subsequently. The essential consideration is that when a totem-
pole configuration is in a logic-low output state, it constrains
a paralleled totem-pole configuration to the logic-low state.
Thus, if A is logic-low in Fig. 2-9(b), output Y will be
constrained to the logic-low state, regardless of the states to
which B, C, and D may be driven.

Note in passing that if an AND-OR gate happens to exhibit Y = ABCD + $\overline{ABCD}$ response, instead of AB + CD response, this is a trouble symptom. It indicates that the OR gate (or its input conductors) developed a short-circuit fault. The troubleshooter observes in this situation that the two AND gates can go logic-high together or logic-low together, but one AND gate alone cannot produce a Y = 1 output.

AND-OR-INVERT Gates

Microprocessors also employ AND-OR-INVERT gates, such as depicted in Fig. 2-10. This arrangement is essentially an AND-OR gate followed by an inverter. It may be regarded as an elaboration of the basic NOR gate; if either of the AND gates has a logic-high output,

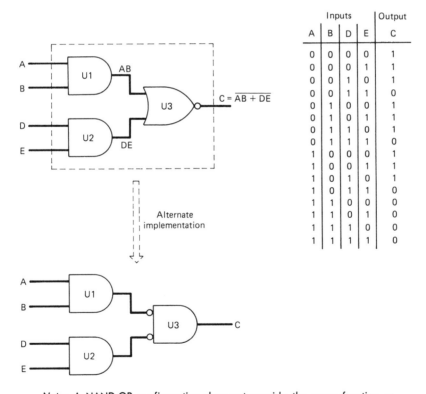

Inputs				Output
A	B	D	E	C
0	0	0	0	1
0	0	0	1	1
0	0	1	0	1
0	0	1	1	0
0	1	0	0	1
0	1	0	1	1
0	1	1	0	1
0	1	1	1	0
1	0	0	0	1
1	0	0	1	1
1	0	1	0	1
1	0	1	1	0
1	1	0	0	0
1	1	0	1	0
1	1	1	0	0
1	1	1	1	0

$C = \overline{AB + DE}$

Alternate implementation

Note: A NAND-OR configuration does not provide the same function as an AND-OR-INVERT configuration. Instead, it provides an AND-NEGATED-OR function. The NEGATED-OR function is the same as the NAND function.

Fig. 2-10. Example of an AND-OR-INVERT gate.

the NOR-gate output will be logic-low. Of course, the NOR-gate output is also logic-low if both of the AND gates have logic-high outputs.

As indicated in the diagram, an AND-OR-INVERT gate can be implemented with a final negated-AND gate, instead of a NOR gate— the truth table for the negated-AND gate is the same as that for a NOR gate. AND-OR-INVERT gates are used in logic circuitry to obtain increased operating flexibility; for example, the gate arrangement in Fig. 2-8 responds to a single control word, whereas an AND-OR-INVERT gate responds to several specific control words.

NAND Implementation

In commercial practice, logic circuitry often employs NAND implementation, as exemplified in Fig. 2-11. Thus, two NAND gates may be configured for the AND function; three NAND gates may be configured for the OR function; five NAND gates may be configured for the XOR function. In each case, at least one of the NAND gates is connected to function as an inverter.

When the inputs of a NAND gate are tied together, the device functions as an inverter because its inputs are constrained to go logic-high together or to go logic-low together. It follows from the NAND truth table that inverter action is thereby obtained. NAND implementation has been widely used because NAND gates were developed early in the history of IC technology. Thus, the NAND implementation got a "head start" on other implementations, and also tended to become entrenched.

Note that in commercial practice, NAND-gate circuitry and inverter circuitry are essentially the same, as seen in Fig. 2-12. The only distinction between the two devices is that the NAND gate employs two inputs, whereas the inverter has only one input. The NAND input transistor is called a multi-emitter transistor. Clamp diodes are commonly used to eliminate undershoot from input waveforms and thereby prevent possible false triggering.

The input transistor operates in the common-base mode; if one of the NAND-gate inputs is driven logic-low, it is thereby effectively short-circuited to ground. In turn, the other input is constrained to the logic-low state—it cannot be driven logic-high because the driving pulse would be effectively short-circuited to ground. This constraint is the basis of NAND-gate response.

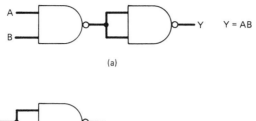

(a)

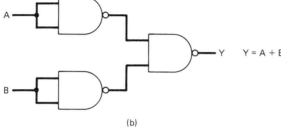

(b)

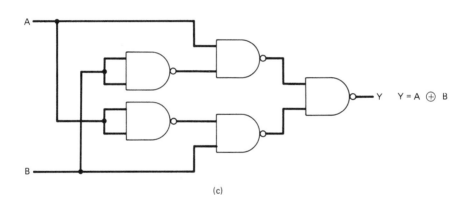

(c)

Fig. 2-11. Gate functions implemented with NAND gates. (a)
AND gate action; (b) OR gate action; (c) XOR gate action.

Observe also in Fig. 2-12 that the two output resistors are connected
in series with each other. This is called the totem-pole arrangement.
Its chief advantage over other output configurations is its high speed
of response. Microprocessors operate at high frequencies, and they
require gates with very small propagation delay. The propagation delay
time of a gate is the elapsed time from application of an input pulse
to the appearance of a corresponding output pulse. A typical NAND
gate has a propagation delay time of 10 nanoseconds.

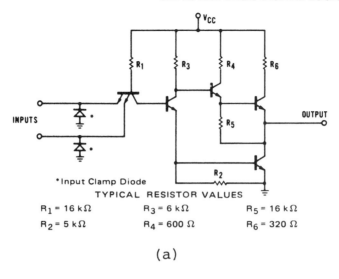

(a)

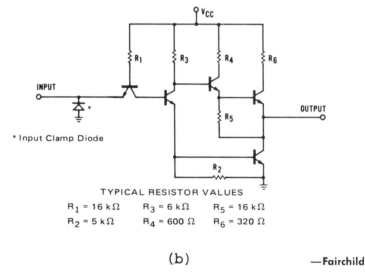

(b)   —Fairchild

Fig. 2-12. Commercial NAND-gate and inverter circuitry. (a) NAND-gate configuration; (b) inverter configuration.

Experimental Project

You can easily construct the inverter arrangement shown in Fig. 2-12(b) from NPN transistors (the clamp diode may be omitted). The inverter can be conveniently constructed on an experimenter's socket, such as the Radio Shack 276-174. All components and devices may be plugged into the rows and columns of holes provided on the socket. The rated V_{cc} supply is 5.1 volts; a 5-volt power supply is adequate.

Note in passing that the inverter input terminal will "look" logic-high if it is allowed to "float." In other words, the input line is normally connected either to a logic-high point or a logic-low point—it does not become open-circuited in normal operation. A floating input terminal "looks" logic-high because the input transistor operates in the common-base mode.

Here is the basis of a common trouble symptom in digital circuitry: if the output of a TTL device such as an inverter is "stuck low," the troubleshooter will suspect that its input may have become open-circuited. When a device becomes "stuck low" or "stuck high," it is unresponsive to input driving pulses, as from a logic pulser. In other words, the device output remains either in a logic-high state (2.4 volts, or somewhat higher), or in a logic-low state (0.4 volt, or somewhat lower).

The two most common faults in digital circuitry are short circuits and open circuits. Note that there are two fundamental types of short circuits: voltage short circuits, and current short circuits. For example,

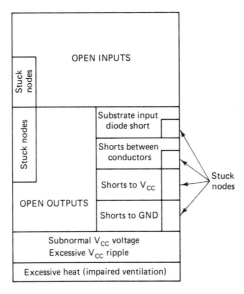

Note: Most digital-circuit faults involve open circuits or short circuits. An open circuit can be tracked down by means of voltage-based troubleshooting methods. A short circuit can be tracked down by means of current-based troubleshooting methods. Both open circuits and short circuits are usually accompanied by abnormal operating temperatures.

Fig. 2-13. Faults in digital circuitry.

if the input lead becomes short-circuited to V_{CC} (Fig. 2-12(b)), a voltage short circuit is present. The input lead is then "stuck high" (it rests at V_{CC} potential); practically no current is drawn by the input transistor from V_{CC}. (See Fig. 2-13.)

Next, if the output lead becomes short-circuited to ground (Fig. 2-12(b)), a current short circuit is present. The output lead is then "stuck low" (it rests at ground potential); heavy current is drawn by the ground through R6 and its associated output transistor. Note that the foregoing example of a voltage short circuit involves high-impedance circuitry; the current short circuit involves low-impedance circuitry. (See also Fig. 2-14.)

Practical Troubleshooting Precaution: If you suspect that a trouble symptom is being caused by a short-circuit somewhere on a micro-computer circuit board, be wary of checking device or component

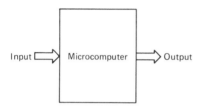

SYSTEMS LEVEL TROUBLESHOOTING

Systems troubleshooting procedures are concerned with abnormal system operation. For example, input/output relations may be checked with a diagnostic program.

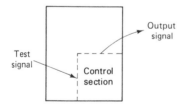

SECTIONAL LEVEL TROUBLESHOOTING

Sectional troubleshooting procedures are concerned with abnormal operation of functional sections. For example, control section operation may be checked with a signature analyzer.

COMPONENT LEVEL TROUBLESHOOTING

Component troubleshooting procedures are concerned with abnormal operation of devices such as a NAND-gate IC. Operation may be checked with a logic probe and pulser.

Note: Diagnostic programs, control sections, signature analyzers, logic probes, and logic pulsers are explained in detail subsequently.

Fig. 2-14. The three basic microcomputer troubleshooting levels.

temperatures with a "finger test." For example, a short circuit inside of an IC can sometimes raise its temperature considerably above the boiling point. If you touch the IC package, a painful burn blister on your finger is the inevitable result.

Troubleshooting Note

The troubleshooter should have available a copy of "Semiconductor Reference Guide," Archer (Radio Shack) Cat. No. 276-4006. This guide describes digital CMOS devices and memories, TTL digital devices, and digital data acquisition and transmission devices. Useful data concerning applications, testing, and handling of devices is included, along with a comprehensive cross-reference substitution listing.

As a practical operating precaution, note that microcomputers are sometimes powered from constant-voltage power supplies. In such a case, it is advisable to always turn on the constant-voltage power supply before turning on the microcomputer. If this order of operation is reversed, it can happen that a starting surge of supply voltage will damage the semiconductor devices in the microcomputer.

Tape Recorder Note

Tape recorders are often used for external storage of programs. When trouble is encountered in "dumping" data from the program memory into the recorder and/or loading data from tape into the program memory, preliminary trouble analysis is made by switching the recorder to its audio playback mode of operation. This quick check provides the following trouble clues:

1. No data may have been recorded on the tape during the "dump" operation.
2. Although data has been recorded on the tape, the recording may be weak.
3. To determine the relative recording level, cross-check against a commercial software cassette.
4. If the recording level is approximately correct, check the setting of the volume control on the recorder.

Microcomputer Troubleshooting Instruments

To anticipate subsequent discussion, a brief listing of microcomputer troubleshooting instruments may be noted:

1. Logic probes, pulsers, current tracers, clips, and comparators are used in troubleshooting at the component level.

2. Digital signature analyzers are utilized in preliminary troubleshooting of microprocessors.

3. Oscilloscopes are used in specialized tests of digital waveforms and in glitch troubleshooting procedures.

4. Logic analyzers (data domain analyzers) are used in microcomputer troubleshooting at the design level.

5. Analog instruments such as digital voltmeters, square-wave generators, and pulse generators also find considerable application in microcomputer troubleshooting procedures.

6. As explained in the last chapter, the recording voltmeter is very helpful when troubleshooting various kinds of malfunctions, and is particularly valuable when tracking down intermittents in microcomputer systems.

IMPORTANT

If the malfunctioning microcomputer has been stored in a damp area, first operate the unit for 100 hours in a warm room—the malfunction will often clear up before the drying-out period is completed.

3

Basic Latches
and Flip-Flops

Latches Configured from Cross-Connected Gates *
Microprocessor Sections * Experimental Project *
Gated Latches * Flip-Flops and Clocks * Master-Slave
Flip-Flops * JK Flip-Flops * Preset and Clear Func-
tions * Troubleshooting Considerations * Artificial
Intelligence

Latches Configured from Cross-Connected Gates

Microprocessors employ large numbers of latches. With reference to Fig. 3-1, a latch provides temporary storage of a binary digit (bit).
Basic latches are configured from cross-connected gates; cross-connection
provides positive feedback, so that the circuit "locks up" in a particular
state. The most fundamental latch is termed a reset-set (RS) latch. NOR
gates or NAND gates are utilized, as shown in the diagram. (See also
Chart 3-1.)

An RS latch stores a pulse applied in complementary form to its
inputs. It retains this stored datum until another pulse is applied in
reversed complementary form to its inputs. Thereupon, the former stored
datum is erased, and the new datum is stored. Observe that an input
datum is in complementary form, and that the stored datum is also in
complementary form.

Truth tables for the RS latches depicted in Fig. 3-1 show that a
complementary input signal does not necessarily have to be applied. In
other words, a 0,0 input signal may be applied—and the RS latch does

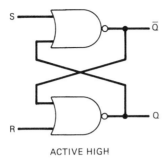

S	R	Q	Q̄
1	0	1	0
0	1	0	1
0	0	Hold	
1	1	invalid	

ACTIVE HIGH

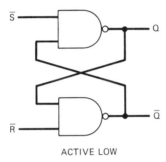

S̄	R̄	Q	Q̄
1	0	0	1
0	1	1	0
0	0	Hold	
1	1	invalid	

ACTIVE LOW

Note: An RS latch is "set" when its Q output is logic-high. The latch is "reset"
when its Q̄ output is logic-high. In the NOR-gate version, the "set"
condition corresponds to S = 1, R = 0. (Q is logic-high when S is
logic-high.) On the other hand, in the NAND-gate version, the "set"
condition corresponds to S̄ = 0, R̄ = 1. (Q is logic-high when S̄ is
logic-low.) In turn, the NOR-gate version is said to be an "active-high"
latch; whereas, the NAND-gate version is said to be an "active-low"
latch. This active-low response is denoted by symbolizing the inputs as
"NOT-S" and "NOT-R."

Fig. 3-1. Two arrangements of the basic RS latch.

not respond; the latch simply remains in its prevailing state. Note,
however, that a 1,1 input signal is invalid, or "forbidden." The reason for
this is that a 1,1 input triggers opposing circuit actions in the RS latch,
with the result that the prevailing state may or may not change,
depending upon component and device tolerances. Therefore, a 1,1 input
signal is never applied to an RS latch (at least, in normal operation).

Next, observe the active-high and active-low RS latch implementations with **OR-NOT** and **NEGATED-OR** gates depicted in Fig. 3-2.
Analysis of the circuit action will show that when a logic-high input is

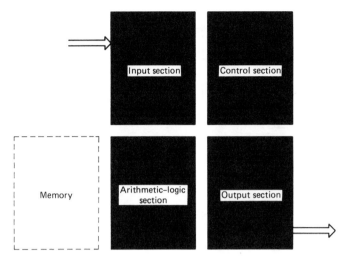

Chart 3-1

Microprocessor Sections

1. *Input Section* accepts data and instructions; in a microcomputer, the data and instructions originate from a keyboard.

2. *Memory Section* may be internal or external, or both; the microprocessor may contain a small memory which is supplemented by a large external memory. Microcomputer operation is based on a program stored in the memory.

3. *Control Section* automatically determines the sequence of data processing operations.

4. *Arithmetic-Logic Section* performs the required data processing operations.

5. *Output Section* drives peripheral devices such as video modules, printers, etc.

applied to the S line of the active-high latch, its Q output will go logic-high. On the other hand, when a logic-low input is applied to the S line of the active-low latch, its Q output will go logic-high.

Note also that an active-high latch will function as an active-low latch if its Q output is treated as a $\overline{Q}$ output, and its $\overline{Q}$ output is treated as a Q output. When this is done, we indicate the S input by $\overline{S}$, and indicate the R input by $\overline{R}$, as a reminder that the configuration now has active-low function. In other words, there is no "hardware" or interconnection distinction between an active-high latch and an active-low latch—it is only a designation of operating mode.

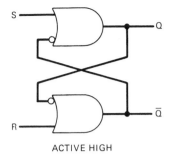

S	R	Q	Q̄
1	0	1	0
0	1	0	1
0	0	Hold	
1	1	invalid	

ACTIVE HIGH

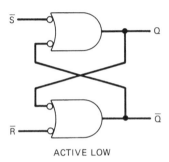

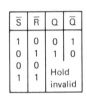

S̄	R̄	Q	Q̄
1	0	0	1
0	1	1	0
0	0	Hold	
1	1	invalid	

ACTIVE LOW

Note: Active-high and active-low RS latches may be configured as shown above. Observe that the active-high latch could also be configured from a pair of A NAND-NOT B GATES. An active-low RS latch may also be configured from a pair of A AND-NOT B gates.

Fig. 3-2. Active-high and active-low RS latch implementations with OR-NOT and NEGATED-OR gates.

Experimental Project

A connection diagram for an experimental RS latch is shown in Fig. 3-3. It employs two of the gates in a 7402 quad two-input NOR-gate IC package. The other two gates are unused at this time. Although not shown in the diagram, each of the NOR gates is connected to V_{CC} and is connected to Gnd inside of the IC package. The current drain is less than 30 mA under any condition of operation, and any small 5-volt power supply may be used.

The following experiments may be made:

1. Connect the R input to Gnd, and connect the S input to V_{CC}. Measure the Q and $\overline{Q}$ output voltages with a dc voltmeter.

2. Connect the S input to Gnd, and connect the R input to V_{CC}. Measure the Q and $\overline{Q}$ output voltages with a dc voltmeter.

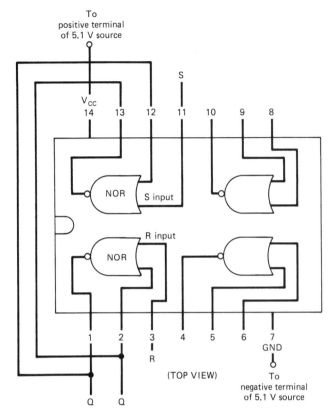

Fig. 3-3. Connection diagram for an experimental RS latch.

Note: A quad two-input NOR-gate IC package such as the Radio Shack 276-1811 may be used. This is the type 7402 TTL NOR gate. The RS latch may be easily constructed on an experimenter's socket, such as the Radio Shack 276-174. Do not use excessive V_{CC} voltage, or the NOR gates may be damaged.

3. Connect the R input to Gnd, and let the S input "float." Measure the Q and $\overline{Q}$ voltages, and measure the "float" voltage at the S input.

4. Let both the R input and the S input "float." Measure the Q and $\overline{Q}$ voltages. Explain the reason for your experimental findings.

Consider next the basic D latch depicted in Fig. 3-4. It is the first step in elaboration of the RS latch. Like the basic RS latch, a D latch is a simple logic storage element. If a logic-high input is applied, this datum is stored in complementary form—the Q output goes logic-high, and the

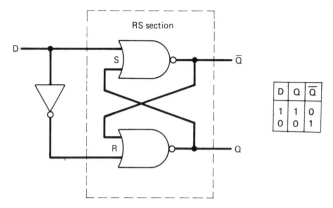

Note: A D (data-input) latch comprises an RS latch with an inverter across its
input terminals. In turn, the D latch operates with only one input
terminal. The drive signal applied to the S input (D input) is
automatically inverted and applied to the R input. In turn, a D latch has
no invalid condition, since a 1,1 input cannot be applied. Neither can a
0,0 input be applied.

Fig. 3-4. Basic D latch arrangement.

$\overline{Q}$ output goes logic-low. Next, if a logic-low input is applied, the stored
datum is erased: the Q output goes logic-low, and the $\overline{Q}$ output goes
logic-high.

Gated Latches

Microprocessors employ various forms of gated latches. A gated latch
(Fig. 3-5), has a gated or strobed input that provides a "window" for data
entry. A strobed input functions to lock out any data that may be present
on the D line, except for the brief duration of strobe pulse. This latch is
called a transparent latch because its Q output follows the D input for the
duration of the gate or strobe pulse. When this control pulse is wide, it is
termed a gating pulse; on the other hand, a comparatively narrow control
pulse is called a strobe pulse.

We say that the data on the D line in Fig. 3-5 is strobed into the latch.
The gated input section is frozen except for the duration of the strobe
pulse. Desired data is called valid data; this valid data will be admitted to
the latch when the gate line is driven logic-high. On the other hand,
undesired data (invalid data) is rejected or frozen out from the latch when
the gate line is driven logic-low. A transparent latch has the advantage
that a single D line can be used to feed more than one latch when the
strobe pulses are suitably staggered.

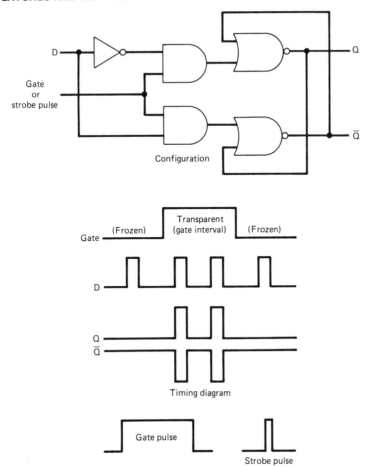

Fig. 3-5. Basic gated (transparent) latch.

Flip-Flops and Clocks

Microprocessors employ both latches and flip-flops. The basic RS latch, or the basic D latch, is not a flip-flop because it is an asynchronous device (it is unclocked). That is, a latch functions at arbitrary times, whenever data pulses may be inputted. On the other hand, we will see that a flip-flop is a synchronous device; it is clocked, and it can change state only on arrival of a clock pulse.* Clock pulses are basically square waves;

---

*A clock pulse theoretically has a rectangular waveshape. In practice, however, the pulses may become distorted in various ways.

they may have a very low repetition rate, as in a scanner-monitor radio, or they may have a very high repetition rate, as in a microcomputer.

Note that the simple arrangement depicted in Fig. 3-6 operates as a flip-flop, inasmuch as the RS latch function is locked in step with the clock input. This is an active-low configuration; the R and S outputs can be complemented only while the clock is logic-low. Note the similarity between the circuits in Figs. 3-5 and 3-6; if the gate or strobe pulse in Fig. 3-5 were replaced by a clock signal, the latch would then be termed a flip-flop. In other words, a gate pulse may occur at any time; whereas, a clock input is a steady square-wave signal.

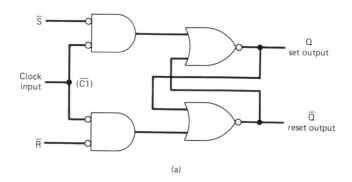

(a)

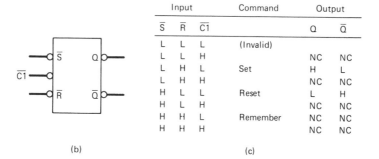

Input			Command	Output	
$\overline{S}$	$\overline{R}$	$\overline{C1}$		Q	$\overline{Q}$
L	L	L	(Invalid)		
L	L	H		NC	NC
L	H	L	Set	H	L
L	H	H		NC	NC
H	L	L	Reset	L	H
H	L	H		NC	NC
H	H	L	Remember	NC	NC
H	H	H		NC	NC

(b)   (c)

NC = no change

Note: The inversion bars over R, S, and CI denote that these inputs are active-low.

Fig. 3-6. Basic clocked RS flip-flop arrangement. (a) Logic diagram; (b) flip-flop symbol; (c) truth table.

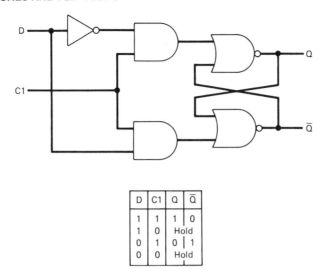

D	C1	Q	Q̄
1	1	1	0
1	0	Hold	
0	1	0	1
0	0	Hold	

Note: This arrangement is active-high. It is very similar to the gated transparent latch depicted in Fig. 3-5. The technical distinction between them is that the transparent latch is controlled by a gating signal; whereas, the clocked D flip-flop is controlled by a clock signal.

Fig. 3-7. Basic clocked D flip-flop arrangement.

It is a small step from the clocked RS flip-flop to the clocked D flip-flop, as seen in Fig. 3-7. Note that if an inverter is placed in series with the clock line, the clock signal becomes active-low. If an inverter is placed in series with the D line, the data signal becomes active-low. Thus, the basic circuit can be slightly modified to operate with the data line active-high and the clock active-low, or with the data line active-low and the clock active-high.

Master-Slave Flip-Flops

Master-slave flip-flops are important building blocks in microprocessor systems. With reference to Fig. 3-8, a master-slave flip-flop contains two gated latches which are clocked. The master flip-flop accepts data from the R and S lines while Clk (Clock) 1 is logic-high; during this time the slave flip-flop is isolated. Next, the slave flip-flop accepts data from the master flip-flop while Clk 2 is logic-high; during this time the master flip-flop is isolated.

Note that Clk 2 is called a subordinate clock; the Clk-2 signal is obtained by passing the Clk-1 signal through an inverter. In turn, the Clk-2 signal is the complement of the Clk-1 signal. An important

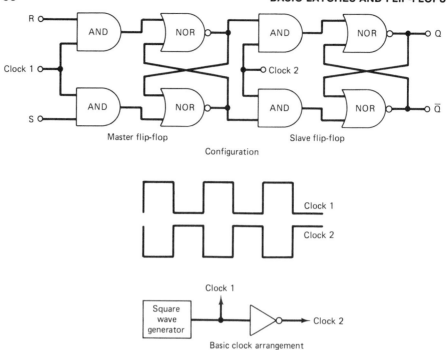

Fig. 3-8. Basic RS flip-flop (master-slave clocked latches).

Note: To follow the circuit action of the RS master-slave flip-flop, assume that
both latches start (are initialized) with their Q outputs logic-low. When
Clk 1 goes logic-high, the master latch will set if S = 1 and R = 0. At this
time, Clk 2 is logic-low, and data cannot be transferred into the slave
latch. Next, when Clk 1 goes logic-low, Clk 2 goes logic-high, and the
data from the master latch is transferred into the slave latch; the slave's
Q output goes logic-high. Since Clk 1 is logic-low at this time, new data
cannot be loaded into the master latch. However, when Clk 1 again
goes logic-high, data may be loaded into the master latch, and the
foregoing cycle is repeated.

operating mode of this master-slave flip-flop is as an RS toggle (RST)
flip-flop (Fig. 3-9). This is the basic toggle (T) flip-flop. It employs
positive feedback whereby the output is complemented on successive
clock pulses.

As seen in the timing diagram, a toggle flip-flop functions not only
as a storage device, but also as a modulus-2 (mod-2) counter; it counts to
two and then recycles. It functions as a divider, inasmuch as it outputs
one pulse for every two input pulses. RST flip-flops may be used in
up-counters and down-counters such as described in the first chapter.
This topic is detailed subsequently.

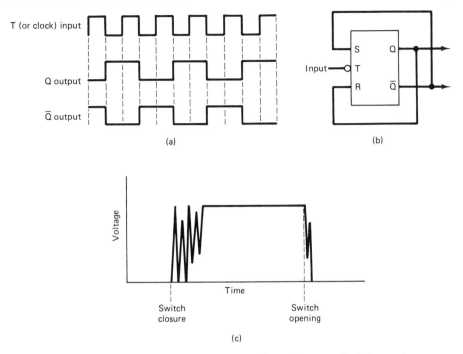

(a)

(b)

(c)

Note: If you attempt to operate a toggle flip-flop with a manual switch, erratic output states will be encountered due to "bounce" inherent in mechanical contacts.

Note: Toggle action is provided only by master-slave flip-flops. In other words, the basic clocked RS flip-flop depicted in Fig. 3-6 cannot be operated in the toggle mode. Toggling becomes available when two basic flip-flops are connected in cascade and clocked from a master clock and a subordinate clock. Observe that the Q-to-R and the $\overline{Q}$-to-S feedback connections in the diagram operate to condition the R and S inputs as required for toggle action.

Fig. 3-9. Basic toggle (T) flip-flop. (a) Timing diagram; (b) configuration of the RST FF; (c) typical mechanical "bounce" contact waveform.

JK Flip-Flops

Microprocessors employ JK flip-flops in various subsections; a typical configuration is shown in Fig. 3-10. (The J input corresponds to an S input, and the K input corresponds to the R input of an RS flip-flop.) With reference to Fig. 3-8, we observe that the R and S inputs of an RS flip-flop should not both be driven logic-high simultaneously. As previously noted, this would be an invalid or "forbidden" mode of operation—the Q and $\overline{Q}$ outputs would be unpredictable.

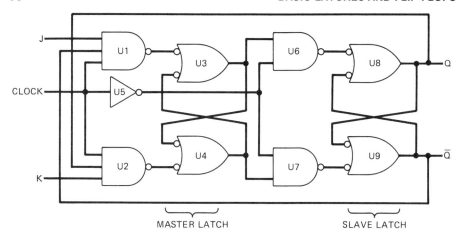

MASTER LATCH　　　　　　　　SLAVE LATCH

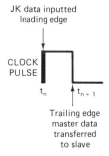

Inputs at t_n		Output at t_{n+1}
J	K	Q_{n+1}
0	0	Q_n
0	1	0
1	0	1
1	1	$\overline{Q}_n$

Note: Edge triggering (as contrasted to simple level triggering) is accomplished by configuring the gate input circuitry so that the master latch is locked out from the J and K lines except for a brief instant as the clock goes high. This narrow "window" results from a transient propagation delay that occurs in the gate input circuitry for the master latch. The slave latch is locked out from the master-latch outputs at t_n. However, the gates to the slave latch are opened at t_{n+1}, and the master-latch output data is then transferred into the slave latch. These circuit actions are explained in greater detail subsequently.

Fig. 3-10. Typical configuration for a JK flip-flop (*Courtesy Hewlett-Packard*).

On the other hand, the JK flip-flop depicted in Fig. 3-10 is free from this limitation; it cannot have an invalid output, even if its J and K inputs are driven logic-high simultaneously. This is a clocked master-slave configuration. As seen in the truth table, if the J and K inputs are both held logic-high, the Q and $\overline{Q}$ outputs toggle in response to the clock signal. This JK toggle arrangement is in very wide use.

Note the conventions that are used in the JK truth table (Fig. 3-10). These conventions denote whether the output referred to occurs before or after the leading edge of the clock waveform. The time before the clock edge is called t_n, and the time after the clock edge is called t_{n+1}. Similarly, the state of the Q output before the clock edge is termed Q_n, and the state of the Q output after the clock edge is termed Q_{n+1}. If the J and K inputs are both 0 before the clock edge, the Q_{n+1} output after the clock edge will be the same as before, or Q_n. On the other hand, if the J and K inputs are both at logic 1, the Q_{n+1} output after the clock edge will be $\overline{Q}_n$; this is the toggle-mode operation of the JK flip-flop.

Observe that the leading (positive) edge-triggered flip-flop in Fig. 3-10 can be converted into a trailing (negative) edge-triggered flip-flop by inserting an inverter in series with the clock input line. Distinction between these two modes of operation is shown in logic diagrams by the symbolism seen in Fig. 3-11. In other words, a "triangle" at the clock input denotes edge-triggering, and positive edge action. However, if the "triangle" is preceded by a "bubble," edge-triggering is denoted with negative edge action.

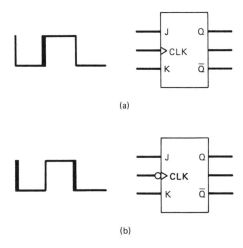

(a)

(b)

Note: The leading edge of the clock waveform is variously termed the rising edge or the positive edge (positive-going edge). The lagging edge of the clock waveform is variously termed the falling edge, the trailing edge, or the negative edge (negative-going edge).

An ideal clock pulse has instantaneous rise and instantaneous fall. On the other hand, practical clock pulses have finite rise and fall times. Excessive rise and/or fall time can be a trouble symptom.

Fig. 3-11. Edge-triggered flip-flop clock-input conventions. (a) Positive edge-triggered flip-flop; (b) negative edge-triggered flip-flop.

By way of comparison, a level-triggered flip-flop inputs data from the J and K lines as long as the clock remains logic-high. In turn, the data on the J and K lines must be valid all the time that the clock is high. This means that the level-triggered flip-flop "uses up" 50 percent of the clock time. A level-triggered flip-flop is sometimes called a one's-catching flip-flop, because false response will occur in case the data on the J and K lines does not remain valid for the entire time that the clock is high.

On the other hand, an edge-triggered flip-flop inputs data from the J and K lines only for the duration of the leading edge in the clock waveform. This is typically a 12-ns interval. Thus, if a 2-MHz clock is used, the edge-triggered flip-flop "uses up" only 5 percent of the clock time, approximately. This is only 0.1 of the time required for loading a level-triggered flip-flop.

Preset and Clear Functions

Many flip-flops are provided with preset and clear functions, as exemplified in Fig. 3-12. A preset line is sometimes called a direct-set line; a clear line is sometimes called a direct-reset line. In this example, the $\overline{S}_D$ line is an active-low preset function; the $\overline{R}_D$ line is an active-low clear function. Observe that when the $\overline{S}_D$ line is driven logic-low, Q will go logic-high, and $\overline{Q}$ will go logic-low. Conversely, when the $\overline{R}_D$ line is driven logic-low, $\overline{Q}$ will go logic-high and Q will go logic-low.

Note particularly that the preset and clear functions are asynchronous, whereas the master and slave sections are synchronous circuits (a clock signal is ordinarily applied at T). The practical result is that the preset input or the clear input takes precedence over the states of A and B, and of C and D. In other words, the flip-flop can be set or reset at any arbitrary time, and independently of the clock. This is just another way of saying that the preset and clear lines will "force" the flip-flop to $Q = 1$ or to $Q = 0$, without regard to the prevailing states of the flip-flop gates.

Troubleshooting Considerations

As previously noted, the clock usually operates at high frequency in a microprocessor system. Although this is a matter of no concern in some troubleshooting procedures, it can make other troubleshooting procedures impractical or impossible. In turn, it is sometimes desirable to stop the clock, or at least to slow it down. To stop the clock, the troubleshooter merely disconnects the clock line from the clock oscillator. In turn, the clock line is connected to ground for a logic-low test, or to V_{CC} for a logic-high test.

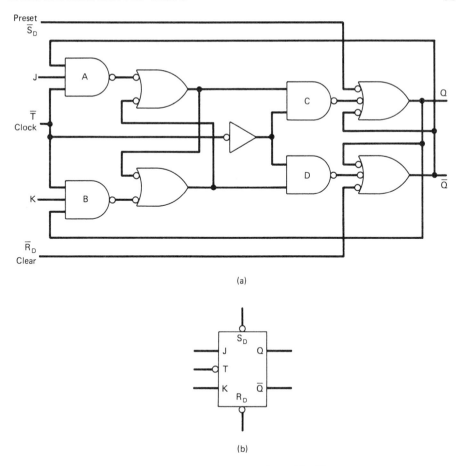

(a)

(b)

Note: The preset line is active-low, and is indicated by $\overline{S}_D$ in the diagram. However, the preset line is indicated by S_D in the logic symbol. An inversion bar is not placed over S_D in the logic symbol because the indication is inside the symbol (beyond the inversion "bubble"). In other words, a 0 on the preset line becomes a 1 past the "bubble." Similarly, the toggle or clock terminal is indicated by $\overline{T}$ in the diagram, but is indicated by T in the logic symbol.

Fig. 3-12. JK flip-flop with preset and clear functions. (a) Configuration; (b) logic symbol.

To slow down the clock, the troubleshooter disconnects the clock line from the clock oscillator and drives the clock line from a clock subber. Specialized clock subbers may be used, or a square-wave generator that provides positive-going output will serve satisfactorily. A specialized clock subber usually provides subordinate clock output. However, in the case of a general-purpose square-wave generator, the troubleshooter may

Voltage-based Tests	DC and/or AC voltage measurements with a voltmeter. Stimulus-response tests with a digital probe and pulser.
Current-based Tests	Stimulus-response tests with a current tracer and logic pulser. IR drop measurements with a microvoltmeter.
Resistance-based Tests	Resistance measurements with an ohmmeter or from voltage/current ratios. Preliminary tests with a continuity checker.
Temperature-based Tests	Temperature measurements with a temperature probe and DVM. Often evaluated on a comparison basis.
Activity-based Tests	Presence or absence of digital activity checked with logic probe, pulser, current tracer, logic clip, or logic comparator.
Substitution Tests	IC interchange or replacement (if mounted in sockets). IC card interchange or replacement. Peripheral replacement tests. Interconnect cable substitution.

Note: In addition to determination of the presence or absence of digital activity, input/output relations are checked with respect to device truth tables. Activity-based tests may also include diagnostic programs. Troubleshooting on the design level generally employs data domain analyzers. Simulation techniques are also utilized.

Note: Data domain analyzers (logic analyzers) are CRT devices that connect into computer circuitry and display data flow in rows and columns of 1's and 0's. In turn, the troubleshooter sees how the system sections run, or what happens when they malfunction. Logic simulation employs simplified circuitry to model the operational channels of complex circuitry, and thereby provide an economical implementation for evaluation tests and design-level troubleshooting.

Fig. 3-13. Overview of digital troubleshooting approaches.

need to use a supplementary inverter if a subordinate clock waveform is required. (See also Figs. 3-13 and 3-14.)

It was noted in the previous chapter that you should guard against possible burns by avoiding "finger tests" of IC operating temperatures on microcomputer circuit boards. However, if you have a DVM with an accessory temperature probe available, this instrument can provide very helpful preliminary troubleshooting data (particularly on a comparative basis). Note that below-normal operating temperatures indicate trouble, just as do above-normal operating temperatures.

Artificial Intelligence

Artificial intelligence denotes performance of functions by a computer which are normally associated with human intelligence, such as learning, reasoning, adapting, self-correction, and automatic improve-

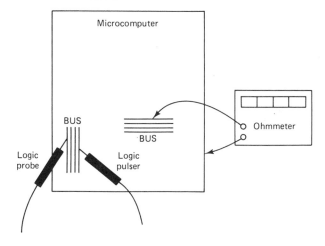

Note: An ohmmeter makes passive tests of bus circuitry. In other words, the V$_{CC}$ supply voltage is turned off when resistance measurements are made. On the other hand, a logic pulser and logic probe make active tests of bus circuitry. The V$_{CC}$ supply voltage is turned on when activity is checked with a logic probe and pulser.

Fig. 3-14. Active tests versus passive tests.

ment. This capability is essentially in a research stage at this time. All of these functions can be modeled to some extent; for example, when a computer adds a pair of numbers, this electronic data processing is a model of (is analogous to) human calculation of a sum.

Although mathematicians can discover new mathematical theorems, even the most advanced computers have been unable to discover new concepts. Computers perform logical operations; however, no computer has been able to develop a new and previously unknown logical operation. A computer can be programmed to play an unbeatable game of checkers, if given the choice of first move. A computer can also be programmed to play a respectable game of chess.

Because a computer can only model mathematical logic, for example, the computer has no intelligence in the human sense of the term. "Intelligent oscilloscopes" and "intelligent terminals" can perform involved calculations with extreme rapidity. However, these are rote operations; thus far, no intelligent terminal has been designed which can perform non-rote human thinking assignments.

It is sometimes said that a computer is intelligent when it calculates the value of pi to more decimal places than ever before. However, this is fundamentally another rote operation—the computer is merely following the step-by-step instructions that have been programmed for it. Again, it is sometimes said that a computer is intelligent when it applies axioms in a heuristic program to prove a theorem. (Heuristics denotes exploratory problem-solving methods in which solutions are achieved through evaluation of the progress made toward the final result.)

Heuristic programs are comparatively long and elaborate. They comprise a set of instructions that simulate the steps followed by mathematicians in their approach to similar problems. The central feature of a heuristic program is a trial-and-error (trial-and-success) processing of the problem. The program includes lines that define "error" and "success." Thus, the computer is not intelligent in the sense that the programmer is intelligent.

Troubleshooting Note

A "bounce" trouble symptom is occasionally encountered in a microcomputer keyboard. This means that when a key is pressed, two or more characters are printed, instead of a single character. When this malfunction occurs, a mechanical fault is first suspected. As an illustration, keys such as utilized with the classical TRS-80 Model I have a pair of contacts located beneath the keybutton. If grime, cigarette ashes, or other foreign substance works its way into the keyway, "bounce" is likely to occur.

The keybutton (keycap) in the exemplified microcomputer can be "popped off" with the aid of a paper clip with its end bent into a hook. The key contacts are thereby exposed, and can be cleaned with a cotton swab moistened with a spray lubricant such as a TV tuner cleaner fluid. Since the contacts are comparatively delicate, application of excessive force should be avoided. When the keycap is replaced, the "bounce" trouble symptom will probably have disappeared.

It is good practice to install a microcomputer in a dust-free location, and to cover the keyboard when it is not in use. Note also that if a book or ash tray happens to drop on the keyboard, damage to the key contacts can be anticipated. It is also good practice to make a habit of striking keys directly from above—not at an acute angle. If a key is struck from an angle, marginal contact may occur, with resulting "bounce."

Note that capacitive switches are also used in keyboards; this type of switch is bounce-free. In most cases, the keybuttons cannot be "popped out," and damage can occur if excessive force is applied in an attempt to remove a keybutton. This is just another way of saying that the service data should be consulted in advance.

Counters and
Associated Circuitry

Basic Microprocessing Devices * Synchronous Versus Asynchronous Counters * Microprocessor Subsections * Experimental Project * Synchronous and Asynchronous Down-Counters * Even- and Odd-Mod Counters * Programmable Counter * BCD Counter * 2421 Counter * Troubleshooting Notes

Basic Microprocessing Devices

We have seen that gates are the fundamental microprocessor building blocks, followed by latches and flip-flops. Counters are also extensively used in microprocessor systems. A prominent example is the program counter in a microcomputer, as depicted in Chart 4-1. The program counter is the "conductor" that "orchestrates" microprocessor data processing. The accumulator in Chart 4-1 is also a type of counter; its activity is directed from the program counter.

Synchronous Versus Asynchronous Counters

It was noted in Chapter 1 how a counter can add or subtract and store sums or differences. Either asynchronous or synchronous counters may be utilized. A basic arrangement for a four-bit ripple-carry binary up-counter is shown in Fig. 4-1. This is an asynchronous configuration (it is unclocked). The pulses to be counted are applied to the clock-input terminal of the first JK master-slave flip-flop. In turn, the Q output from the first flip-flop is fed to the clock input of the second flip-flop, and so on.

MICROPROCESSOR SUBSECTIONS

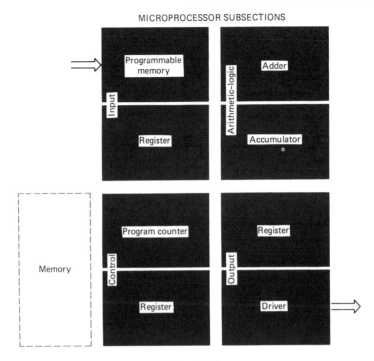

Chart 4-1

Microprocessor Subsections

1. *Programmable Memory* receives binary data from a keyboard or equivalent source.

2. *Register* provides temporary storage of binary data pending utilization.

3. *Program Counter* reads out the stored program word by word as prearranged.

4. *Register* provides temporary storage; most of the activity on the bus lines consists of data transfer from one register to another.

5. *Adder* processes data read out from memory; it adds binary numbers.

6. *Accumulator* adds one sum to a following sum to form the total sum.

7. *Register* provides temporary storage under direction of the control section.

8. *Driver* energizes peripherals such as a video monitor, printer, etc.

Observe that the up-counter also functions as a frequency divider. Thus, FF1 outputs one pulse for every two input pulses; FF2 outputs one pulse for every four input pulses; FF3 outputs one pulse for every eight input pulses; and so on. This configuration is called a ripple-carry counter because a carry bit lags the input pulse, and the final readout is not obtained until ripple carry is completed. As an

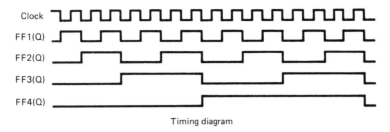

Timing diagram

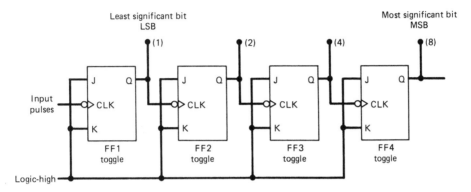

Note: This is an asynchronous up-counter. It is unclocked, although it will count clock pulses if the input is connected to a clock line. The FF clock inputs are used as trigger inputs to the toggles.

Note: This arrangement is also called a mod-16 (modulo-16 or modulus-16) counter because it sequences through 16 states. It may also be termed a $2 \times 2 \times 2 \times 2$ counter, because each flip-flop sequences through two states.

Note: Binary numbers are conventionally written with the most significant bit in the lefthand place; for example, 1 is the MSB in the binary number 1000. However, counter circuitry is commonly drawn with the most significant FF in the right-hand position. Accordingly, the binary number 1000 would read out 0001 in a counter diagram. The reader must keep in mind that readouts are "backward" in conventional counter diagrams.

Fig. 4-1. Basic arrangement for a four-bit ripple-carry binary up-counter.

illustration, if the readout is 0111, and a pulse is inputted, a carry bit from FF1 must ripple through FF2 and FF3 and into FF4 before the readout is finalized. This is the type of counter that was noted in Chapter 1 for binary addition.

Consider next the four-bit synchronous binary up-counter depicted in Fig. 4-2. A synchronous counter is configured to operate in step

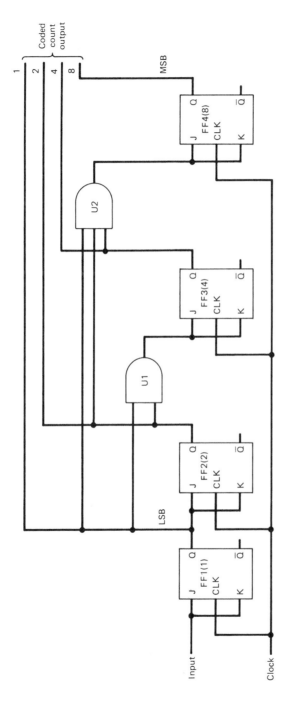

Fig. 4-2. A basic configuration for a four-bit synchronous binary up-counter.

Note: Level-triggered flip-flops are used in this example, although edge-triggered flip-flops could be utilized, as in Fig. 4-1. Master-slave flip-flops are required in either case, to obtain toggle action. Observe that the J and K inputs may be either logic-low or logic-high in the synchronous flip-flop, whereas the J and K inputs are continuously maintained logic-high in the asynchronous flip-flop. Recall that when the J and K inputs are both logic-low, the Q and Q̄ outputs do not toggle; the flip-flop remains in its previous state although it is being clocked.

Note: FF4 outputs the MSB. In this example, the MSB has a weight of 8. If only two FF's were employed in the counter, FF2 would output the MSB, and the MSB would have a weight of 2. Weight and significant position are unrelated characteristics—the most significant bit is outputted by the final FF in a counter, regardless of the weight that might be assigned to this bit.

Note: A counter is an example of sequential logic, whereas its individual gates are examples of combinational logic. In other words, the output states of a counter depend upon its previous inputs; however, the output state of a gate depends only upon its present inputs.

70

with clock pulses, and also to change the state of all flip-flops simultaneously (instead of ripple state changes), thereby providing much faster counter action. In a synchronous counter, the output from each flip-flop is connected to all more-significant-bit inputs via gates. Each gate selectively determines when each MSB flip-flop is to change state (toggle) on the next clock pulse. In turn, all flip-flops can change state simultaneously, without waiting for a ripple carry.

Note that a small setup time is required at the input to FF1 in Fig. 4-2. In other words, the master-slave flip-flop cannot accept data while the clock is low. Although the flip-flop accepts data as soon as the clock goes high, this data must not be changed (must remain valid) as long as the clock is high. Otherwise, a false count will result. Thus, the setup time in this example is equal to the time that the clock is high.

Setup time is also involved in the operation of the counter depicted in Fig. 4-1, although this setup time is comparatively short. Since edge-triggered flip-flops are used, the setup time is roughly equal to the rise time of the clock-signal trailing edge. However, for the data to be valid, it must be applied to the input terminal slightly before the clock edge arrives. Thus, if a flip-flop is rated for 10 ns setup time, the input data should lead the clock edge by at least 10 ns.

Note in passing that we will sometimes encounter $J\overline{K}$ flip-flops, as shown in Fig. 4-3. This device is the same as a JK flip-flop with an inverter included in series with the $\overline{K}$ input. In turn, it has the same function as a JK flip-flop, provided that the signal on the K line is inverted. Observe, also, that the $J\overline{K}$ flip-flop operates as a D flip-flop if the J and $\overline{K}$ terminals are tied together.

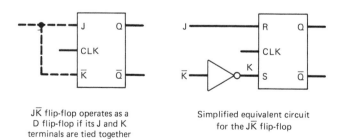

JK̄ flip-flop operates as a
D flip-flop if its J and K
terminals are tied together

Simplified equivalent circuit
for the JK̄ flip-flop

Note: The simplified equivalent circuit is essentially a D flip-flop in which the
$\overline{K}$ input is unconnected to the J input. Thus, it differs from a true D
flip-flop in that two inputs are provided. After the $\overline{K}$ input passes
through the inverter, it becomes a so-called K input which is applied to
the S input of the RS flip-flop.

Fig. 4-3. The JK̄ flip-flop arrangement.

Experimental Project

It is instructive to assemble the asynchronous up-counter arrangement depicted in Fig. 4-4. Note that the flip-flops in the 7476 IC package have separate presets, clears, and clocks. The preset and clear inputs are tied to V_{CC} so that they can be disregarded in this experiment. The J and K inputs are tied to V_{CC} to obtain toggling in response to input pulses. Since the input pulses are applied to the lefthand

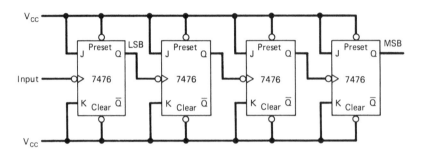

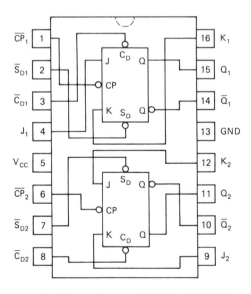

Note: This up-counter is configured from two 7476 dual JK flip-flop packages. These are 16-pin IC packages, as shown in the pinout diagram. The counter may be easily assembled on an experimenter's socket, such as the Archer (Radio Shack) 276-174.

Fig. 4-4. Experimental asynchronous up-counter arrangement.

flip-flop, the readout will be "backwards," with respect to conventional binary-number notation.

Note that the start-up states of the flip-flop are unpredictable. However, the counter will be cleared by the time that 16 input pulses have been applied. The Q outputs can be checked by means of a dc voltmeter, or with a digital-logic probe. Any small 5-volt power supply will serve satisfactorily as a V_{CC} source. The counter can be driven from a low-frequency square-wave generator that provides positive-going output.

In theory, the counter could be operated by connecting a test lead to the input terminal, and then touching the lead to Gnd, removing the lead from Gnd, then touching it to Gnd again, and so on. The floating input "looks" logic-high, and touching the test lead to Gnd drives the input logic-low. In practice, you are likely to find that this manual mode of triggering often results in false counts. The reason for this is that mechanical contacts are likely to make and break erratically (to produce an extremely rapid "burst" of logic-high's and logic-low's).

Synchronous and Asynchronous Down-Counters

Microprocessors also use down-counters, such as shown in Fig. 4-5. This is an example of a four-bit ripple-carry binary down counter. Down-counting is accomplished by feeding the $\overline{Q}$ output from each flip-flop to the Clk input of the following flip-flop. The timing diagram shows the count starting at 15 (1111), and clocking down to 1 (1). However, the starting count (initialization) could be chosen at any value from 15 to 0. As detailed subsequently, initialization is accomplished by means of selective preset and clear signals.

A synchronous down-counter can be configured from the arrangement in Fig. 4-2 by employing the $\overline{Q}$ outputs instead of the Q outputs from the flip-flops. In turn, the timing diagram becomes similar to that shown in Fig. 4-5. Initialization of the synchronous down-counter is accomplished as noted above—by means of selective preset and clear signals. The initialization signals are applied in parallel (broadside) to the flip-flops prior to the counting cycle.

Even- and Odd-Mod Counters

Observe that the four-bit counter depicted in Fig. 4-1 is a mod-16 counter, or, it is an even-mod counter. On the other hand, the mod-

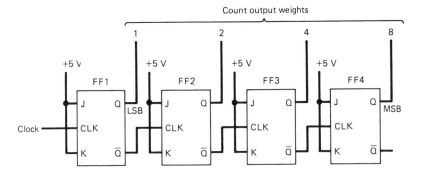

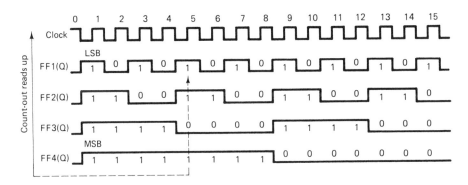

Note: This is a four-bit counter because it has four outputs—the readout contains a maximum of four bits. It is a mod-16 (modulo-16 or modulus-16) counter because it reverts to 0 in the counting sequence after starting at a maximum value of 16-1.

Fig. 4-5. Basic arrangement for an asynchronous four-bit ripple-carry binary down-counter.

3 counter shown in Fig. 4-6(a) is an odd-mod counter. As seen in the truth table, this counter cycles through three readouts. Observe that it would function as a mod-4 counter if the feedback line FF3 $\overline{Q}$ to FF1 J were omitted (J would then float and remain logic-high). However, when FF2 Q goes logic-high, the feedback line conditions FF1 J to prevent toggling on the next clock pulse.

Recall that when J = 0 and K = 1, a JK flip-flop will go to Q = 0 on the next clock pulse. Thus, when FF2 Q goes logic-high, its inputs are conditioned for a Q = 0 output on the next clock pulse, or, the cycle of the mod-3 counter is now terminated, and the count will start anew from FF1 = 0 and FF2 = 0. In practice, the mod-3 counter is usually provided with preset and reset inputs; these are asynchronous functions that override the clock.

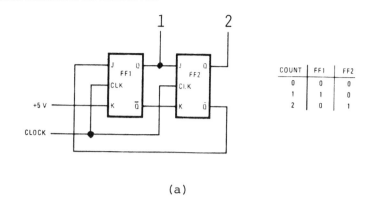

(a)

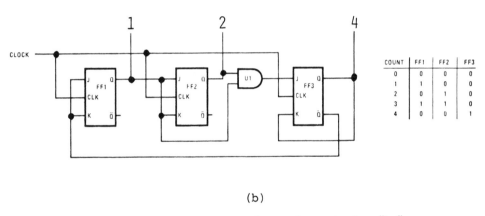

(b)

Note: These are synchronous counters that employ master-slave flip-flops.
      Although level-triggered flip-flops are shown in the diagrams, edge-
      triggered flip-flops may be used. All odd-mod counters are basically
      even-mod counters supplemented with one or more feedback loops.

Fig. 4-6. Odd-modulo counters. (a) Mod-3 configuration; (b)
mod-5 configuration (*Courtesy, Hewlett-Packard*).

Next, with reference to Fig. 4-6(b), we observe that this mod-5
counter is basically a mod-8 counter with two feedback loops. One
loop is from FF3 $\overline{Q}$ to FF1 JK, and the other loop is from FF3 Q
to FF3 K. Note that when FF3 Q goes logic-high (on count 4), feedback
from $\overline{Q}$ FF3 to FF1 JK conditions the FF1 inputs from J = 1 and
K = 1 to J = 0 and K = 0. In turn, FF1 will not change its output
state on the next clock pulse.

Observe also that when the readout is 001, FF3 J is zero, and FF3
K is 1 (via feedback from FF3 Q to FF3 K). As previously noted, when
J = 0 and K = 1, the flip-flop will go to Q = 0 on the next clock

pulse. Accordingly, the cycle of the mod-5 counter is now terminated, and the count will start anew from FF1 = 0, FF2 = 0, and FF3 = 0. Note that AND gate U1 serves the same function in the mod-5 counter as AND-gate U1 in the mod-16 counter depicted in Fig. 4-2.

Mod-7 and mod-11 counter configurations are shown in Fig. 4-7. The mod-7 arrangement employs three feedback loops with three

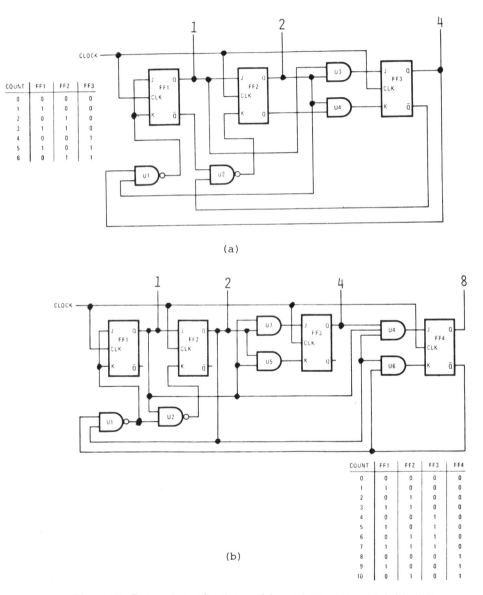

(a)

(b)

Fig. 4-7. Examples of other odd-mod counters. (a) Mod-7 configuration; (b) mod-11 configuration (*Courtesy, Hewlett-Packard*).

more gates in comparison with a mod-5 counter. These circuit actions operate to terminate the count cycle after readout 6 and to return the readout to 000. Note that the mod-11 configuration employs two feedback loops with four flip-flops and six gates. The count cycle terminates after readout 10, with return of the readout to 0000.

Programmable Counter

Microprocessors generally include programmable counters, such as depicted in Fig. 4-8. A programmable counter has facilities for modification of its count cycle by means of a control signal. The most widely used programming signals are related to presetting the counter to a certain readout (thus changing the modulus of the counter), and also to the control of whether the counter will stop at a certain readout or resets and starts its counting cycle anew.

With reference to Fig. 4-8, a typical configuration is shown for a programmable counter with preset inputs. It is basically a 4-bit up-counter that can be preset to any desired count between 0 and 15 via gates U1 through U4, by "enabling" the load signal line (placing it logic-low). For operation as a mod-7 counter, a preset count of 8 is

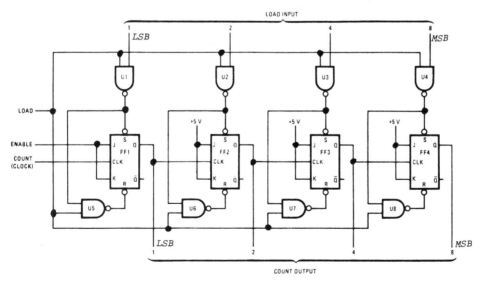

Note: A mod-10 counter is also called a BCD (binary coded decimal) counter. It cycles through 10 states. BCD counters are particularly important in microprocessor systems wherein a decimal count is employed. This topic is detailed subsequently.

Fig. 4-8. Basic configuration for a programmable counter with preset inputs (*Courtesy, Hewlett-Packard*).

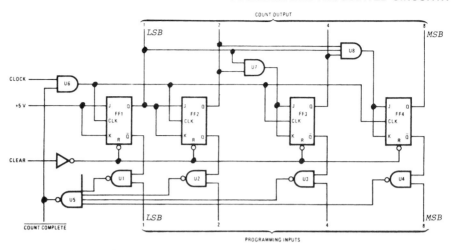

Note: This programmable counter is limited to the up-count mode, and to the 8421 code. For example, other configurations are required to count in the 2421, XS3, or XS3 Gray Codes.

Fig. 4-9. Programmable counter with preselection of final count (*Courtesy, Hewlett-Packard*).

employed and it is allowed to count to 15. Observe that at the count of 15, the counter must be preset to 8 again (prior to the next clock pulse); this is accomplished by means of additional load control circuitry (not shown in the diagram).

Next, a programmable counter configuration that provides preselection of its final readout is depicted in Fig. 4-9. This is fundamentally a synchronous 4-bit up-counter whose modulus can be selected with the programming inputs via gates U1 through U4; however, this programming is accomplished so that the final count (instead of the starting count) is determined. Basically, gates U1 through U4 function to make a digital comparison; when the counter output matches the programming inputs, the clock is stopped and counting ceases. At this point, the Count Complete signal can be utilized to reset the counter, or the readout can be stored for future use.

BCD Counter

As noted previously, binary coded decimal (BCD) counters are of special importance in microprocessor systems. A typical synchronous BCD up-counter configuration is shown in Fig. 4-10. A BCD counter may be either synchronous or asynchronous; the synchronous version is depicted in the diagram. A BCD counter is similar to any 4-bit counter

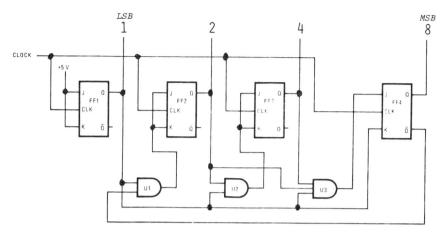

Note: This is a mod-10 counter because it sequences through 10 states.

Fig. 4-10. A binary-coded-decimal counter configuration (*Courtesy, Hewlett-Packard*).

with mod-10 operation. The arrangement in Fig. 4-10 utilizes the 8421 code in an up-counting mode.

Observe that to maintain FF2 in the 0 state on the next clock pulse after the 1001 state, $\overline{Q}$ of FF4 is connected to gate U1. The $\overline{Q}$ output of FF4 is logic 0; thus the J and K inputs to FF2 are logic 0, and FF2 does not change to logic 1 at the next clock pulse edge. Furthermore, to reset FF4 to 0, Q of FF1 is connected directly to K of FF4. In turn, the K input is alternately high and low during the counts of 1 through 6, but the J input of FF4 is continuously low, so that FF4 remains in the 0 state.

Note that at count 7, all inputs to U3 become high, and there is a high signal at both J and K of FF4. Accordingly, with the next clock pulse (count 8), FF4 toggles to the 1 state. FF4 remains in the 1 state after one more clock pulse (count 9), because Q of FF1 is now 0, thus removing the logic 1 from both J and K of FF4. At count 9, Q of FF1 goes to 1 again, and thus FF4 has a high K input although its J input is still low. Consequently, on the next clock pulse, FF4 resets back to the 0 state.

2421 Counter

Microprocessors sometimes employ the 2421 (2′421) code, in addition to the 8421 code. The 8421 code counters are most extensively used because they have the simplest hardware and utilize the flip-flops with maximum efficiency (count to the highest readout with a given number of flip-flops). A 2421 synchronous counter configuration is exemplified in Fig. 4-11. It is a 2421 code counter.

Note that the distinction between the 2421 counter and an 8421 counter is in the gating circuitry between the flip-flops. (Compare Fig.

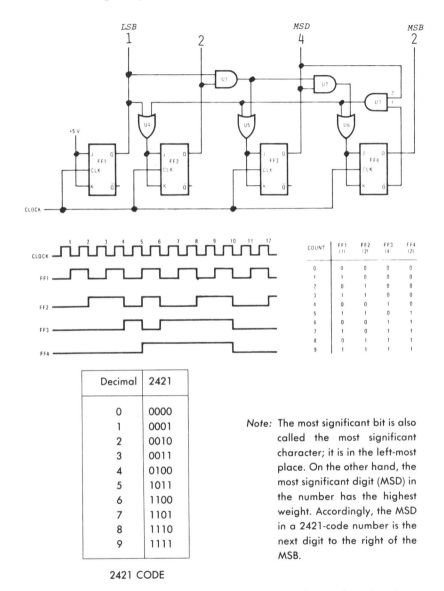

Decimal	2421
0	0000
1	0001
2	0010
3	0011
4	0100
5	1011
6	1100
7	1101
8	1110
9	1111

2421 CODE

Note: The most significant bit is also called the most significant character; it is in the left-most place. On the other hand, the most significant digit (MSD) in the number has the highest weight. Accordingly, the MSD in a 2421-code number is the next digit to the right of the MSB.

Note: This is sometimes called a 2'421 counter to denote that 2' is the MSB, and that 2 is the next least significant bit.

Fig. 4-11. Synchronous 2421 counter configuration (*Courtesy, Hewlett-Packard*).

4-11 with Fig. 4-10.) The 2421 code is a BCD code; however, instead of the MSB place having a weight of 8, the MSB place in the 2421 code has a weight of 2. In turn, decimal 5 has a value of 0101 in straight binary code; whereas, it has a value of 1011 in the 2421 code. In other words, $2+0+2+1 = 5$.

The 2421 code is used when the nine's complement is required by a microprocessor. The nine's complement is obtained by taking the one's complement of the 2421 number. As an illustration, the nine's complement of 4 (0100) is equal to 5 (1011); 1011 is the one's complement of 0100. The nine's complement is sometimes used to perform subtraction with binary adders. The XS3 code (Fig. 4-12) is also used to obtain the nine's complement of a decimal digit; the XS3 code is obtained by adding 3 to the values of the straight (natural) binary code.

The Gray code is also shown in Fig. 4-12. This code is used in microprocessors for analog-to-digital (A-D) conversion. The distinctive feature of the Gray code is that there is only one bit change from

EXCESS 3 CODE	
DECIMAL	BINARY CODE
0	0011
1	0100
2	0101
3	0110
4	0111
5	1000
6	1001
7	1010
8	1011
9	1100

DECIMAL	GRAY CODE $a_3a_2a_1a_0$
0	0000
1	0001
2	0011
3	0010
4	0110
5	0111
6	0101
7	0100
8	1100
9	1101
10	1111
11	1110
12	1010
13	1011
14	1001
15	1000

Note: The XS3 code is the same as the basic binary code except that 3 (11) is added to each basic binary number. Thus, an XS3-code number has an MSB and an LSB; the MSB is also the MSD. On the other hand, the Gray code is not quantitatively related to the basic binary code. A Gray-code number has an MSB and an LSB; however, it has no MSD.

Fig. 4-12. Excess 3 code and Gray code.

one count to the next. This characteristic permits A-D systems to be designed so that the inherent error is limited to one count. Also, 180° ambiguity is eliminated in representation of rotational motion by the Gray code. Note the following terminology used in characterizing codes, and data in general:

1 is called a binary number, or binary digit, or bit

0 is also called a binary number, or binary digit, or bit

10 is an example of a digital word, or word, or bit pattern

1101 is an example of a nibble (four-bit word)

10111010 is an example of a byte (eight-bit word)

Troubleshooting Notes

Counter troubleshooting is facilitated by use of a programmable logic pulser. In other words, the programmable pulser can be set for 1, 17, 125, 251, or other number of output pulses that may be desired.

Logic Probe	A logic probe is applied in a digital circuit to indicate logic-high and logic-low states, bad levels, single pulses, or pulse trains.
Logic Pulser	A logic pulser is a miniature pulse generator that drives high nodes instantaneously low, and drives low nodes instantaneously high.
Current Tracer	A current tracer locates low-impedance circuit faults by sensing changes in magnetic field intensity along conductors carrying digital pulses.
Logic Clip	A logic clip reads the high or low states on all pins of a digital IC simultaneously. It shows if a device is or is not obeying its truth table.
Logic Comparator	A logic comparator checks the response of a suspect IC against that of a known good IC. It provides a comparison quick test.
Oscilloscope	An oscilloscope is used to a comparatively limited extent in digital troubleshooting procedures. However, it finds application in measurements of rise time and in tracking down narrow glitches.
Voltmeter	A voltmeter is another instrument that is used to a comparatively limited extent in digital troubleshooting procedures. However, it finds application in V_{cc} measurement and bad-level measurements.
Ohmmeter	An ohmmeter finds application as a continuity tester. Some modern ohmmeters include built-in logic-probe features. An ohmmeter can also be used in "wipe" tests of TTL digital devices.

Fig. 4-13. Features of basic digital troubleshooting instruments.

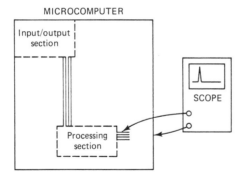

Note: Data processing errors can be caused by spurious pulses called glitches. Glitches result from device defects in most cases. Very narrow glitches are difficult to identify unless a high-performance oscilloscope is used. Logic analyzers sometimes include built-in glitch detectors.

Fig. 4-14. A high-performance oscilloscope is used to track down very narrow glitches.

This saves much time, particularly when high counts need to be verified. In other words, a 129 readout would require 129 operations with a single-shot pulser; whereas, it requires only one programming operation and one application operation when a programmable pulser is used.

Counter troubleshooting is also facilitated by use of a logic clip. This is an indicating device that plugs over an IC, and indicates the logic states at all pins by LED's. It allows up to 16 signals to be observed simultaneously. On the other hand, if a simple logic probe were used, the troubleshooter would have to make 16 separate checks. Much time and effort is thereby saved when checking counter operation. (See also Figs. 4-13 and 4-14.)

External Interference

"Tough dog" troubleshooting situations sometimes result from external interference. As an illustration, a video monitor produces comparatively strong stay fields which can cause erratic operation of nearby logic circuitry. In a typical case history, a microcomputer system malfunctioned when the video monitor was located to the left of the logic unit, although operation was normal when the video monitor was located to the right of the logic unit. Note in passing that large-screen video monitors have more intense stray fields than do small-screen video monitors.

Shift-Register
Circuitry and Operation

Basic Microprocessor Organization * Shift Register
Principles * Weighted Coding * Shift Register Circuitry *
Experimental Project * Feedback Shift Register * Uni-
versal Shift Register * Self Correcting Ring Counter *
Pseudo-Random Binary Sequence Generator * Typical
Microprocessor System Faults

Basic Microprocessor Organization

Basic microprocessor organization is depicted in Fig. 5-1.
Microcomputer organization concerns interconnection of peripheral
equipment to the microprocessor. The microprocessor comprises five
principal sections: input, control, memory, arithmetic, and output
sections. As indicated in the diagram, the arithmetic (or arithmetic-
logic) unit employs shift registers.

Shift-Register Principles

A shift register consists of a series of interconnected flip-flops. In
turn, it has a superficial resemblance to a counter. On the other hand,
shift-register action is fundamentally different from counter action.
When a data bit is entered into the first FF of a shift register, it proceeds
from one FF to the next each time that a clock pulse occurs, as indicated
in Fig. 5-1.

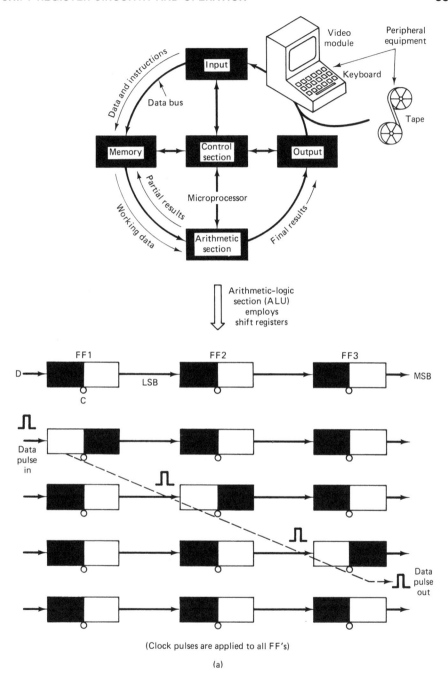

(a)

Note: A typical microcomputer utilizes 80 integrated circuits.

Fig. 5-1(a). Basic microcomputer organization.

Fig. 5-1(b). Typical microcomputer keyboard with keypad.
(*Courtesy, Radio Shack, a Division of Tandy Corporation*).

As previously noted, the weight of a data bit is multiplied by two each time that it is shifted one place to the right. The data bit is stored in the flip-flops until it is clocked out of the most significant FF. Thus, a shift register also functions as a serial memory. This function is as follows:

1. Let all FF's in the shift register have the same weight, 1. In turn, the combined number of 1's in the register represents the stored number.
2. If the register contains two 1 bits, the number 2 has been stored. To store the number 3, one more bit must be entered.
3. To enter the number 3 into the shift register, four clock pulses must be applied, and the D input must be suitably driven, as shown in Fig. 5-2.
4. If the shift register is initially cleared (all FF's reset to 0, the three data bits indicated in Fig. 5-2 will be shifted through the register, and the FF's will have the following logic states at the end of four clock pulses:

    $FF1 = 0$ $FF2 = 1$ $FF3 = 1$ $FF4 = 1$

5. The foregoing readout is $0111 = 3$. Note that this arrangement can store five different numbers: 0, 1, 2, 3, and 4.

Inasmuch as the bits in the foregoing example were loaded one after another and were then shifted from one FF to another, this is an operation of loading serial data; the circuit that accomplishes this operation is called a 4-bit serially loaded shift register (in this example). A shift register may have hundreds of flip-flops; in turn, we may designate a 400-bit serially loaded shift register, for example.

The alternative to serial loading of a shift register is parallel loading, as seen in Fig. 5-2. For parallel loading, a separate line is

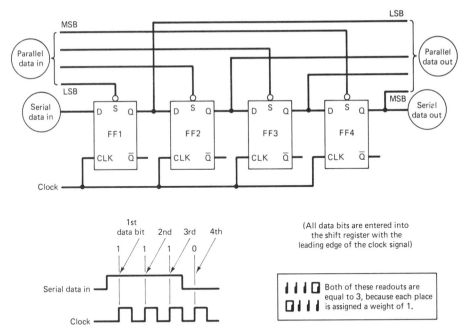

Fig. 5-2. Shifting of data into and out of a register (*Courtesy, Hewlett-Packard*).

connected to the preset input of each FF. In turn, all data bits are simultaneously loaded by setting the pertinent FF's to logic 1 via their preset inputs. This is an asynchronous operation, and is independent of the clock. Note that the data on the preset inputs is called parallel data.

It is evident that just as the data bits can be loaded into the shift register in the parallel mode or in the serial mode, so can the data be read out in the parallel mode or in the serial mode. A parallel readout is accomplished by simultaneously sampling the data at the outputs of each FF in Fig. 5-2. On the other hand, a serial readout is accomplished by shifting the data through the FF's and sampling at the output of FF4.

If data is loaded serially into the register and is read out in parallel, the register is said to be functioning as a serial-to-parallel converter. Conversely, if the data is loaded in parallel into the register and is read out in series, the register is said to be functioning as a parallel-to-serial converter. With reference to Fig. 5-1, either serial data flow or parallel data flow may occur in the data bus.

Weighted Coding

Four bits can be stored in the Fig. 5-2 shift register. Five bits can be stored in the Fig. 5-3 shift register. Unless we employ 1,2,4,8,16 weighting, however, it soon becomes impractical to store larger numbers. An example of weighted coding is shown in the diagram: the number 3 in a weighted shift register becomes equal to 6 when shifted one place to the left. A 5-bit weighted shift register can store

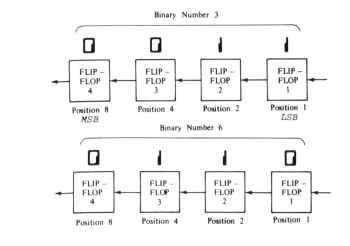

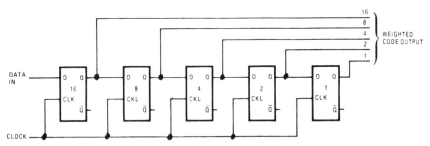

Note: The 8421 binary code has weights that also apply to the binary coded decimal (BCD) code. The BCD code employs 4 bits; the value of these bits corresponds to the value of a corresponding decimal digit from 0 through 9. Eight FF's are used to store a two-digit decimal number in BCD code. For example, decimal number 19 corresponds to binary 10011 and corresponds to BCD 00011001.

Fig. 5-3. Example of weighted coding of flip-flops in a shift register (*Courtesy, Hewlett-Packard*).

any number up to 31, or if we include 0, up to 32 numbers. This compares to six numbers (including 0), if the nonweighted code is used.

Shift-Register Circuitry

As seen in Fig. 5-4, shift registers can be configured from D flip-flops, or from JK flip-flops; they can also be configured from RS flip-flops. In any case, master-slave flip-flops must be used; they may be

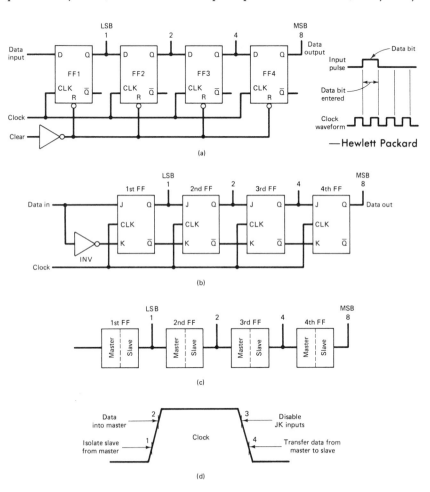

Note: A shift register is an example of sequential logic because its output states depend upon its previous input states. On the other hand, an AND-OR-INVERT gate is an example of combinational logic, since its output state depends only upon its present input state.

Fig. 5-4. Basic shift register. (a) D flip-flop arrangement; (b) JK flip-flop arrangement; (c) flip-flops are master-slave devices; (d) edge-trigger action.

level-triggered, but in most cases are edge-triggered, as exemplified in the diagram. All types of edge-triggered flip-flops have a setup time (in the 10's of nanoseconds) which must be observed. In other words, the data bit must arrive at the data input terminal approximately 10 ns before the clock edge to ensure that valid data will be loaded. This setup time is depicted in Fig. 5-2 as the lag between the clock edge and the leading edge of the serial data waveform.

Experimental Project

An instructive experimental serial-in parallel-out shift-register project is depicted in Fig. 5-5. It employs a pair of type 7474 dual D flip-flops. The shift register can be assembled easily on an experimenter's socket. Observe that each D flip-flop has direct-set and direct-clear inputs; these are asynchronous preset and reset functions. They are active-low, and if permitted to float, will be effectively out of the circuit.

The 7474 flip-flop is a master-slave device and is positive-edge-triggered. A low-frequency square-wave generator with positive-going output may be used to clock the Fig. 5-5 shift register; the outputs can be checked with a logic probe. Observe that the data input will be logic-low if it is connected to ground; it will go logic-high if it is permitted to float. If the data input line is left floating, FF1 will load a 1 on each clock pulse, and FF4 will output a 1 on each clock pulse.

Register action can be followed with static stimulus tests, as follows:

1. Ground the clock line and float the data line.
2. Float the clock line. This loads a 1 into FF1.
3. Ground the clock line. This transfers the 1 from the master section to the slave section of FF1.
4. Ground the data line. This prevents FF1 from loading a new 1 bit.
5. Float the clock line. This loads the 1 from FF1 into FF2.
6. Ground the clock line. This transfers the 1 from the master section to the slave section of FF2.
7. Check the flip-flop output states with a logic probe.
8. Repeat floating and grounding connections of the clock line, and check the flip-flop output states.

Feedback Shift Register

Microprocessors often employ feedback shift registers. A simple configuration is shown in Fig. 5-6. It is also called a ring counter or a timing slot generator. If a digital word is being recirculated in

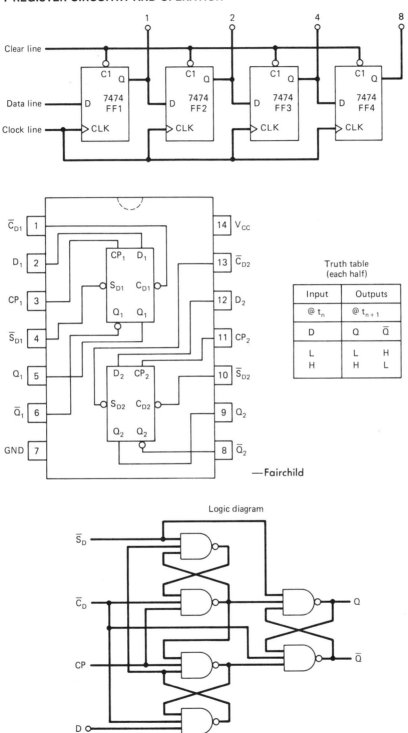

Truth table
(each half)

Input	Outputs	
@ t_n	@ t_{n+1}	
D	Q	$\overline{Q}$
L	L	H
H	H	L

—Fairchild

Logic diagram

Fig. 5-5. Experimental serial-in parallel-out shift register.

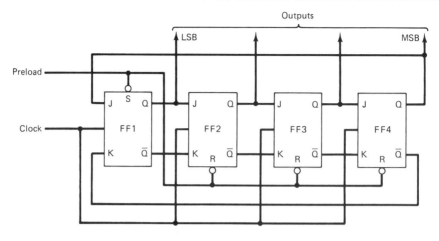

State	Flip-flop 1 2 3 4	
1	1 0 0 0	◄──Preloaded
2	0 1 0 0	
3	0 0 1 0	
4	0 0 0 1	

(Return to State 1)

Note: This feedback shift register (ring counter or timing-slot generator) is a mod-4 counter that cycles 1 bit through 4 states. It outputs four ring words listed in the truth table. This is an example of the basic ring code.

Fig. 5-6. A simple feedback shift-register configuration with preload line and parallel output.

a feedback shift register, it is termed a serial memory or an accumulator, depending upon the associated circuitry. A data bit in a feedback shift register will continue to recirculate as long as the register is clocked, unless the FF's are cleared.

The arrangement in Fig. 5-6 is provided with a preload line. Observe that this line connects to the set input of the first FF, and to the reset inputs of the other three FF's. These are asynchronous control inputs. If the preload line is driven logic-low, FF1 is set to 1, and the other three FF's are reset to 0. Then, when the preload line is held logic-high, the preload 1 bit in FF1 is clocked indefinitely and recirculated through the shift register.

This ring counter or timing-slot generator is often used to control a sequence of events which must occur one after another. As a simple illustration, the scanning sequence in a scanner-monitor radio is determined by the timing slot generator. Ring counters are also employed in timing operations for data processing in microcomputers. This topic is explained in greater detail subsequently. At this time, we will note the ring code which consists of the ring words 0001, 0010, 0100, and 1000 (see the truth table in Fig. 5-6). They are called ring words because they are outputted by the basic ring counter.

Universal Shift Register

Arithmetic operations in microprocessors variously require left-shifting, right-shifting, serial loading/serial unloading, serial loading/parallel unloading, parallel loading/serial unloading, parallel loading/parallel unloading. This flexibility is provided by the universal shift register, exemplified in Fig. 5-7. Thus, a universal shift register provides conversion of data-flow modes; it can operate as a serial-parallel converter, or as a parallel-serial converter.

Master-slave RS flip-flops are utilized in the example of Fig. 5-7. Although the clock inputs to the flip-flops are active-low, the system clock is effectively active-high due to the input NOR gate. Similarly, although the Clear inputs to the flip-flops are active-low, the system Clear signal is effectively active-high due to the input inverter. Observe that when Mode Control S_0 is driven logic-high, the Shift-Left serial input is enabled. Conversely, when Mode Control S_1 is driven logic-high, the Shift-Right serial input is enabled.

Note also that the parallel inputs in Fig. 5-7 are enabled when Mode Controls S_0 and S_1 are both driven logic-low. The parallel outputs are not gated, and are active continually. Observe that when Mode Control S_0 and S_1 are both driven logic-high at the same time, the clock signal is overridden. Effectively, this condition stops the clock for the duration of $S_1 = 1$ and $S_0 = 1$. The Clear function is asynchronous and can be activated at any time, independently of the clock.

Self-Correcting Ring Counter

Microprocessors employ ring counters to sequence other logic circuits or various equipment through specified operations. As an illustration, a ring counter can sequence a machine tool station on an assembly line. Again, it can sequence a digital calculator through the process of addition. Shift registers and counters have various characteristics in common, although they perform distinctive functions.

Observe that if a flip-flop in a ring counter such as shown in Fig. 5-6 becomes erroneously set due to a noise pulse or other anomaly, a "special state" or erroneous sequence is thereby established. This

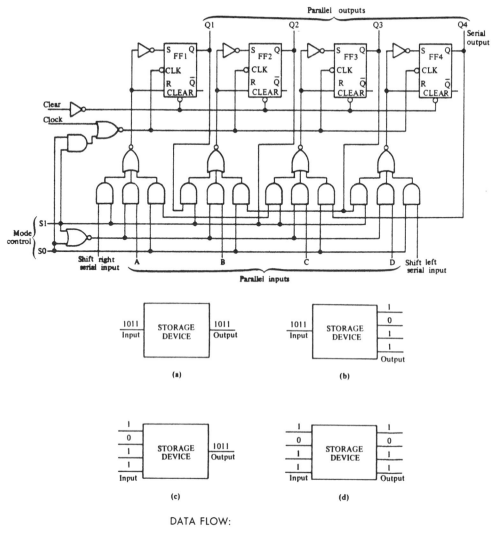

DATA FLOW:

    (a) Serial Input/Serial Output
    (b) Serial Input/Parallel Output
    (c) Parallel Input/Serial Output
    (d) Parallel Input/Parallel Output

Fig. 5-7. Configuration for a universal left-right serial-parallel shift register (*Courtesy, Hewlett-Packard*).

"special state" will continue to recirculate, resulting in system malfunction. Therefore, self-correcting ring counters are of practical interest. This form of counter has a limited period of malfunction if a "special state" occurs, and quickly returns to its correct ring word.

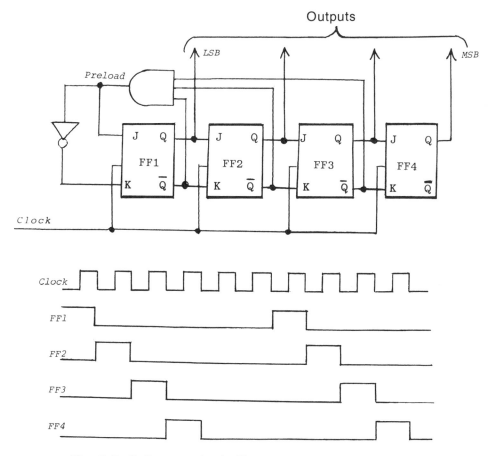

Fig. 5-8. Self-correcting/self-preloading ring counter configuration.

A self-correcting ring counter is depicted in Fig. 5-8. We will note that this is also a self-preloading configuration. In other words, when the readout is 1,000, the $\overline{Q}$ outputs of FF1, FF2, and FF3 are logic-high. In turn, the AND gate loads a 1 into FF1, and the ring-counting cycle resumes on the next clock pulse. In effect, the configuration employs three feedback loops; when all three loops go logic-high, the counter automatically preloads.

Next, suppose that a "special state" happens to arise, and that the ring word 0110 is shifting through the flip-flops. This erroneous ring word will clock through the flip-flops and out of the FF4 Q output until the $\overline{Q}$ outputs of FF1, FF2, and FF3 are all 1's. Thereupon, the AND gate preloads FF1 with a 1, and FF4 Q is (or goes to) 0. At this point, the normal ring-counting action resumes.

Pseudo-Random Binary Sequence Generator

Microprocessor troubleshooting techniques often employ checkouts with pseudo-random binary sequence signals (PRBS signals). A PRBS signal displays the properties of a random output signal, but repeats every 2^n-1 bits (where n is the number of flip-flops in the shift register). In turn, a PRBS generator outputs 2^n-1 states that appear to occur in random order, particularly if n is large. When generating a PRBS signal, the shift register operates in a closed-loop mode wherein the input to the first stage is provided via an XOR feedback path from later stages.

An example of a PRBS generator configuration is shown in Fig. 5-9. It produces all possible 15-bit sequences; since the register is

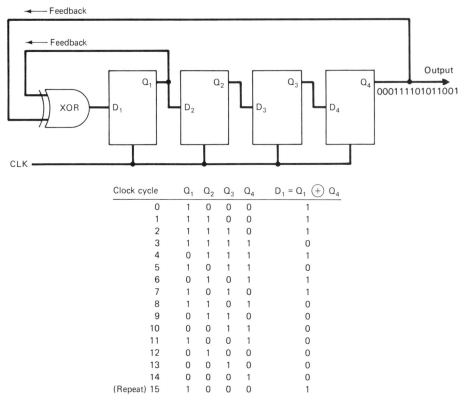

Clock cycle	Q_1	Q_2	Q_3	Q_4	$D_1 = Q_1 \oplus Q_4$
0	1	0	0	0	1
1	1	1	0	0	1
2	1	1	1	0	1
3	1	1	1	1	0
4	0	1	1	1	1
5	1	0	1	1	0
6	0	1	0	1	1
7	1	0	1	0	1
8	1	1	0	1	0
9	0	1	1	0	0
10	0	0	1	1	0
11	1	0	0	1	0
12	0	1	0	0	0
13	0	0	1	0	0
14	0	0	0	1	0
(Repeat) 15	1	0	0	0	1

Note: The XOR gate has a logic-HIGH output if one of its inputs is logic-HIGH and its other input is logic-LOW. The XOR gate has a logic-LOW output if both of its inputs are logic-HIGH, or if both of its inputs are logic-LOW.

Fig. 5-9. Feedback shift register configured to generate a 15-bit PRBS signal.

preloaded ($Q_1 = 1$), a train of 15 zeros is excluded. In other words, the generator provides all possible non-zero 4-bit words in a sequence that repeats indefinitely. Note that an all-zero 4-bit output is excluded because it would have no utility in microprocessor testing.

When a PRBS signal is inputted by a microprocessor, data compression results; this is a display technique that minimizes the time and effort required to examine an entire data record. The PRBS data compression process converts binary words into hexadecimal ("funny hex") words. The characteristic "funny hex" word that appears at a given microprocessor node is called a node signature. A node signature has meaning only with respect to the corresponding node signature in a normally functioning microprocessor system.

This is just another way of saying that if a node signature fails to correspond to the normal node signature, it indicates only that a fault is present. That is, an abnormal node signature provides no diagnostic information, per se. PRBS testing is essentially a go/no-go test technique. For this reason, a "funny hex" character set is used in signature analysis (to avoid confusion with the more traditional hex applications). This "funny hex" character set is: 0, 1, 2, 3, 4, 5, 6, 7, 8, 9, A, B, C, F, H, P, U. By way of comparison, the conventional hex character set is: 0, 1, 2, 3, 4, 5, 6, 7, 8, 9, A, B, C, D, E, F.

A PRBS signal is so-called because it produces predictable patterns that have useful random characteristics. Note that a completely random pattern would have no predictable property; in turn, it could not develop a fixed digital signature such as 27AU at a microprocessor node. Observe next the PRBS generator arrangement shown in Fig. 5-10. It is provided with an input terminal which is used to feed in external data, as from a microprocessor node, and to mix this external data with the PRBS signal in the generator network.

As an illustration, a 1010101000100101 signal from a microprocessor node might be fed into the PRBS generator in Fig. 5-10 and mixed with the feedback signals from Q1 and Q4. This mixture changes the contents of the generator (changes its remainder pattern), and thereby provides a "funny hex" signature. Thus, a normal signal on a microprocessor node might produce the register contents 1100, or a readout of F. On the other hand, if there is a 1-bit error in the signal on the microprocessor node, the register contents would be changed, perhaps to 1011 (a readout of C).

In other words, the normal input signal in this example produces the remainder:

$$Q1 = 1 \quad Q2 = 1 \quad Q3 = 0 \quad Q4 = 0$$

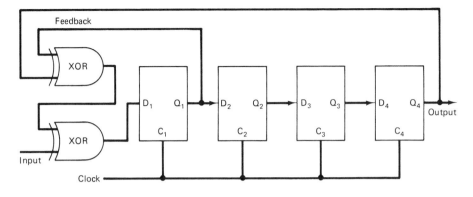

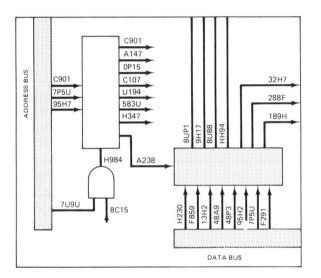

Example of specified "funny hex" signatures for a microprocessor system that has been designed for signature analysis (Courtesy, B&K Precision, a Division of Dynascan Corporation).

Fig. 5-10. Feedback shift register provided with an input terminal for developing a digital signature.

However, when the 1-bit error occurs, the erroneous input signal produces the abnormal remainder:

$$Q1 = 1 \quad Q2 = 0 \quad Q3 = 1 \quad Q4 = 1$$

The "funny hex" outputs from the register are applied to a decoder which in turn energizes 7-segment readout devices, as depicted in Fig. 5-11. Single-bit errors, even in a very long data stream, will always

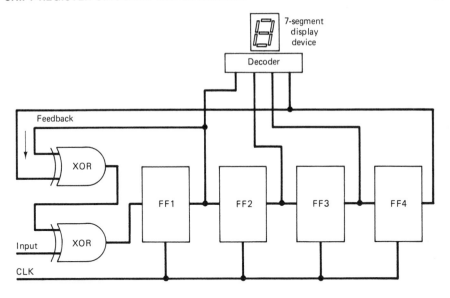

Remainder				Readout
0	0	0	0	*0*
1	0	0	0	*1*
0	1	0	0	*2*
1	1	0	0	*3*
0	0	1	0	*4*
1	0	1	0	*5*
0	1	1	0	*6*
1	1	1	0	*7*
0	0	0	1	*8*
1	0	0	1	*9*
0	1	0	1	*A*
1	1	0	1	*C*
0	0	1	1	*F*
1	0	1	1	*H*
0	1	1	1	*P*
1	1	1	1	*U*

(a)

Fig. 5-11. Example of feedback shift register and application.
(a) Logic diagram; (b) a signature multimeter for microprocessor
troubleshooting (*Courtesy, Hewlett-Packard*).

be caught by the signature analyzer shown in Fig. 5-11. Thus, if a
64-bit word on a microprocessor node is checked with this arrangement,
the readout might be P. On the other hand, if there is a 1-bit error
in this 64-bit word, the readout will be changed, as to 5.

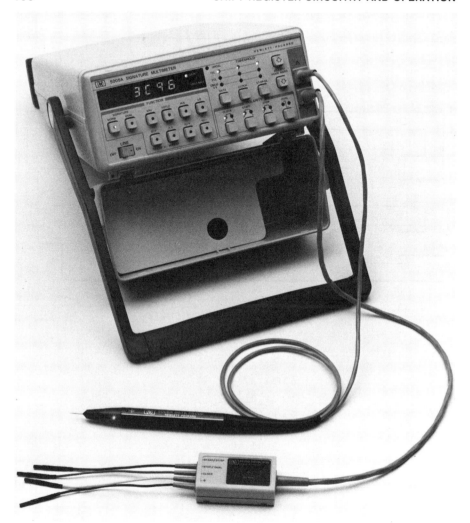

Fig. 5-11(b) (*continued*)

An incorrect signature informs the troubleshooter that there is a malfunction associated with the node under test. Consider next the possible occurrence of more than one error in the foregoing 64-bit word. In such a case, there is a remote possibility that one error could cancel the other error, and restore a correct signature. Although the probability of error cancellation is small, it does exist—for this reason, additional test circuitry is provided in practice.

Typical Microprocessor System Faults

At this point, it is helpful to note typical faults that occur in microprocessor systems. These include: poor connection, printed-circuit conductor shorted to ground, printed-circuit conductor shorted to V_{CC}, break in PC conductor, solder bridge or whisker(s) between PC conductors, internal defect in microprocessor (MPU), internal defect in an IC connected to the MPU, marginal and/or noisy V_{CC} voltage, fault in a peripheral device, or a grounding system defect.

A "sneaky" source of malfunction is called the solder-ball short circuit. Solder balls are generally formed during automatic soldering of PC board connections—the small spheres of solder are "sprayed" into the air and tend to fall back on the PC board and stick to its surface. Sometimes all of the solder balls are not removed—if a ball eventually breaks loose and starts rolling around the circuit board inside of the microcomputer, it is possible for puzzling trouble symptoms to occur. Accordingly, this is an odd-ball trouble condition that should be kept in mind.

IMPORTANT

Particular brands and models of microcomputers tend to develop certain kinds of malfunctions. In turn, it is good practice to keep a file of troubleshooting data in this regard. Then, when the next job comes along on a brand and model which is on file, the fault can possibly be identified immediately.

Adders
and Subtracters

Microprocessing Arithmetic Devices * Half and Full Adders * Boolean Algebra * Serial Adder * Parallel Adder * BCD Adder * 2's Complement Adder/Subtracter * Algebraic Addition/Subtraction * Troubleshooting Notes

Microprocessing Arithmetic Devices

Mathematical and logical operations are accomplished in the arithmetic-logic unit (ALU) of a microprocessor. Addition and subtraction are an aspect of these data-processing procedures, as indicated in Fig. 6-1. As previously noted, multiplication is essentially a process of repeated addition, and division is fundamentally a process of repeated subtraction. An ALU processes both positive and negative binary numbers, and also binary fractions.

Half and Full Adders

An XOR gate functions as a mod-2 summer; it forms the sum of two bits, but rejects the carry (if any). A half adder comprises a mod-2 summer with an AND gate to retain a carry, as depicted in Fig. 6-2. The half adder has two inputs and two outputs; it provides parallel addition, inasmuch as the input bits A and B are applied simultaneously, and not sequentially as in the case of a serial adder.

Next, a full adder comprises two half adders with an OR gate, as shown in Fig. 6-3. The full adder provides for simultaneous inputting of

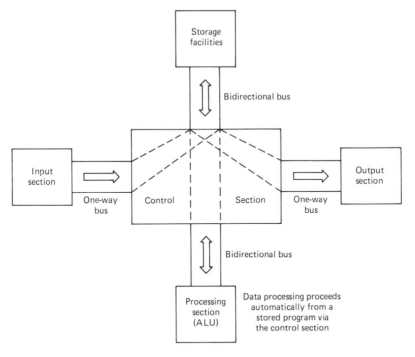

Note: Circuitry for addition and subtraction is included in the arithmetic-logic
unit (ALU) of the processing section. The central processing unit (CPU)
also contains registers and input-output ports.

Fig. 6-1. Typical data channels in a microcomputer.

three binary digits (addend, augend, and carry-in), and outputs
corresponding sum and carry digits. This is another example of parallel
addition, inasmuch as the input bits A, B, and C′ are simultaneously
applied to the full adder.

A logic-flow diagram for the full adder is shown in Fig. 6-4. Since
there are two outputs, two logic equations are required to define the
circuit section.

Boolean Algebra

Observe that Fig. 6-4 exemplifies relations between binary arithmetic and Boolean algebra. In other words, binary arithmetic is
concerned with numerical relations in addition and subtraction
operations (and related mathematical operations). On the other hand,
Boolean algebra is concerned with operators such as AND, OR, NOT,

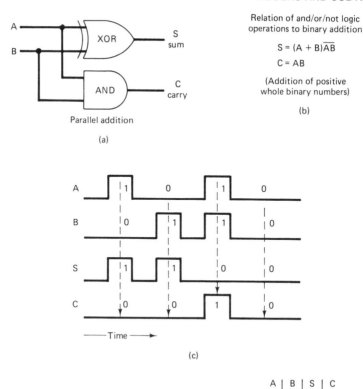

Relation of and/or/not logic
operations to binary addition

$$S = (A + B)\overline{AB}$$

$$C = AB$$

(Addition of positive
whole binary numbers)

(b)

Parallel addition

(a)

(c)

A	B	S	C
0	0	0	0
0	1	1	0
1	0	1	0
1	1	0	1

$0 + 0 = 0$
$1 + 0 = 1$
$1 + 1 = 1$ and 1 to carry

(d)   (e)

Note: A half adder is an example of combinational logic, because its output
states depend only upon its present input states.

Fig. 6-2. Half adder. (a) Logic diagram; (b) logic equations;
(c) timing diagram; (d) binary addition rules; (e) truth table.

EXCEPT, IF . . . , THEN . . . , and related logical operations. Since
binary arithmetic and Boolean algebra have a logical common core,
binary arithmetical processes have corresponding Boolean algebraic
processes.

Boolean algebra is concerned with variables, such as A and B, which
are restricted to values of 1 or 0. Thus, if the value of A is not 1, its value is
necessarily 0. The five Boolean postulates corresponding to the AND
operator are:

$$A = 1 \text{ (if } A \neq 0)$$
$$0 \cdot 0 = 0$$
$$1 \cdot 1 = 1$$

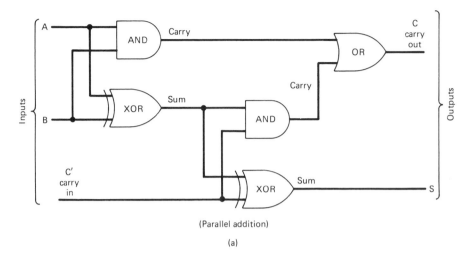

(Parallel addition)

(a)

A	B	C'	S	C
0	0	0	0	0
0	0	1	1	0
0	1	0	1	0
0	1	1	0	1
1	0	0	1	0
1	0	1	0	1
1	1	0	0	1
1	1	1	1	1

(b)

Relation of and/or/not logic
operations to binary addition

LOGIC EQUATIONS:

$S = \overline{A}\overline{B}C' + \overline{A}B\overline{C}' + A\overline{B}\overline{C}' + ABC'$

$C = AB + AC' + BC' + ABC'$

(Addition of positive
whole binary numbers)

(c)

Note: Adders can process mixed numbers such as 1.1, 10.11, 0.011, and so
on. Some computer systems employ fixed-point arithmetic, in which
correct location of the binary point (or decimal point) is the
programmer's responsibility. Other computer systems employ floating-
point arithmetic, wherein the computer keeps track of the binary point
(or decimal point).

Fig. 6-3. Full adder. (a) Logic diagram; (b) truth table;
(c) logic equations.

$$\frac{1 \cdot 0 = 0}{\overline{1} = 0}$$

These five Boolean postulates, which define the function of the AND
operator may be stated in dual form to define the function of the OR
operator:

$$A = 0 \ (\text{if } A \neq 1)$$
$$0 + 0 = 0$$
$$1 + 1 = 1$$
$$\frac{1 + 0 = 1}{\overline{0} = 1}$$

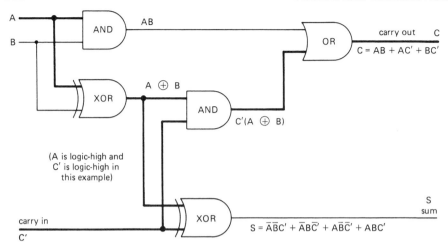

Note: A logic flow chart sets forth the procedures and details of the steps that are involved in the solution of a problem, and their order of arrangement in logical terms. In this example, heavy lines are employed to indicate solution of the problem in addition wherein $A = 1$, $B = 0$, and $C' = 1$.

Note: The logic circuit is an electronic model of the mathematical operation of binary addition.

Fig. 6-4. A logic flow diagram for a full adder.

Boolean algebra has three properties, which are also properties of general algebra:

$$AB = BA \qquad\qquad AB = BA \text{ is a } commutative \text{ property.}$$
$$A(BC) = AB(C) \qquad A(BC) = AB(C) \text{ is an } associative \text{ property.}$$
$$A(B+C) = AB + AC \qquad A(B+C) = AB + AC \text{ is a } distributive \text{ property.}$$

These three algebraic properties may be stated in dual form:

$$A + B = B + A$$
$$A + (B+C) = (A+B) + C$$
$$A + BC = (A+B)(A+C)$$

Five theorems define the application of Boolean operators to variables:

$$A \cdot 0 = 0$$
$$A \cdot 1 = A$$
$$A \cdot A = A$$
$$\overline{\overline{A}} = A$$

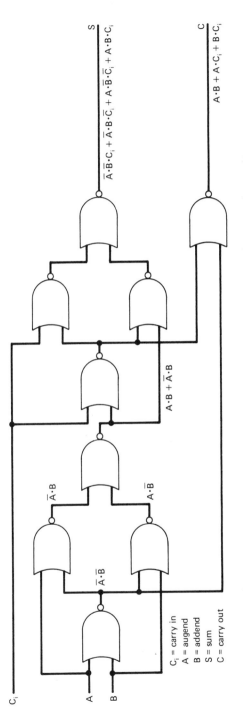

$\overline{A} \cdot \overline{B} \cdot C_i + \overline{A} \cdot B \cdot \overline{C_i} + A \cdot \overline{B} \cdot \overline{C_i} + A \cdot B \cdot C_i$ S

$A \cdot B + A \cdot C_i + B \cdot C_i$ C

$A \cdot B + \overline{A} \cdot B$

$\overline{A} \cdot B$

$A \cdot \overline{B}$

$\overline{A} \cdot \overline{B}$

C_i

A

B

C_i = carry in
A = augend
B = addend
S = sum
C = carry out

Note: This adder configuration includes nine gates, whereas the configuration depicted in Fig. 6-4 employs five gates. Stated otherwise, the NOR implementation requires more hardware to obtain the same end result. Observe that although the S and C logic equations are the same in either case, their derivations are quite different for the two implementations. The basic distinction between them is the *exclusive-or* function in Fig. 6-4, and the *inclusive-or* function in Fig. 6-5.

Fig. 6-5. NOR gate implementation for a full adder.

These five theorems may be stated in dual form:

$$A + 0 = A$$
$$A + 1 = 1$$
$$A + A = A$$
$$A + \overline{A} = 1$$
$$A = \overline{\overline{A}}$$

The full adder depicted in Fig. 6-2 may be implemented with NOR gates, as shown in Fig. 6-5. Observe that the same logic equations apply in either case. It follows from prior discussion that a full adder may also be implemented with NAND gates. Note in passing that implementation with either NOR or NAND gates is possible inasmuch as these gates include an inverter. Thus, AND implementation is not possible. However, it is evident that each NOR gate in Fig. 6-5 may be replaced with a negated-AND gate.

Serial Adder

A primitive serial adder (up-counter) was discussed in the first chapter. A more elaborate serial adder employs two registers and a full adder, as shown in Fig. 6-6. The augend is contained in the A register, and the addend is contained in the B register. In most arrangements, the A register and the B register are parallel-loaded. The addition process starts by clocking the LSBs from the A and B registers into the full adder. In turn, a sum bit appears at the S output, and a carry-out may appear at the C_o output.

The sum bit is clocked into the sum register in the MSB place, and the carry-out bit (if any) is clocked into the D flip-flop where its flow is delayed for one clock cycle. This addition process is then repeated for the next-most-significant bits in the A and B registers. These bits are summed with the carry-in bit (if any), and the corresponding sum bit appears at the S output; a carry-out bit may appear at the C_o output.

Next, this sum bit is clocked into the sum register in the MSB place, and the previous LSB is simultaneously clocked (shifted) to the less significant place in the sum register. Also, the carry-out bit (if any) is clocked into the D flip-flop. Then, this addition cycle is repeated until the A and B registers have been unloaded and the last carry-out bit has been clocked into the sum register.

The addition of 1011 and 1001 is exemplified in Fig. 6-6. Note that the process is completed two clock cycles after the A and B registers have been unloaded. Observe also that the first sum-register input bit undergoes sequential shifts, so that it finally occupies the LSB place in the register. The delay flip-flop is typically a clocked JK master-slave FF with an input inverter for operation as a D flip-flop.

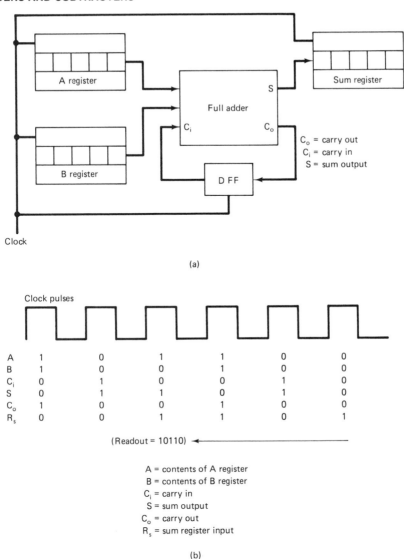

(a)

Clock pulses

A	1	0	1	1	0	0
B	1	0	0	1	0	0
C_i	0	1	0	0	1	0
S	0	1	1	0	1	0
C_o	1	0	0	1	0	0
R_s	0	0	1	1	0	1

(Readout = 10110) ◄──────────────────

A = contents of A register
B = contents of B register
C_i = carry in
S = sum output
C_o = carry out
R_s = sum register input

(b)

Fig. 6-6. Basic serial adder arrangement. (a) Block diagram;
(b) addition of 1011 and 1001.

Another arrangement of the basic serial adder is shown in Fig. 6-7. Here, the A register is configured as a recirculating shift register, or accumulator, so that it does double duty. The accumulator functions as an addend register and as a sum register. It initially contains the addend, and it finally contains the sum at the termination of the addition process. Note also that this type of serial adder will accept successive addends and augends, and their grand total will be indicated by the accumulator, as exemplified in Fig. 6-8.

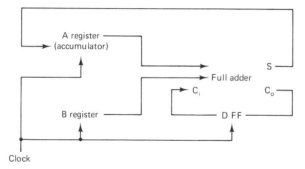

Note: An accumulator is a 4-, 8-, 12-, 16-, or 32-bit register that provides temporary storage. The accumulator (ACC) may be cleared (contents replaced with 0's), or rotated. When an ACC is rotated, its contents are recirculated; that is, its contents are clocked out and are simultaneously clocked back into the ACC. This circuit action is basically that of a serial memory.

Fig. 6-7. Basic serial adder with the A register operating also as a sum-register accumulator.

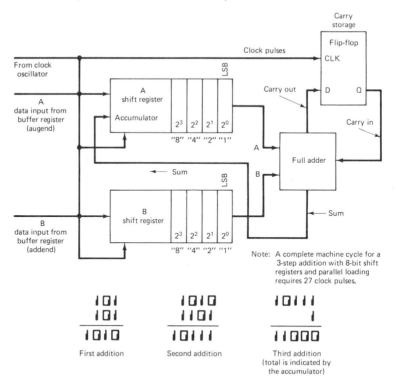

Note: A complete machine cycle for a 3-step addition with 8-bit shift registers and parallel loading requires 27 clock pulses.

Fig. 6-8. Example of addition of three binary numbers by a serial adder.

Parallel Adder

A parallel adder processes data more rapidly than a serial adder. The parallel adder sums all the digits in an addend and augend simultaneously, as contrasted with sequential or serial addition. A typical four-bit parallel adder is shown in Fig. 6-9. It comprises four full adders with carry-out from a less significant adder connected to the carry-in terminal of the next most significant adder. In turn, the carry process lags the

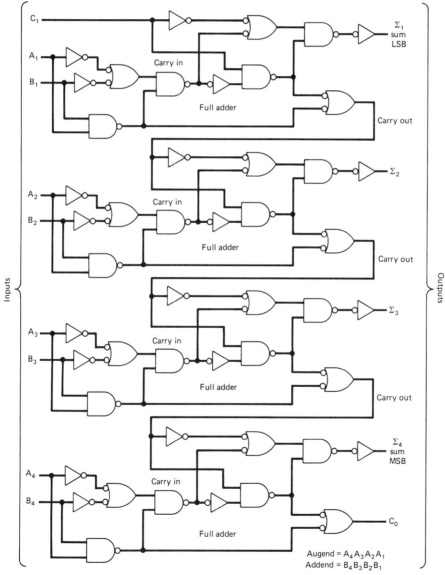

Fig. 6-9. A four-bit parallel-adder configuration with ripple carry.

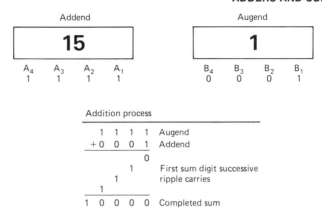

Fig. 6-10. Four basic propagation delay periods are involved in the addition of 15 + 1.

summing process; this is called ripple carry and the final sum usually lags the initial sum output by one or more propagation delay periods.

With reference to Fig. 6-10, four propagation delay periods are involved in the addition of 15 + 1, when the arrangement of Fig. 6-9 is employed. This disadvantage can be reduced by including a look-ahead carry adder in the configuration, so that look-ahead carry is used instead of ripple carry. This topic is explained in greater detail subsequently.

BCD Adder

Binary coded decimal (BCD) adders are often used in calculators and other microprocessor-based digital equipment. A BCD adder is not basically different from the binary adders previously described. However, a BCD adder has its circuitry arranged to process data in BCD format, instead of binary format. As an illustration, decimal 13 is processed as 0001 0011 in BCD format; whereas, it is processed as 1101 in straight binary format.

A configuration for a BCD adder stage is depicted in Fig. 6-11. Note that although a 4-bit binary full-adder circuit will add numbers whose sum is as large as 15, without generating a carry-out, a BCD adder circuit must generate a carry-out whenever the sum exceeds 9 (in order to properly relate to the decimal system). Also, the BCD adder must subtract 10 from the primary sum in order to obtain the final sum whenever a carry-out is generated.

To subtract 10 from a primary sum, the 2's complement of 10 is added to the primary sum. Stated otherwise, the 2's complement of 1010 is 0110 (0101 + 1). Observe that whenever the output from U1 in Fig. 6-11 goes logic-high, $A_4A_3A_2A_1$ in the correcting adder equals 0110. In turn, 0110 is added to the primary sum, thereby forming the final sum. This final sum is the valid BCD number in answer to the problem.

Ripple carry is employed in the basic BCD adder arrangement of Fig. 6-11. In turn, several propagation delays are usually involved. Look-ahead carry circuitry may also be included in BCD adder configurations, as in straight binary adder configurations. Look-ahead carry circuitry speeds up data processing by minimizing the propagation delays that are required to obtain the final sum.

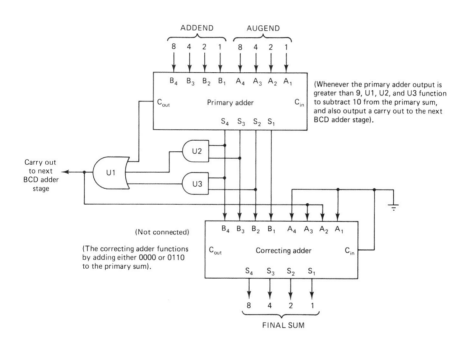

Fig. 6-11. Configuration of a BCD adder stage.

2's Complement Adder/Subtracter

Although dedicated subtractor hardware can be used in an ALU, most microcomputers employ a 2's complement adder/subtractor in order to accomplish either addition or subtraction with a minimum number of gates. With reference to Fig. 6-12, a controlled inverter is employed to form 2's complements; it is also called a true/complement zero-one element. It consists of an XOR gate with data inputted to one terminal and a control signal (invert signal) inputted to the other

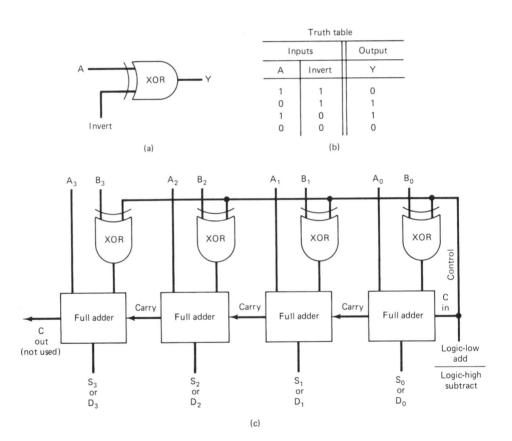

Note: The adder processes mixed numbers in the same manner as whole numbers. For example, 1.01 + 10.1 = 11.11; or, 1.25 + 2.5 = 3.75. Observe, however, that the programmer must keep track of the binary point (decimal point).

Fig. 6-12. Controlled-inverter adder/subtracter configuration. (a) XOR gate operates as a controlled inverter; (b) truth table; (c) controlled-inverter adder/subtracter configuration.

terminal. Accordingly, as seen in the truth table, a controlled inverter can transmit either the input bit or its 1's complement.

A controlled inverter (also called a programmed inverter) is combined with full adders as shown in Fig. 6-12 to form a 2's complement adder/subtracter. When the invert control input is driven logic-low, the B input bits flow into the full adders and their sum is formed with respect to the A bits.

On the other hand, when the invert control input is driven logic-high, the carry-in input is also driven logic-high, and the B bits are complemented before they flow into the full adders. Since a 1 carry-in bit was entered, the 2's complement of the B bits is added to the A bits. Accordingly, the difference between the A bits and the B bits is outputted as $D_3 D_2 D_1 D_0$.

Algebraic Addition/Subtraction

Algebraic addition and subtraction involves the processing of both positive and negative numbers. For example, $+2$ added to $+3$ is equal to $+5$; $+2$ added to -3 is equal to -1; $+2$ subtracted from $+3$ is equal to $+1$; $+2$ added to -3 is equal to -1; $+2$ subtracted from -3 is equal to -5; -2 added to -3 is equal to -5; -3 subtracted from -2 is equal to $+1$. With reference to Fig. 6-13, the controlled-inverter adder/subtracter can process either positive or negative inputs.

Observe in Fig. 6-14 that each negative number is the 2's complement of its corresponding positive number. Thus, the 1's complement of 0001 is 1110, and the 2's complement of 0001 is 1111. Similarly, the 1's complement of 0010 is 1101, and the 2's complement of 0010 is 1110. The sign bit of 0001 is 0, and the sign bit of 1111 is 1. (The sign bit is the leading bit.) Note the examples of algebraic addition and subtraction in Fig. 6-14. (See also Chart 6-1.)

Troubleshooting Notes

Adders or adder/subtracters can develop various kinds of malfunctions. For example, an adder/subtracter may provide correct sums, but incorrect differences. Again, it may provide correct sums of positive numbers, but incorrect sums of negative numbers. Or, an incorrect sum bit might always appear in the fifth place; an incorrect difference bit might always appear in the seventh place. These trouble symptoms relate to a troubleshooting technique called diagnostic programming. They are specifically related to particular circuit actions in an adder/subtracter.

When the troubleshooter runs a diagnostic program, he notes the incorrect data that appears in the adder/subtracter output, and visualizes

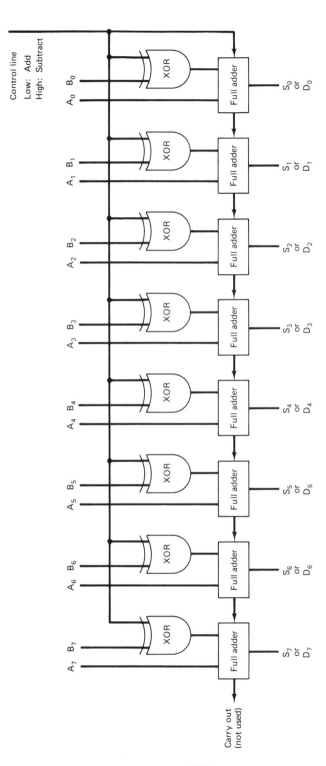

(Algebraic addition or subtraction is provided when the A and B inputs are in 2's complement code)

Fig. 6-13. Algebraic addition or subtraction is provided by a controlled-inverter adder/subtracter.

116

1100	1101	1110	1111	0000	0001	0010	0011	0100	(2's complement number notation)

$$-4 \quad -3 \quad -2 \quad -1 \quad 0 \quad 1 \quad 2 \quad 3 \quad 4$$

(Decimal number notation)

Positive and negative numbers in 2's complement number notation
(each negative number is the 2's complement of its
corresponding positive number, and vice versa)

Note: In the algebraic addition or subtraction process, the leading bit in a number is a *sign bit*. The sign bit is 1 for minus and 0 for plus. For example, -3 is 1101 in 2's complement number notation; the leading 1 denotes that the number is negative, and 101 denotes number 3. Again, 4 is 0100 in 2's complement number notation; the leading 0 denotes that the number is positive, and 100 denotes number 4.

In 8-bit 2's complement number notation, -2 is represented by 11111110; or, 11111110 is the 8-bit 2's complement of 00000010. The leading 1 in 11111110 denotes that the number is negative in an algebraic addition or subtraction process.

Example: The algebraic addition of $-24 +17$ with the controlled-inverter adder/subtracter in Fig. 6-13 employs an augend of 11101000 and an addend of 00010001; or, $A_7A_6A_5A_4A_3A_2A_1A_0 = 11101000$, and $B_7B_6B_5B_4B_3B_2B_1B_0 = 00010001$. The control line is held logic-low for algebraic addition, with the result that the sum 11111001 is outputted. The leading bit (sign bit) denotes that the sum is negative. Since the 2's complement of 11111001 is 00000111, the algebraic sum is -111, or -7 (decimal).

Again, the algebraic subtraction of -24 and $+17$ with the controlled-inverter adder/subtracter in Fig. 6-13 employs a minuend of 11101000 and a subtrahend of 00010001; or, $A_7A_6A_5A_4A_3A_2A_1A_0 = 11101000$, and $B_7B_6B_5B_4B_3B_2B_1B_0 = 00010001$.

The control line is held logic-high for algebraic subtraction, with the result that the difference 11010111 is outputted. The leading bit (sign bit) denotes that the difference is negative. Since the 2's complement of 11010111 is 00101001, the algebraic difference is -101001, or -41 (decimal).

Fig. 6-14. Examples of algebraic addition and subtraction in the 2's complement number code.

a logic-flow diagram. He relates the incorrect data to particular processing steps in the logic-flow diagram. In turn, he narrows down the trouble possibilities, and proceeds to associated electrical tests. As previously noted, a digital circuit fault may be tracked down to a failure inside of an IC package, or it may be localized to a defect in the external circuitry. (See also Fig. 6-15.)

Chart 6-1

Other Adder and Subtracter Circuits

Troubleshooters will also encounter an occasional obsolescent adder and/or subtracter arrangement. Therefore, it is necessary to be knowledgeable concerning this area of logic circuitry.

Addition and subtraction by 1's complements has been extensively employed in older designs. These operations are exemplified below:

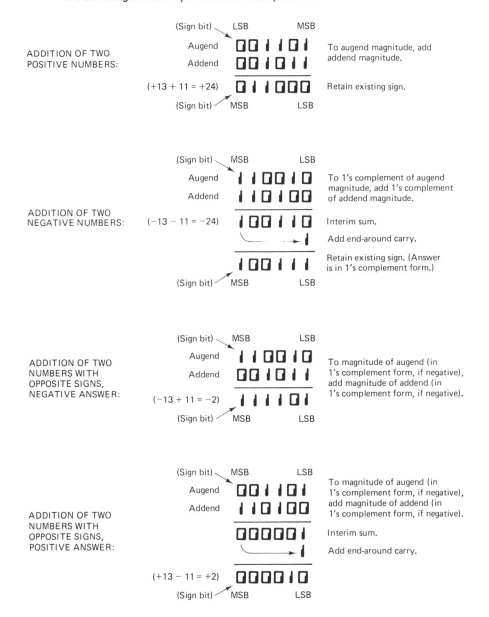

ADDITION OF TWO
POSITIVE NUMBERS:

(Sign bit)   LSB   MSB
Augend   0 0 1 1 0 1   To augend magnitude, add
Addend   0 0 1 0 1 1   addend magnitude.

(+13 + 11 = +24)   0 1 1 0 0 0   Retain existing sign.
(Sign bit)   MSB   LSB

ADDITION OF TWO
NEGATIVE NUMBERS:

(Sign bit)   MSB   LSB
Augend   1 1 0 0 1 0   To 1's complement of augend
Addend   1 1 0 1 0 0   magnitude, add 1's complement
                           of addend magnitude.

(−13 − 11 = −24)   1 0 0 1 1 0   Interim sum.

                           1   Add end-around carry.

           1 0 0 1 1 1   Retain existing sign. (Answer
                           is in 1's complement form.)
(Sign bit)   MSB   LSB

ADDITION OF TWO
NUMBERS WITH
OPPOSITE SIGNS,
NEGATIVE ANSWER:

(Sign bit)   MSB   LSB
Augend   1 1 0 0 1 0   To magnitude of augend (in
Addend   0 0 1 0 1 1   1's complement form, if negative),
                           add magnitude of addend (in
(−13 + 11 = −2)   1 1 1 1 0 1   1's complement form, if negative).
(Sign bit)   MSB   LSB

ADDITION OF TWO
NUMBERS WITH
OPPOSITE SIGNS,
POSITIVE ANSWER:

(Sign bit)   MSB   LSB
Augend   0 0 1 1 0 1   To magnitude of augend (in
Addend   1 1 0 1 0 0   1's complement form, if negative),
                           add magnitude of addend (in
                           1's complement form, if negative).

           0 0 0 0 0 1   Interim sum.

                           1   Add end-around carry.

(+13 − 11 = +2)   0 0 0 0 1 0
(Sign bit)   MSB   LSB

Positive binary numbers are stored in a computer memory in binary code with a 0 in the sign position preceding the number to indicate the positive sign. Negative binary numbers are stored in a computer memory in complement form with a 1 in the sign position to indicate the negative sign. Addition of binary numbers is accomplished independently of positive and negative signs. When an end-around carry is generated, it is added to the LSB of the interim sum. Subtraction of a pair of binary numbers requires that the subtrahend be complemented before addition is performed, regardless of the sign of the subtrahend. Note that all of the foregoing examples are instances of addition by the 1's complement method. In effect, however, "Addition of two positive numbers" and "Addition of two negative numbers" would be regarded as examples of conventional addition, whereas "Addition of two numbers with opposite signs, negative answer," and "Addition of two numbers with opposite signs, positive answer," would be regarded as examples of conventional subtraction. Observe also that negative answers are obtained in 1's complement form.

The foregoing method of addition and subtraction is called the sign-and-magnitude mode of processing. A typical sign-and-magnitude adder/subtracter arrangement is shown below:

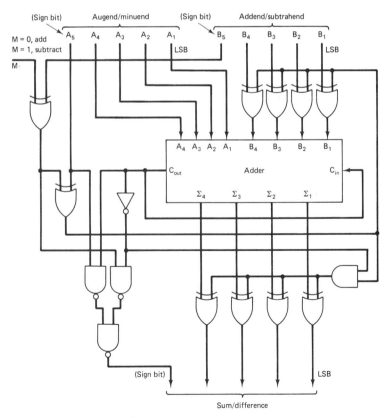

Chart 6-1 (*continued*)

Next, a typical 9's complement BCD subtracter arrangement is shown below:

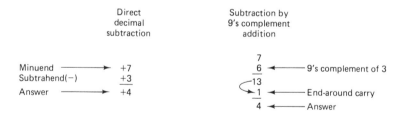

(1 indicates positive
result: 0 indicates
negative result.)

The 9's complement of any number is calculated by subtracting each decimal digit from 9. For example, the 9's complement of 30 is equal to 69, as shown below:

$$
\begin{array}{r}
99 \\
- 30 \\
\hline
69
\end{array}
$$
 ◄——— 9's complement of 30

Calculation of a 9's complement.

Direct decimal subtraction	Subtraction by 9's complement addition

Minuend ———► +7
Subtrahend(−) +3
Answer ———► +4

$$
\begin{array}{r}
7 \\
6 \\
\hline
13 \\
1 \\
\hline
4
\end{array}
$$

7
6 ◄——— 9's complement of 3
13
1 ◄——— End-around carry
4 ◄——— Answer

Subtraction by 9's complement addition.

The 9's complement of a number can be used in subtraction; thus, the 9's complement of the subtrahend is added to the minuend, as shown above. An end-around carry is always generated, and it is added to the least significant digit.

Peripheral Difficulties

Trouble symptoms may be caused by malfunctioning or misadjustment of peripheral equipment such as a tape recorder or a video monitor. Various types of personal computers employ a TV receiver as a video monitor. It follows that trouble symptoms will result from improper adjustment of the channel-selector switch, contrast, brightness, and fine-tuning controls. Note also that an antenna/computer switch is often provided—the switch must be set to "computer" for proper operation as a video monitor.

When a tape cassette program fails to load into the computer, the trouble is often due to an incorrect setting of the cassette volume control. Either too high or too low a setting will result in malfunction. If the tape recorder has a tone control, it should be set to "treble." Note also that the tape may be deteriorated (try loading a known good tape); the head(s) may need cleaning, demagnetization, or replacement. Interconnecting cables occasionally become defective (or incorrectly connected).

In locations where TV station field strength is high, interference can occur, with resulting mixed displays of computer data and TV programs ("ghosts"). In such a case, computer output should be switched to another channel. For example, a typical personal computer provides a choice of operation on either channel 3 or channel 4.

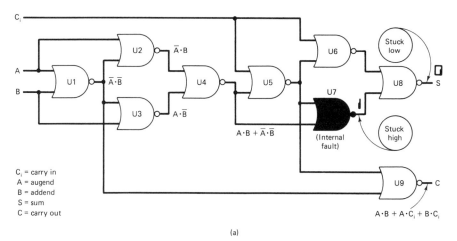

(a)

Note: In this example, U7 has developed an internal fault whereby its output is stuck logic-high and cannot be driven logic-low. In turn, the S output is stuck logic-low. On the other hand, the C output is unaffected by the fault, and the carry output obeys its logic equation.

Fig. 6-15(a). Example of IC failure in an adder circuit.

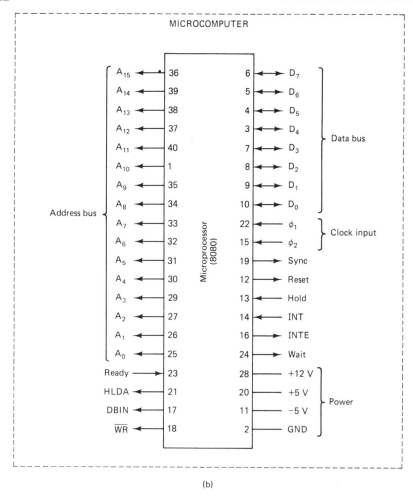

(b)

Note: The microprocessor is usually mounted in an IC socket. In turn, it is comparatively easy to make a substitution test of the microprocessor chip. Observe, however, that adequate care should be taken to ensure that one or more pins are not accidentally bent under the IC package.

Fig. 6-15(b). The microprocessor chip must be replaced if an internal adder failure occurs.

Power-Up Precautions

Note that some personal computers require a specified power-up sequence to avoid difficulties and/or possible equipment damage. For example, a typical computer used with a color-TV receiver requires all accessories to be turned on before the computer is turned on. In other words, a tape recorder, printer, and TV receiver should be turned on before the computer is turned on. By the same token, the computer must be turned off before inserting or removing a ROM cartridge (computer program package), in this same example. Otherwise, the ROM cartridge may be damaged.

Note also that excessive line-voltage fluctuation can result in computer malfunction. For example, the computer may "hang up," with resulting loss of keyboard control if the line voltage dips excessively or is interrupted. A *reset* button may be provided to regain keyboard control; otherwise, the computer must be turned off and then turned back on again. (Check your operating instructions—in some cases, the computer must not be turned back on again for 30 seconds.)

It was previously noted that a personal computer may be operated from a constant-voltage power transformer. This type of transformer provides good control of line voltage, and "smooths out" fluctuations. To repeat a very important precaution, the computer should not be turned on until after the constant-voltage transformer has been turned on. Otherwise, damage to the semiconductor devices in the computer could result.

Multiplication and Division Operations

Microprocessor ALU Section

An ALU typically comprises arithmetic circuits, logic circuits, registers, and switching circuits, as depicted in Fig. 7-1. These circuits seldom operate independently. For example, we know that an arithmetic operation often involves shifting, which is a logical operation. The logic circuits generally operate with respect to AND, OR, XOR, and Complement instructions. Results of a logical instruction are routed to the A (augend) register.

Shift-and-Add Multiplier Action

It was previously noted that multiplication consists of repeated addition. As an illustration, it is seen in Fig. 7-2 that 13 is multiplied by 11 if we add eleven 13's; or we could add thirteen 11's. When we use the common longhand method of multiplication, we do not always recognize that we are employing a shift-and-add technique. In other words, when we multiply 13 by 11, our first partial product is 13. Our second partial product is evidently 130—but we do not write it explicitly. Instead, we write the second partial product as 13, with a shift one place to the left. This left shift effectively multiplies 13 by 10, and we are actually writing 130.

Similarly binary multiplication involves shift-and-add operations. With reference to Fig. 7-2, each partial product is either a repetition of the multiplicand, or is a row of zeros, in the conventional method of binary multiplication. Each partial product is shifted one place to the left, with

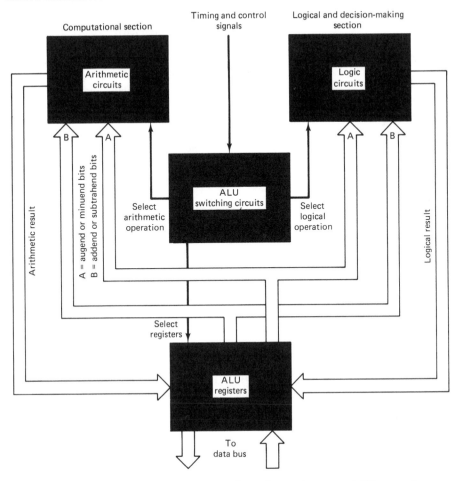

Fig. 7-1. The arithmetic-logic unit performs addition, subtraction, multiplication, and division.

respect to the preceding partial product. In turn, each shift is equivalent to multiplying the partial product by 2. Thus, 1101 equals 13, but 11010 equals 26.

Observe that we are using the same method when we multiply 1101 by 1011 as we do when we multiplied 13 by 11. In other words, when we multiply 1101 by 1011, we are taking 1101 a total of 1011 times, and then adding the 1101's. In the conventional method of binary multiplication, all of the partial products are added together at the same time. However, as shown in Fig. 7-2, an alternate method is often used in microcomputers for reasons of economy. Thus, the first two partial products may be added to obtain a partial sum, to which the third and fourth partial products are added (with incidental shifts) to obtain the final sum which is the product.

DECIMAL MULTIPLICATION

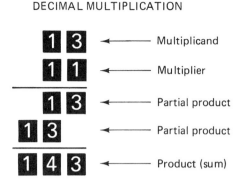

In this example, 13 is multiplied by 11. Multiplication is accomplished by taking 13 eleven times, and adding the eleven 13's. The first partial product represents taking 13 once. The second partial product represents taking 13 ten times. Note that shifting 13 one place to the left effectively multiplies it by ten. Finally, when the eleven 13's are added, their sum, 143, represents the product of 13 × 11.

BINARY MULTIPLICATION
(Conventional Method)

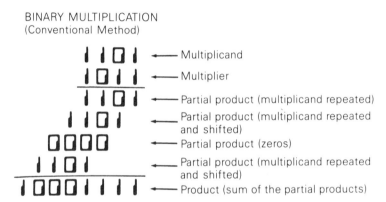

BINARY MULTIPLICATION
(Alternate Method Often
Used in Microcomputers)

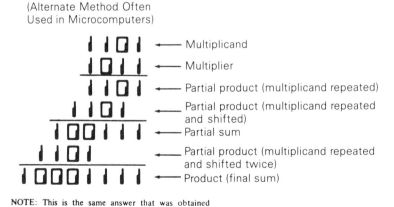

NOTE: This is the same answer that was obtained by conventional multiplication.

Fig. 7-2. Examples of shift-and-add multiplication.

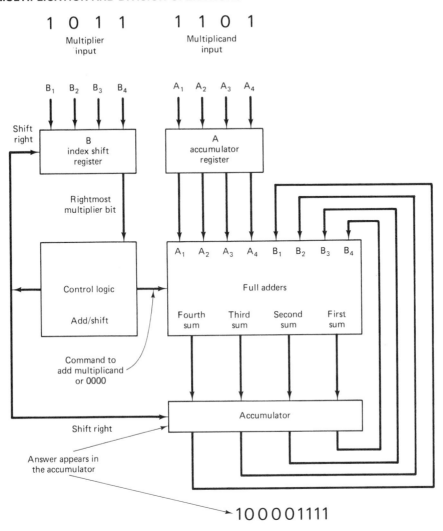

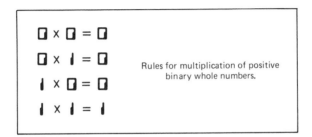

Fig. 7-3. Shift-and-add multiplier arrangement.

A basic shift-and-add multiplier arrangement is depicted in Fig. 7-3. It comprises a shift register called the B or index register in which the multiplier is temporarily stored; it also contains a register called the A or accumulator register in which the multiplicand is temporarily stored. Also, the multiplier comprises full adders and a shift register called the accumulator into which the product is outputted; a control logic section "orchestrates" performance of the multiplier sections.

Next, observe the steps that are followed in multiplication of 1101 by 1011. First, the multiplier and the multiplicand are loaded into the B and A registers, respectively. The accumulator is automatically cleared, in

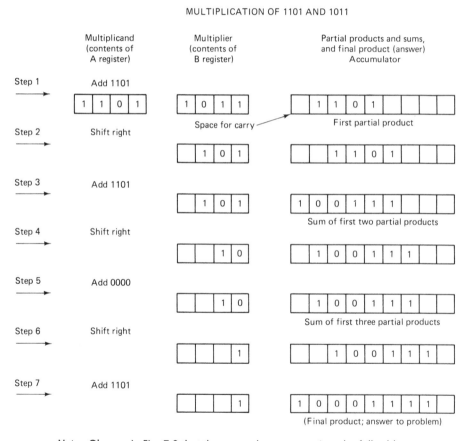

MULTIPLICATION OF 1101 AND 1011

Note: Observe in Fig. 7-3 that the accumulator outputs into the full adders. This permits the multiplicand to be added to the first partial product, and finally to be added to the sum of the first three partial products.

Fig. 7-4. Example of accumulator operation in multiplication of 1101 and 1011 (*Courtesy, Hewlett-Packard*).

preparation for the ensuing process. Next the control logic (add-shift logic) checks the rightmost digit in the multiplier; this digit is a 1, whereupon the control logic instructs the adder to add the multiplicand 1011 to the contents of the index register: 1011. In turn, the first partial product, 1101, is temporarily stored in the accumulator.

After this first addition is completed, the control logic then shifts the contents of both the B register and the accumulator by one place to the right. Next, the control logic checks the rightmost digit in the multiplier register; again, this digit is a 1, and again the multiplicand is added to the first partial product. The resulting sum, 100111 is temporarily stored in the accumulator. This is the sum of the first two partial products, or the partial sum that was noted in Fig. 7-2.

We observe in Fig. 7-4 that the foregoing operation is followed by shifting the contents of both the B register and the accumulator by one place to the right. The control logic then checks the rightmost digit in the multiplier register; this time, however, the multiplier digit is a 0, and nothing is to be added to the partial sum. Accordingly, the sum of the first three partial products is the same as the sum of the first two partial products.

Next, the contents of both the B register and the accumulator are shifted by one place to the right. The control logic checks the rightmost digit in the multiplier register; this digit is a 1, and again the multiplicand is added to the sum of the first three partial products. Accordingly, the final product 10001111 appears in the accumulator, and the calculation is complete.

BCD Multiplication

Just as BCD addition is often employed, so too is BCD multiplication. To minimize hardware, partial products are "diagonally" repositioned in the shift registers, and are then added to form the BCD sum. With reference to Fig. 7-5, "diagonal" multiplication is exemplified for a pair of decimal numbers (this makes the "action" easier to follow). The diagram compares "diagonal" multiplication with conventional multiplication.

Observe that "diagonal" multiplication consists in "rewriting" each partial product from a horizontal format to a "diagonal" format, including a right shift. In turn, when the repositioned digits are added, the same answer is obtained as in conventional multiplication. An example of "diagonal" multiplication with BCD notation is shown in Fig. 7-6, along with its conventional counterpart.

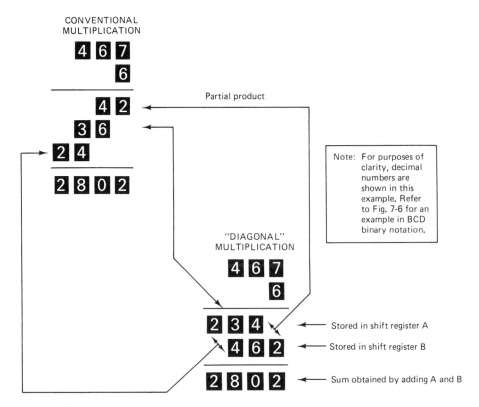

Note: For purposes of clarity, decimal numbers are shown in this example. Refer to Fig. 7-6 for an example in BCD binary notation.

Note: When binary coded decimal (BCD) numbers are multiplied, the product is formed by a BCD adder in combination with two shift registers. "Diagonal" multiplication is often employed, as shown above. Thus, the partial product 42 is stored with the 4 in the A register, and the 2 in the B register with a right shift. Similarly, the partial products 36 and 24 are stored "diagonally." Finally, the BCD adder forms the sum of the partial products to calculate the product. "Diagonal" multiplication minimizes hardware, because only two registers are required.

Fig. 7-5. "Diagonal" multiplication is often used in microprocessors.

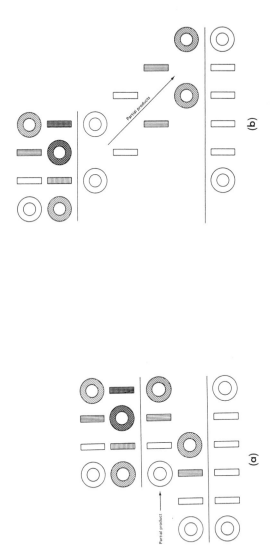

(a)

(b)

Note (a): In these examples, multiplicand and multiplier digits are identified by shading, so that their placements in the partial products are evident. In the (a) algorithm, horizontal placement is shown; in the (b) algorithm, "diagonal" placement is shown.

Note (b): Either of the multiplication methods yields the same answer for binary whole numbers. Either method will also yield the same answer for binary mixed numbers. For example, $1.01 \times 1.1 = 1.111 = 1\text{-}7/8$. If the multiplier and the multiplicand have the same sign, the product is positive; if the multiplier and multiplicand have opposite signs, the answer is negative. The programmer may or may not have the responsibility of "keeping track" of binary points and product signs.

Fig. 7-6. Multiplication of BCD numbers. (a) Conventional format; (b) "diagonal" format.

0000 0000	0000 0001	0000 0010	0000 0011	0000 0100	0000 0101	0000 0110	0000 0111	0000 1000	0000 1001
0000 0001	0000 0001	0000 0010	0000 0011	0000 0100	0000 0101	0000 0110	0000 0111	0000 1000	0000 1001
0000 0010	0000 0010	0000 0100	0000 0110	0000 1000	0001 0000	0001 0010	0001 0100	0001 0110	0001 1000
0000 0011	0000 0011	0000 0110	0000 1001	0001 0010	0001 0101	0001 1000	0010 0001	0010 0100	0010 0111
0000 0100	0000 0100	0000 1000	0001 0010	0001 0110	0010 0000	0010 0100	0010 1000	0011 0010	0011 0110
0000 0101	0000 0101	0001 0000	0001 0101	0010 0000	0010 0101	0011 0000	0011 0101	0100 0000	0100 0101
0000 0110	0000 0110	0001 0010	0001 1000	0010 0100	0011 0000	0011 0110	0100 0010	0100 1000	0101 0100
0000 0111	0000 0111	0001 0100	0010 0001	0010 1000	0011 0101	0100 0010	0100 1001	0101 0110	0110 0011
0000 1000	0000 1000	0001 0110	0010 0100	0011 0010	0100 0000	0100 1000	0101 0110	0110 0100	0111 0010
0000 1001	0000 1001	0001 1000	0010 0111	0011 0110	0100 0101	0101 0100	0110 0011	0111 0010	1000 0001

Example:
Decimal 7 × 5 = 35
BCD 0000 0111 × 0000 0101 = 0011 0101

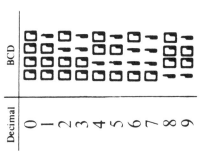

Decimal	BCD
0	0000
1	0001
2	0010
3	0011
4	0100
5	0101
6	0110
7	0111
8	1000
9	1001

Fig. 7-7. Multiplication table for BCD numbers 0000 through 1001.

Look-Up Tables

Another widely used method of BCD multiplication employs look-up tables, as depicted in Fig. 7-7. This table contains all possible multiples of two numbers between 0 and 9; the entries are permanently stored in a read-only memory (ROM) which functions as a look-up table. Thus, the product of any two digits can be directly read out of the ROM in BCD code. In turn, BCD multiplication is reduced to repeated BCD addition.

Shift-and-Subtract Divider Action

Inasmuch as division is the opposite of multiplication, it can be accomplished by means of repeated subtraction of the divisor from the dividend. As an illustration, 10 "goes into" 40 four times, as shown in Fig. 7-8. The shift-and-subtract operations of division in the decimal

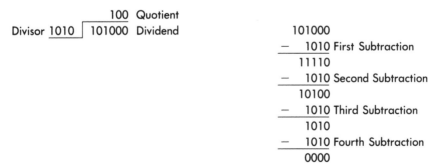

DIVISION OF DECIMAL NUMBERS BY REPEATED SUBTRACTION OF THE DIVISOR

```
            4  Quotient
Divisor 10 | 40  Dividend              40
                                    − 10 First Subtraction
                                      30
                                    − 10 Second Subtraction
                                      20
                                    − 10 Third Subtraction
                                      10
                                    − 10 Fourth Subtraction
                                      00
```

DIVISION OF BINARY NUMBERS BY REPEATED SUBTRACTION OF THE DIVISOR

```
              100  Quotient
Divisor 1010 | 101000  Dividend          101000
                                       −   1010 First Subtraction
                                         11110
                                       −   1010 Second Subtraction
                                         10100
                                       −   1010 Third Subtraction
                                          1010
                                       −   1010 Fourth Subtraction
                                          0000
```

Fig. 7-8. Ten "goes into" 40 four times, as shown by repeated subtraction.

system and in the binary system are exemplified in Fig. 7-9. The binary-system example is similar to the ALU operation in a microcomputer.

Stated otherwise, if 2526 is divided by 6 in an ALU, the 6 will not be subtracted from 2526 a total of 421 times. Instead, the 6 will be shifted and then subtracted; this reduces the number of operations that are required. Observe in Fig. 7-9 that if 10 were subtracted 25 times from 110010, the same answer (11001) would be obtained as by shifting 10 and performing

DIVISION WITH WHOLE NUMBERS

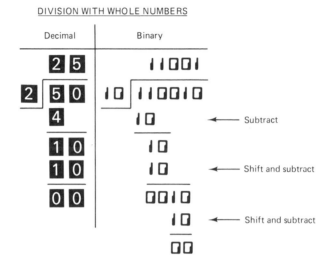

EXAMPLES OF CONTINUED FRACTIONS

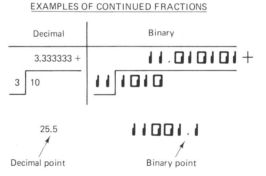

Note: Division is performed in the same manner with mixed binary numbers as with whole binary numbers. The programmer may or may not have the responsibility of "keeping track" of the binary point. If the dividend and the divisor have the same sign, the quotient is positive. On the other hand, if the dividend and the divisor have opposite signs, the quotient is negative.

Fig. 7-9. Division operations in the decimal system and in the binary system.

three subtractions. Note also that if a remainder is left when binary whole numbers are divided, the division process may be continued to determine the value of the remainder (fractional).

Continued Fractions

In the case of continued fractions, an exact value cannot be obtained for the remainder, although the value may be determined as precisely as desired by continuing the division process. To anticipate subsequent discussion, the operator often enters large numbers as a power of ten, and the result of an arithmetic operation may be displayed as a power of ten. This is called scientific notation. For example, $1234 = 1.234 \times 10^3$, and $0.001234 = 1.234 \times 10^{-3}$.

Observe the example of binary division by subtraction and shifting, with a fractional remainder, as depicted in Fig. 7-10. This is much the same procedure that is used to divide decimal 2526 by decimal 6. On the other hand, there are two incidental considerations: If we perform a longhand division, 600 will be chosen in the first subtraction (top example). The longhand operator chooses the position of the divisor. A microprocessor, however, does not have the ability to examine the problem in this manner; the microprocessor must start with the highest possible value of the divisor, by shifting left as far as possible.

After the highest possible value of the divisor has been determined, the microprocessor must perform three trial subtractions; on each unsuccessful subtraction (a subtraction that yields a negative difference), the divisor must then be shifted right until it is in the position with which we started. Evidently the end result will be the same, although more steps are required. Observe also that three additional 0 bits will be stored in the leftmost position of the quotient: 000101.1; in turn, more space is required in the quotient register.

To avoid waste of steps and register space, one traditional technique requires that the decimal point in the dividend and divisor be adjusted (scaled) before the numbers are inputted to the computer; this scaling operation ensures that the divisor will be larger than the dividend, so that the leftmost digits can be aligned. This operation is similar to the scaling of decimal points. For example, when we divide 20.40 by 1.57, we shift the decimal points two places to the right, so that the division process employs 2040 divided by 157.

Again, with reference to the top example in Fig. 7-10, the longhand operator chooses when to shift from 600 to 60 in order to avoid a negative result. A computer may not have the ability to judge whether the result of the next subtraction will be positive or negative, and it simply proceeds to

```
        421
  6 ⟌ 2526
        24
        12
        12
         6
         6
         0
```

BASIC CONCEPT OF DATA PROCESSING BY
THE ALU IN THE OPERATION OF DIVISION

	6 ⟌ 2526	Add to Quotient ↓	Quotient (Total) ↓
	600	100	100
	1926		
	600	100	200
	1326		
	600	100	300
	726		
	600	100	400
	126		
	60	10	410
	66		
	60	10	420
	6		
	6	1	421
	0		

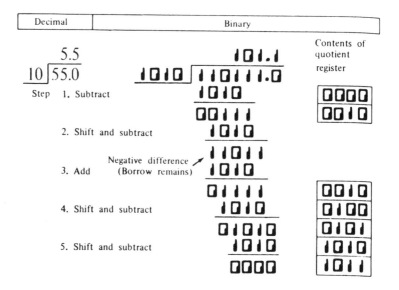

a. Divisor is subtracted from dividend.
b. If the difference is a positive number, put 1 in the rightmost digit position of the quotient register; however, if the difference is a negative number, add the divisor back to the dividend.
c. Shift the quotient left by one digit and shift the divisor right by one digit (or shift the dividend left by one digit).
d. Repeat steps a, b, and c.
e. Continue steps a through d until a subtraction yields a difference of all 0 bits, or until required accuracy of answer is obtained, or until all available bit positions in the quotient register are filled.

Fig. 7-10. Illustrative examples of division by a microprocessor (*Courtesy, Hewlett-Packard*).

try to subtract. If it subtracts the divisor and the difference is negative (as indicated by a remaining borrow), it must add the divisor back in. Auxiliary circuitry must be provided to detect the negative result.

Divider Hardware

Hardware to implement the foregoing division algorithm is much the same as for multiplication (Figs. 7-3 and 7-4). The dividend is loaded into the accumulator, indexed left, and the divisor is loaded into the A register. During the division process, the adder element must be able to subtract and add; the shifting is accomplished in the accumulator by moving the dividend to the left. As the dividend is shifted left, the right end of the accumulator is vacated and it may be used for storage of the quotient.

In the foregoing example of binary division, subtraction was direct; however, in a configuration such as the multiplier under discussion, subtraction is ordinarily accomplished by the 2's complement method. Also, a sign bit is included with all numbers, so that division can be performed with negative numbers, as well as with positive numbers and fractions.

Note that when BCD division is employed, the look-up table in Fig. 7-7 may be utilized, much as in BCD multiplication. Thus, in BCD division, the leftmost digits in the dividend and the divisor are used to obtain estimated trial quotients by which the divisor may be multiplied. This method is essentially similar to the basic longhand method, wherein the trial quotient is estimated and then utilized to multiply the divisor.

We may also note that still other division algorithms are employed. The method that has been discussed is called the restoring method; in addition, we will encounter the nonrestoring method and the comparison method. Both of the latter methods are somewhat more sophisticated; they are also more efficient, and in turn are more popular with microcomputer designers.

The nonrestoring method and the comparison method use the same principle of repeated subtractions and shifting; however, the nonrestoring method allows any subtraction of the divisor that yields a negative difference to take place, whereupon it shifts the dividend (or divisor), and proceeds to carry out several additions of the divisor back to the dividend. The magnitude of the quotient is decreased with each addition.

On the other hand, the comparison method performs a comparison of the anticipated magnitude of the difference obtained in the next subtraction with the magnitude of the divisor. If this comparison indicates that a negative number would result from the next subtraction, that subtraction will be inhibited, with a shift being carried out instead.

Besides the four basic operations of addition, subtraction, multiplication, and division, microprocessors also perform various other mathematical operations. Operations such as extraction of square root, computation of logarithms, and computation of trigonometric functions, are all executed with the same logic circuits previously described, using appropriate algorithms. An algorithm is often an iterative process wherein a step or a sequence of steps is repeated over and over until the desired accuracy of results is obtained.

Troubleshooting Approach

Microcomputer troubleshooting may be very easy in some cases, and very difficult in others. It was previously noted that trouble symptoms can be caused by obvious faults, such as a cable or connector that makes poor contact at a keyboard, video monitor, tape recorder, or other peripheral. When a faulty interconnect is suspected, the troubleshooter usually makes a substitution test.

Trouble symptoms can also be caused by malfunction in a peripheral, such as a tape recorder. This situation is suspected when an operation that involves the tape recorder proceeds abnormally. In this situation, the troubleshooter usually starts with a substitution test. If a substitution test is not feasible at the time, he cross-checks the suspect recorder with microphone input to determine whether voice recording and playback occurs normally. Note that various recorders require different settings of their volume controls to provide optimum operation in a microcomputer system.

More difficult troubleshooting situations are encountered when a defect occurs in a device such as a tape interface, a video divider chain, a video processing device, a multiplexer, or a memory. In such a case, the troubleshooter needs to know how the system operates, so that he can make suitable tests and thereby narrow down the trouble area. As previously noted, diagnostic programs are often helpful—but only if the troubleshooter understands what their results signify.

The troubleshooter needs to know, for example, that there are typically half a dozen data-conversion steps involved from keyboard input to video-monitor output. As explained in greater detail subsequently, these involve keyboard switching operations, encoding of the keyboard signals into American Standard Code for Information Interchange (ASCII), BCD to binary conversion, CPU processing, with CPU binary output conversion to ASCII, followed by ASCII to alphanumeric conversion and display on the video-monitor screen of the alphanumeric letters, numerals, and punctuation marks.

More difficult troubleshooting problems are generally analyzed with reference to a block diagram for the microcomputer. The system block diagram sets forth all of the key devices and components, along with their interconnecting buses. For example a widely used microcomputer employs a keyboard, video monitor, tape recorder, and power supply, with three basic peripheral interconnect cables. The recorder interconnect cable includes three lines, any one of which could develop a defect, for example.

The Inside Story

Continuing analysis of the data-conversion steps that are involved from keyboard input to video-monitor output leads the troubleshooter inside the microcomputer (typically, inside the keyboard housing). If he understands system operations, he can refer to the block diagram to identify the various buses—often on the basis of tests with logic pulsers and probes. A typical microcomputer employs an address bus, a data bus, a video-address bus, timing and control buses, clock lines, and power lines. Although these terms may seem strange, we will become "at home" with them as we proceed through the following chapters.

ASCII Code

At this point, it is helpful to briefly note the ASCII code tabulated in Fig. 7-11. When an operator enters data via a keyboard, the data is automatically converted into ASCII form for transmission to the CPU. Conversely, when the processor transmits data to a printer, ASCII code is automatically converted into mechanical operations. This code includes 128 numerals, letters, symbols, and special control codes which are designated by 7-bit binary numbers.

With reference to Fig. 7-11, the numeral 5 is designated by 011 0101; the letter K is designated by 100 1011; the percent symbol is designated by 010 0101; the start of the text is designated by 000 0010; and so on. Code conversions are accomplished by means of combinational-logic circuits called encoders and decoders. This topic is explained in greater detail subsequently. (See also Fig. 7-12.)

COLUMN		0	1	2	3	4	5	6	7
	BITS 4321 765 →	000	001	010	011	100	101	110	111
ROW									
0	0000	NUL	DLE	SP	0	@	P	\	p
1	0001	SOH	DC1	!	1	A	Q	a	q
2	0010	STX	DC2	''	2	B	R	b	r
3	0011	ETX	DC3	#	3	C	S	c	s
4	0100	EOT	DC4	$	4	D	T	d	t
5	0101	ENQ	NAK	%	5	E	U	e	u
6	0110	ACK	SYN	&	6	F	V	f	v
7	0111	BEL	ETB	'	7	G	W	g	w
8	1000	BS	CAN	(	8	H	X	h	x
9	1001	HT	EM	)	9	I	Y	i	y
10	1010	LF	SUB	*	:	J	Z	j	z
11	1011	VT	ESC	+	;	K	[	k	}
12	1100	FF	FS	,	<	L	\	l	¦
13	1101	CR	GS	—	=	M	]	m	{
14	1110	SO	RS	.	>	N	⌒	n	~
15	1111	SI	US	/	?	O	—	o	DEL

bits
7-- ---1

Example: Code for A = | 100 | 0001 |

LEGEND for Control Codes in Columns 0 and 1:

NUL	*Null*	*DLE*	*Data link Escape*
SOH	*Start of Heading*	*DC1*	*Device Control 1*
STX	*Start of Text*	*DC2*	*Device Control 2*
ETX	*End of Text*	*DC3*	*Device Control 3*
EOT	*End of Transmission*	*DC4*	*Device Control 4*
ENQ	*Enquiry*	*NAK*	*Negative Acknowledge*
ACK	*Acknowledge*	*SYN*	*Synchronous Idle*
BEL	*Bell [audible signal]*	*ETB*	*End of Transmission Block*
BS	*Backspace*	*CAN*	*Cancel*
HT	*Horizontal Tabulation [punched card skip]*	*EM*	*End of Medium*
LF	*Line Feed*	*SUB*	*Substitute*
VT	*Vertical Tabulation*	*ESC*	*Escape*
FF	*Form Feed*	*FS*	*File Separator*
CR	*Carriage Return*	*GS*	*Group Separator*
SO	*Shift Out*	*RS*	*Record Separator*
SI	*Shift In*	*US*	*Unit Separator*
		DEL	*Delete*

Fig. 7-11. American Standard Code for Information Interchange (ASCII) (*Courtesy, Hewlett-Packard*).

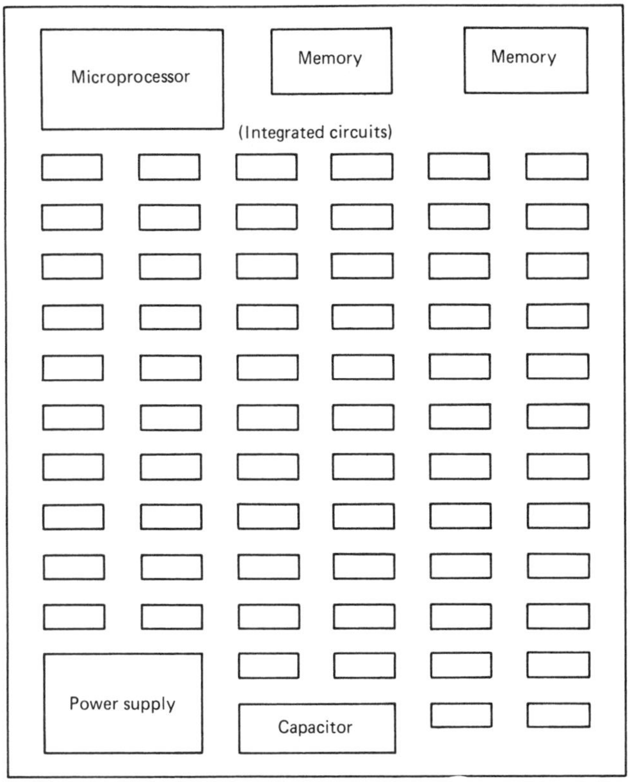

Note: The troubleshooter can identify the various IC packages from the service manual for the microcomputer. Each package may also have a type number marked on it. If a light is placed behind the board, the PC conductors can be followed from the component side.

Fig. 7-12. Logic board layout for a simple microcomputer.

8

Encoders
and Decoders

Microprocessor Bus Activity * 2-to-4-Line Decoder *
Binary Number Decoder * 1-out-of-16 Decoder * 2'421-
to-8421 Converter * Keyboard-to-BCD Encoder *
Binary-to-Seven-Segment Encoder * Priority Encoder *
Troubleshooting Considerations * Low Impedance Gate
Inputs

Microprocessor Bus Activity

Virtually all microprocessor systems used in microcomputers are bus-organized, as depicted in Fig. 8-1. The CPU operates with three principal buses, called the address bus, the data bus, and the control bus. The address bus transmits binary numbers from the CPU to the memory. However, these binary-number addresses cannot be directly used by the memory circuitry. First, an address must be decoded before the relevant register in the memory can be unloaded. (See also Chart 8-1.)

A typical memory comprises a large number of registers; each register contains a digital word. The memory ordinarily includes an on-chip decoder (decoder circuitry on the same integrated circuit as the memory). A decoder provides processed addressing of memory registers and minimizes the number lines required in the address bus. We will find, for example, that eight address lines can select any one out of 256 registers in a memory when an address decoder is used.

Another aspect of a bus-organized microprocessor system is shown in Fig. 8-2. A keyboard is provided for the programmer. Before the output signals from the keyboard enter the data bus, they pass through an

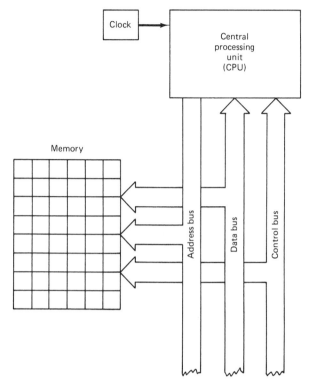

Note: The clock operates at approximately 2 MHz in a typical microcomputer.

Fig. 8-1. Partial plan of a bus-organized microprocessor system.

interface device and are encoded into ASCII format. Since the CPU generally processes numerical data in straight binary code, the ASCII words must be decoded into binary words at the CPU input. Still other types of encoders and decoders are employed in various microprocessor systems.

2-to-4-Line Decoder

A decoder is a device that converts coded data into another form, as a binary number to decimal number decoder, for example. Decimal-to-binary and binary-to-decimal decoders are also called converters. Decoders are used to convert BCD code to a 7-segment format for display of decimal digits, and so on. Memory address decoders were previously noted. A decoder/driver comprises a decoder circuit with an output stage for driving a solid-state display, or other device.

Chart 8-1

Basic Microprocessor Capabilities and Terminal Arrangements

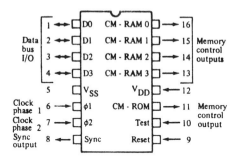

The Intel 4004 microprocessor features a 4-bit parallel CPU with 46 instructions. It can directly address 4000 8-bit instruction words of memory and 5120 bits of data storage RAM. Up to 16 4-bit input ports and 16 4-bit output port can also be directly addressed. Sixteen index registers are built in. It operates at clock rates up to 750 kHz.

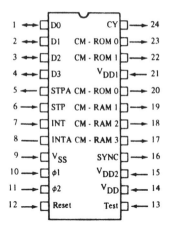

The 4040 microprocessor features a 4-bit parallel CPU with 60 instructions. It can directly address 4000 8-bit instruction words of program memory or 8000 with bank switching, and 5120 bits of data storage RAM. Up to 16 4-bit ports can also be addressed directly. Twenty-four randomly accessible index registers are built in. It operates at clock rates up to 750 kHz.

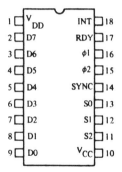

The Intel 8008 8-bit microprocessor features an 8-bit address and data bus that, by time multiplexing, allows control information, 14-bit addresses, and 8-bit data bytes to be transmitted between the CPU and the external memory. The 14-bit address permits direct addressing of 16,000 words of memory. It provides state signals, cycle control signals, and a synchronizing signal to peripheral circuits. It operates with a 500-khz clock.

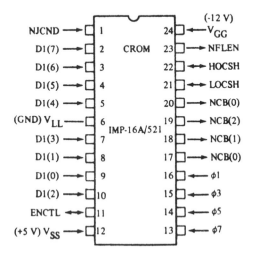

The 8080 microprocessor features an 8-bit, bidirectional, 3-state data bus and a separate 16-bit 3-state address bus. The 16-bit address bus permits direct addressing of 65,000 words of memory. Six timing and control outputs are available, whereas 4 control units and 2 clock signals are required. The microprocessor operates with a 2-MHz clock.

The National Semiconductor Corporation's IMP microprocessor has a CPU that is configured around the control read only memory (CROM) device and one or more register and arithmetic logic unit (RALU) devices. A CROM provides storage for 100 microinstructions of 23 bits each, program sequencing, subroutine execution, and translation of microinstructions into RALU commands. Each RALU provides 96 bits of storage; 4-bits in each of 7 general registers; a status register; and a 16-word last-in/first-out (LIFO) stack. The RALU also contains provisions for: an arithmetic-logic unit to perform ADD, AND, OR, XOR operations; a shift register; an input/output (I/O) data multiplexer to an external data bus; and a 4-bit, time-multiplexed command bus for RALU control.

Chart 8-1 (*continued*)

1	A_{11}	A_{10}	40
2	A_{12}	A_9	39
3	A_{13}	A_8	38
4	A_{14}	A_7	37
5	A_{15}	A_6	36
6	ϕ	A_5	35
7	D_4	A_4	34
8	D_3	A_3	33
9	D_5	A_2	32
10	D_6	A_1	31
11	-5 V Z80	A_0	30
12	D_2	GND	29
13	D_7	$\overline{RFSH}$	28
14	D_0	$\overline{MI}$	27
15	D_1	$\overline{RESET}$	26
16	$\overline{INT}$	$\overline{BUSRQ}$	25
17	$\overline{NMI}$	$\overline{WAIT}$	24
18	$\overline{HALT}$	$\overline{BUSAK}$	23
19	$\overline{MREQ}$	$\overline{WR}$	22
20	$\overline{IORQ}$	$\overline{RD}$	21

The Zilog Z80 microprocessor is an "8-bit" device in which most data is processed in one-byte segments. It has an 8-bit bidirectional, 3-state data bus and a separate 16-bit 3-state address bus. There are 14 general-purpose registers and several special-purpose registers included in the IC. The microprocessor operates with a 2-MHz clock.

Chart 8-1 (*continued*)

A simple 2-to-4-line decoder is shown in Fig. 8-3. Observe that the two inputs A and B together can have only the four different states listed in the truth table (comprising 0 to 3 in binary code), whereby a 2-input decoder can have only four unique outputs. Since a different output gate is enabled by each binary state, there can be as many output gates as there are different input states. A 3-input decoder can have eight unique outputs, a 4-input decoder can have 16 unique outputs, and so on.

BCD-to-Decimal Decoder

Next, observe the BCD-to-decimal decoder shown in Fig. 8-4. This widely used arrangement has four inputs, which could be decoded into 16 unique outputs. However, since the BCD code utilizes only the counts from 0000 to 1001, this decoder is limited to 10 output gates. Observe that the inputs include a strobe line in this example. A strobe pulse enables the decoder for a fixed period only and locks out the 8421 lines except for the strobe duration.

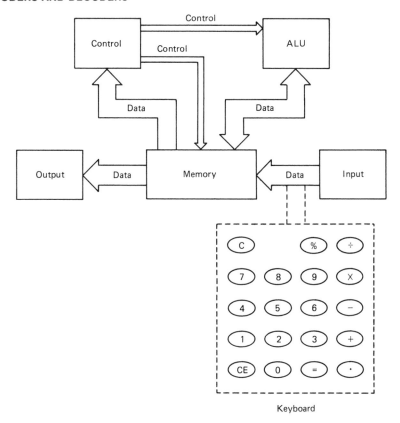

Keyboard

Note: The ASCII code includes 128 numerals, letters, symbols, and special control codes which are designated by 7-bit binary numbers, as explained in the previous chapter. Thus, the numeral 5 on the keyboard is designated by the ASCII code word 011 0101; the letter K on the alphabetic keyboard (not shown) is designated by the ASCII code word 100 1011. The percent symbol on the keyboard is designated by the ASCII code word 010 0101.

Fig. 8-2. Data flow is indicated by broad arrows; control-signal flow is indicated by narrow arrows.

Note in Fig. 8-4 that false data rejection capability is not provided. In other words, if an illegal input code, such as 1010 or 1011 happens to occur, the decoder will respond with some irrelevant output. As an illustration, a 1010 input will cause output lines 2 and 8 to go logic-high. The basic decoder configuration can be elaborated, if desired, to prevent any gate from going logic-high in response to an illegal input.

Binary Number Decoder

A decoder configuration for converting binary numbers stored in a shift register into decimal numbers is depicted in Fig. 8-5. One AND gate

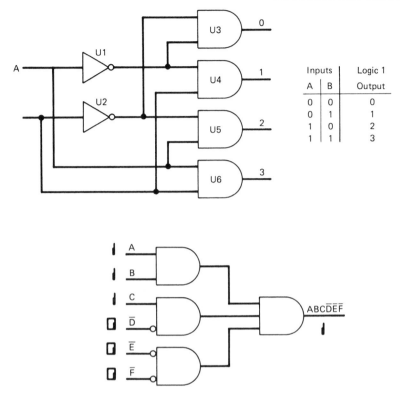

Note: This decoder configuration exemplifies processing of four inputs in order to select a specified single output. Since there are four input lines, there are 64 possible input state combinations. Of these 64 combinations, only ABCDEF represents a logic-high output.

Fig. 8-3. A 2-to-4-line decoder arrangement. (*Courtesy, Hewlett-Packard*).

is provided for each number that is to be decoded. When a particular binary number is stored in the shift register, all inputs to the corresponding decimal AND gate go logic-high. Observe that for each stored binary number, every flip-flop has either its Q output or its $\overline{\text{Q}}$ output logic-high.

In addition to decimal-digit outputs, the arrangement in Fig. 8-5 exemplifies supplementary gates for decoding the numbers 30 and 31. Thus, if the binary number 11111 (decimal 31) is stored, the Q output for each flip-flop is 1. For the binary number 00000 (decimal 0), the $\overline{\text{Q}}$ output for each flip-flop is 1. In turn, to decode binary 31, the five inputs to U12 must be the five Q outputs from the register. Conversely, to decode binary 0, the five inputs to U1 must be the five $\overline{\text{Q}}$ outputs from the register.

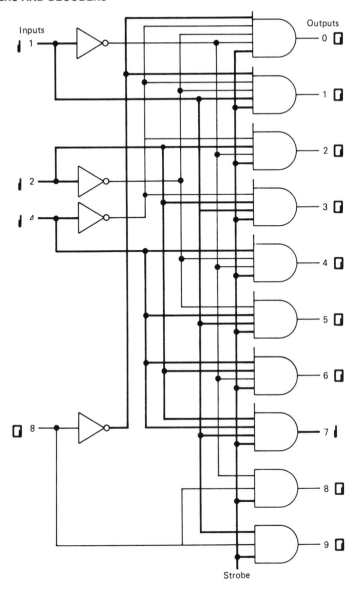

Inputs

Outputs

Note: This arrangement is also called a code converter.

Fig. 8-4. Example of a BCD-to-decimal decoder (*Courtesy, Hewlett-Packard*).

Observe in Fig. 8-5 that this decoder configuration is unresponsive to illegal inputs—false outputs do not occur regardless of the input states. In other words, this decoder can output decimal values from 0 through 9, and can also output the two decimal numbers 30 and 31. On the other

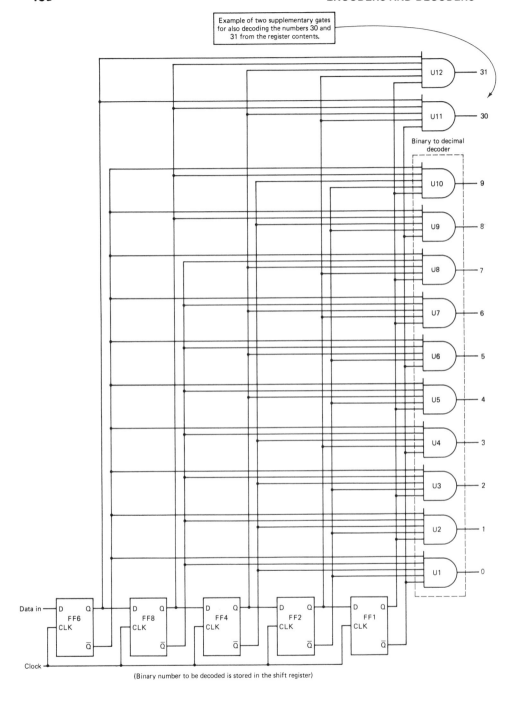

Fig. 8-5. Configuration for decoding binary coded numbers
(*Courtesy, Hewlett-Packard*).

hand, the decoder is unresponsive to register contents such as 1100 or 1011. This type of decoder can be designed to decode all numbers from 0 through 31, if desired, if 32 AND gates are employed.

1-out-of-16 Decoder

Next, a widely used 1-out-of-16 decoder configuration is depicted in Fig. 8-6. It utilizes 16 AND gates with four buffers and four inverters. In the example cited, a binary number 1001 is inputted and the corre-

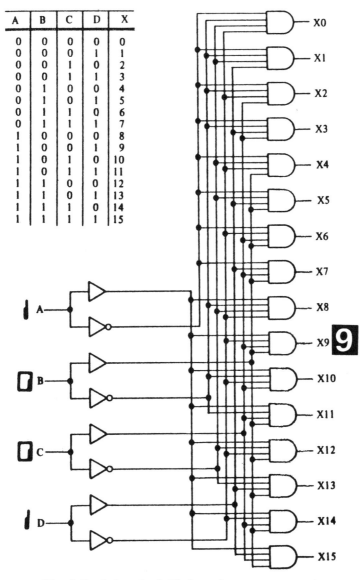

A	B	C	D	X
0	0	0	0	0
0	0	0	1	1
0	0	1	0	2
0	0	1	1	3
0	1	0	0	4
0	1	0	1	5
0	1	1	0	6
0	1	1	1	7
1	0	0	0	8
1	0	0	1	9
1	0	1	0	10
1	0	1	1	11
1	1	0	0	12
1	1	0	1	13
1	1	1	0	14
1	1	1	1	15

Fig. 8-6. A 1-out-of-16 decoder arrangement.

sponding decimal digit 9 is outputted. Note that since there are four input lines, 16 (2^4) input state combinations can be accommodated. There are no illegal states to be contended with.

2'421-to-8421 Code Converter

A decoder configuration for converting from 2'421 code to BCD code words is shown in Fig. 8-7. As previously noted, the 2'421 code is similar to the 8421 code, except that the MSB position in the 2'421 code has a weight of 2. Thus, 1111 has a decimal value of 9 in 2'421 code, but 1001 has a decimal value of 9 in the 8421 BCD code. The first five digits in the 2'421 code are the same as in the 8421 BCD code, but the remaining five digits are different.

With reference to Fig. 8-7, observes that if the 2'421 word 1111 is inputted, the LSB feeds through. The next-most-significant digit produces a 0 output, as does the third digit. However, the fourth digit (the MSB) produces a 1 output, and the BCD output word is 1001. This is a

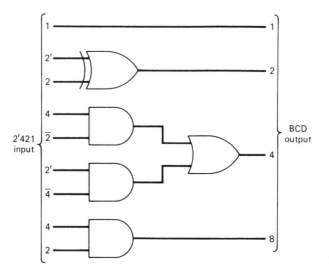

Note: The $\overline{2}$ input signal to the decoder is provided by passing the 2 signal through an inverter. Similarly, the $\overline{4}$ input signal is obtained by passing the 4 signal through an inverter.

Note: The 2421 code is used to obtain the 9's complement of a binary number. Thus, the 9's complement is obtained by taking the 1's complement of the 2421 number.

Fig. 8-7. A logic circuit for converting from 2'421 to 8421 BCD code.

comparatively simple example wherein only five gates are required in the decoder logic diagram. Other more complex codes require numerous gates and generally employ read-only memories (ROMs), as detailed subsequently.

Keyboard-to-BCD Encoder

Encoders are similar to decoders, except that an encoder has a single input and several outputs. For example, the encoder arrangement shown in Fig. 8-8 inputs a pulse from a keyboard switch that represents a decimal digit; in turn, the encoder outputs an 8421 BCD signal that corresponds to the decimal digit. Four OR gates are employed; they are related to the data-processing operation by the logic equations:

$$1 = 1 + 3 + 5 + 7 + 9$$
$$2 = 2 + 3 + 6 + 7$$
$$4 = 4 + 5 + 6 + 7$$
$$8 = 8 + 9$$

In other words, 8421 is the BCD number corresponding to a combination of the decimal digits 0, 1, 2, 3, 4, 5, 6, 7, 8, 9. The logic equations state that the BCD LSB output shall be logic-high whenever

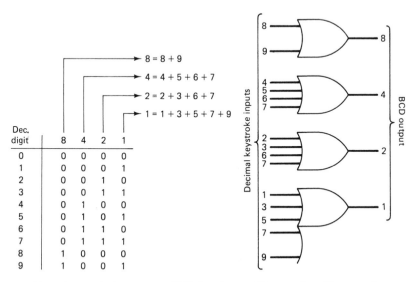

Note: In a typical system, an ASCII decoder would be employed between the keyboard and the bus lines in a microcomputer. Thus, the decimal keystroke signals would be transmitted to the CPU in ASCII code.

Fig. 8-8. An encoder that inputs keystrokes from a decimal keyboard and outputs binary coded decimal signals.

the decimal digit is 1, or 3, or 5, or 7, or 9, as listed in the truth table. The next-most-significant digit shall be logic-high whenever the decimal digit is 2, or 3, or 6, or 7, and so on. Since only OR relations are involved, the encoder comprises only OR gates.

Binary-to-Seven-Segment Encoder

A decimal/7-segment diode matrix encoder is exemplified in Fig. 8-9. This arrangement has ten input lines corresponding to the decimal digits. It has seven output lines (a through g) which correspond to the segments in a 7-segment display device. This display device represents a single decimal digit. When an encoder input line is energized, current flows into particular output lines in accordance with the diodes that interconnect the input and output lines.

In the example of Fig. 8-9, the decimal/7-input line is energized, and in turn the output a,b,c lines are energized. Accordingly, the numeral 7 is displayed. Observe that the encoder diodes permit current flow in only one direction. In turn, an input current is "steered" into particular output lines. As an illustration, when the decimal/7-input line is energized, forward current flows into the a, b, and c output lines. On the other hand, current flow is blocked from the d, e, f, and g output lines.

Priority Encoder

A widely used priority encoder arrangement is shown in Fig. 8-10. It is utilized to control access of peripheral devices to a microcomputer input/output channel, so that the device with the highest assigned priority gains access first. In this example, eight input lines and three output lines are provided. Note that if one input line is activated, the circuit operates as an 8-line-to-binary encoder. Thus if input line $\overline{5}$ is activated, a 101 count is outputted to the microcomputer.

Next, suppose that input lines $\overline{3}$, $\overline{6}$, and $\overline{7}$ are activated. In turn, the encoder outputs a binary count representing the highest-order line ($\overline{7}$), or the binary count 111 is outputted. Observe also that since all inputs are active-low, control output $\overline{EO}$ is logic-low and control output $\overline{GS}$ is logic-high while there is no signal input to the encoder. On the other hand, as soon as any input line is activated, control output $\overline{EO}$ goes logic-high and control output $\overline{GS}$ goes logic-low.

Troubleshooting Considerations

TTL devices can overheat and become damaged if required to conduct excessive current. Therefore, troubleshooting procedures must

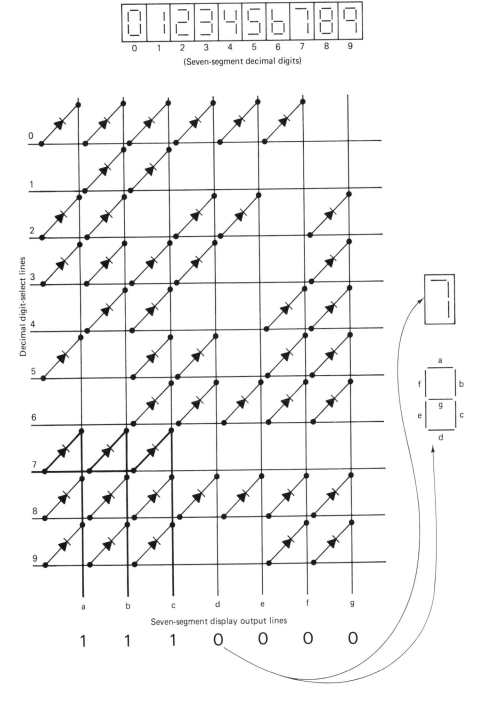

(Seven-segment decimal digits)

Seven-segment display output lines

Note: This diode matrix is an example of a read-only memory (ROM).

Fig. 8-9. A decimal/7-segment diode matrix encoder.

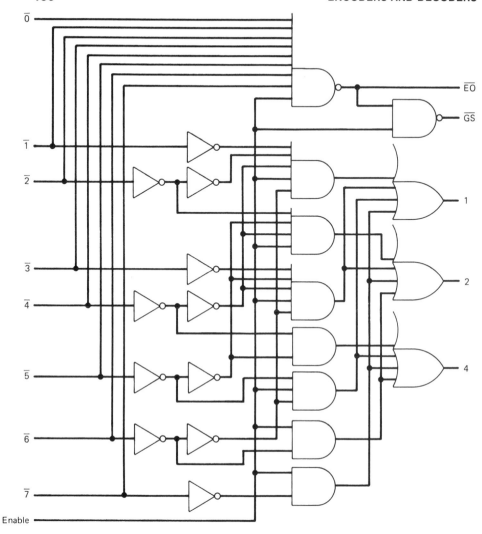

Note: This configuration is an elaborated 8-line-to-binary encoder. It includes an Enable control line whereby input data flow can be enabled or inhibited. The eight input lines produce a 421-binary output, and also develop an Enable Output ($\overline{EO}$) signal and a Gate or Strobe ($\overline{GS}$) signal for control of access to the microcomputer input/output channel by peripheral devices.

Fig. 8-10. A priority encoder arrangement (*Courtesy, Hewlett-Packard*).

observe suitable overload precautions. For example, when making static-stimulus tests, it is often desired to force a logic-low node logic-high, so that the response of subsequent circuitry can be checked. As shown in Fig.

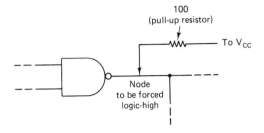

Note: When static stimulus tests are made, V_CC is often used as a logic-high
source. However, it is poor practice to apply V_CC directly to a node which
is resting in a logic-low state. Excessive current flow is likely to damage
the logic-low device (NAND gate in this example). Therefore, the
troubleshooter should employ a series pull-up resistor when forcing a
logic-low node logic-high.

**Fig. 8-11. A pull-up resistor should be used when a node is to
be forced logic-high.**

8-11, a current-limiting pull-up resistor should be used in series with a
test lead to V_CC when a logic-low node is to be forced logic-high.

Note that a commercial logic pulser can drive 750 mA into a logic-
low node while forcing it logic-high. Although this current value would
be highly abnormal in static-stimulus tests, it will not damage a TTL
device inasmuch as the pulse width is limited to 300 ns. Thus, the energy
content of the high-current pulse is comparatively small.

As previously noted, an EO output is active-high; on the other hand,
an $\overline{EO}$ output is active-low. The bar over the EO is read NOT EO. When
working with microcomputer circuitry, $\overline{EO}$ may also be written EO*.
This is also read NOT EO; an asterisk may be used instead of a bar
because computer printouts write asterisks better than bars. In turn, the
troubleshooter should keep this alternative notation in mind and thereby
avoid confusion.

Low-Impedance Gate Inputs

In most cases, gate inputs have sufficiently high input impedance
that they can be pulsed to an opposite logic state with a commercial logic
pulser. However, as shown in Fig. 8-12, there are a few circuit situations
that can be confusing to the beginner. Observe that the V_CC line has a very
low impedance; in turn, it cannot be driven logic-low with a commercial
logic pulser. Of course, the A input in Fig. 8-12(a) should not be forced
logic-low by connecting it to ground, inasmuch as this connection would
short-circuit the V_CC supply.

Although the V_CC voltage cannot be driven logic-low with a logic
pulser in Fig. 8-12(a), a substantial current pulse can be injected. In other

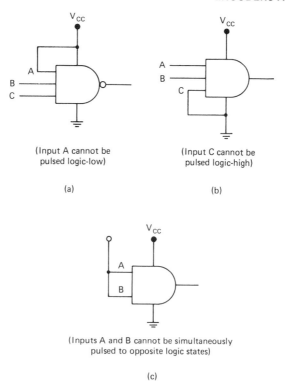

(Input A cannot be
pulsed logic-low)

(a)

(Input C cannot be
pulsed logic-high)

(b)

(Inputs A and B cannot be simultaneously
pulsed to opposite logic states)

(c)

Fig. 8-12. Inputs that cannot be pulsed to the opposite logic
state. (a) An input returned to V_{CC}; (b) an input returned to ground;
(c) inputs tied together.

words, a current tracer will show that a logic pulser injects a pulse current
into the V_{CC} line; this pulse current can be traced through the low-
impedance V_{CC} circuitry with a current tracer. In an elaborate system, the
troubleshooter will note that there is a great deal of current pulse activity
on the V_{CC} line, although its voltage remains essentially constant.

With reference to Fig. 8-12(b) the C input to the gate cannot be pulsed
logic-high with a commercial logic pulser; the impedance of the ground
bus is too low to permit a pulse-voltage test. On the other hand, a current
tracer will show that a logic pulser injects a pulse current into the ground
bus. The troubleshooter will also note that there is considerable current
pulse activity on the ground bus in an elaborate system.

When inputs are tied together, as exemplified in Fig. 8-12(c), they
can be simultaneously pulsed logic-high or logic-low; however, it is
evident that the inputs cannot be simultaneously pulsed to opposite logic
states. If the troubleshooter should need to make this type of test, he must

razor-cut one of the PC conductors, so that it is temporarily open-circuited. Then, after tests are completed, the slit in the PC conductor must be repaired with a small drop of solder. (See also Fig. 8-13.)

GENERAL PRECAUTIONS

1. Keep track of the various mounting screws and their proper locations. It is good foresight to color-code individual screws and insertion points with a toothpick and poster paints.

2. Keep track of spacers, retaining rings, and springs. Color-code items that could cause confusion on reassembly.

3. The logic board may mate with an edge connector, or it may have an interconnect cable. Take care not to place undue stress on interconnect cables.

4. When you turn a logic board over, remember that a device or component which was to the left of a "landmark" will now be to the right of the "landmark." (Or, if it was above the "landmark," it will now be below the "landmark.")

5. Take more than usual care to avoid accidental short circuits between device pins or between PC conductors with instrument test tips, or with tools.

6. Check the service manual for the microcomputer to determine correct procedures in adjusting the power supplies.

7. Make certain that all socketed devices are fully inserted into their sockets.

8. Do not touch any CMOS device or replace it unless your hand is at ground potential.

SPECIALIZED PRECAUTIONS

1. Check the service manual for the microcomputer to determine the correct sequence of operation in adjustment or replacement of mechanical components.

2. Check the service manual for any special instructions in analysis of CPU trouble symptoms.

3. If the microcomputer has been previously serviced, try to obtain a report of the malfunction and what was done to correct it.

4. Comparison tests against a similar microcomputer in normal operating condition can be very helpful—but only for steady-state conditions. Remember that the clocks are not synchronized.

Fig. 8-13. Precautions in troubleshooting microcomputer logic boards.

Multiplexers
and Demultiplexers

Microprocessor Bus Lines * Eight-Channel Multiplexer Arrangement * Eight-Channel Demultiplexer Arrangement * Three-State Buffers * Virtual Multiplexer * Multiplexed Seven-Segment Display * Troubleshooting Notes * Novel Scanning-Action Quick Test * Disassembly Precautions * Measure V_{CC} First

Microprocessor Bus Lines

As previously noted, microprocessors are bus-organized digital systems. With reference to Fig. 9-1, a typical microprocessor arrangement employs an address bus, a data bus, timing and control buses, clock lines, and power lines. Note that the data bus in this example consists of eight wires (lines) for bidirectional data flow. The external data bus typically comprises PC conductors on the microcomputer circuit board. This external data bus connects to pins of various IC's, and thence to internal data buses. An internal data bus consists of microinterconnects inside of an IC.

When data is being fed into a microcomputer from several sources, the bus lines must be energized from only one source at a time. In turn, means are required to select a desired source and to exclude the other sources. Data from one source may be admitted for a certain period of time, and then the data from another source may be admitted for a following period of time. This process is called multiplexing.

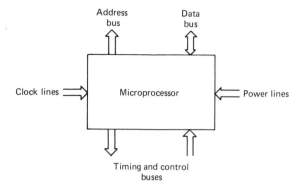

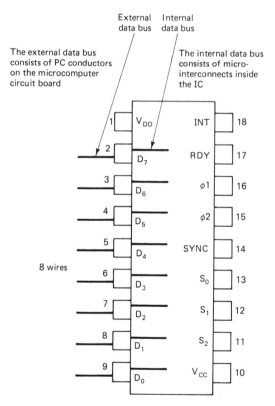

Fig. 9-1. A microprocessor is a bus-organized system.

Eight-Channel Multiplexer Arrangement

With reference to Fig. 9-2, the information on data line D3 is being multiplexed into the output line T. Observe that the Inhibit line is logic-low, and that the binary address 110 is being applied to control

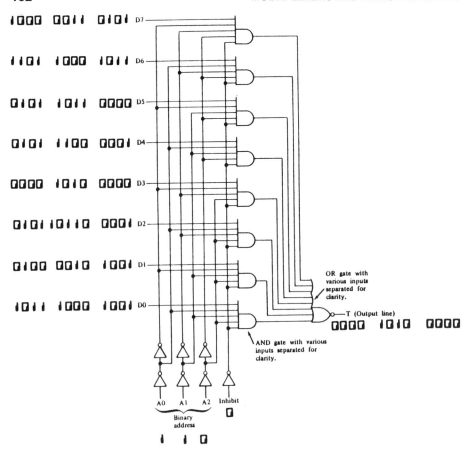

Fig. 9-2. An eight-channel multiplexer arrangement with eight data inputs, one data output, and three control inputs (*Courtesy, Hewlett-Packard*).

inputs $A_0A_1A_2$. In turn, all inputs to the AND gate connected to data line D3 are logic-high; on the other hand not all of the inputs to any other AND gate are logic-high at this time. Accordingly, the information on data line D3 is channeled through the multiplexer and into the output line T.

Basically, multiplexing is a processing of signals from multiple sources into a lesser number of outputs. As an illustration, other widely used multiplexer arrangements can multiplex 4 or 16 lines into one output line; word multiplexers can be used, for example, to multiplex three 4-bit-wide parallel words into a single 4-bit-wide output. In other words, a multiplexer may have several output lines, although by definition it will have a greater number of input lines.

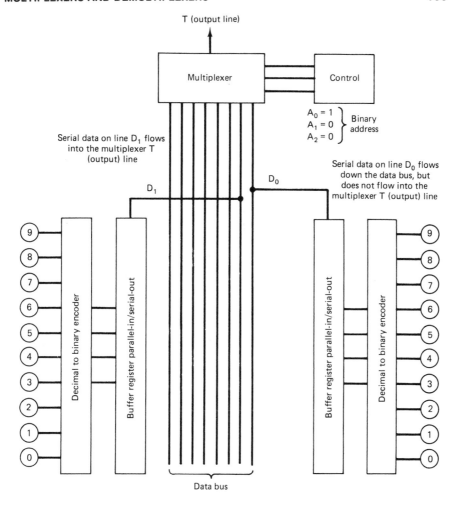

Fig. 9-3. Example of multiplexer operation.

In the example of Fig. 9-2, the multiplexer may be inhibited (disabled) at any time by driving the Inhibit input logic-high. The binary address may be changed at any time to channel some other data lines through the multiplexer. If the Inhibit line is maintained logic-low, and a binary address such as 110 is continuously applied, the multiplexer is said to function as a data selector. These terms are often used interchangeably. An example of multiplexer operation is shown in Fig. 9-3.

Eight-Channel Demultiplexer Arrangement

A demultiplexer directs data from a single input into one of several outputs as determined by a binary address applied to the control inputs.

With reference to Fig. 9-4, the data on the input line is channeled through the demultiplexer into output D4 due to application of the binary address 100 to control inputs $A_0A_1A_2$. We observe that the demultiplexer in Fig. 9-4 has a single input, whereas the multiplexer in Fig. 9-2 has a single output.

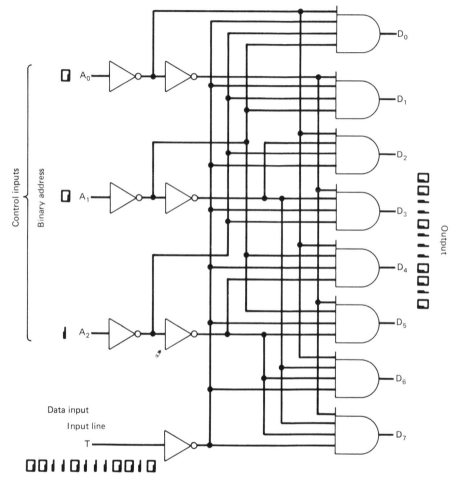

Note: Instead of being demultiplexed first to one output channel, then to another output channel, and then to still another output channel, the data on the single input line can be continuously channeled into a given output line by maintaining a fixed binary address on the control inputs. For example, if the address 100 is continuously maintained, output line D4 will be continuously active. When used in this manner, the demultiplexer is called a data distributor.

Fig. 9-4. A demultiplexer arrangement with a single data input, eight data outputs, and three control inputs (*Courtesy, Hewlett-Packard*).

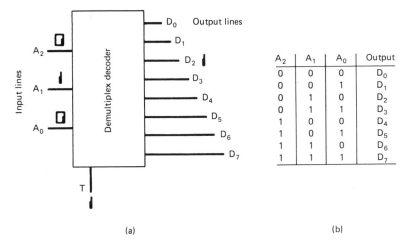

Fig. 9-5. Demultiplexer in decoder application. (a) Input and output lines; (b) truth table.

With reference to Fig. 9-5, a demultiplexer may also be operated as a decoder. Thus, if line T is continuously maintained logic-high, the binary address $A_0A_1A_2$ will determine which of the output lines will go logic-high. In this example, $A_0A_1A_2 = 010$, and output line D2 goes logic-high. Stated otherwise, the demultiplexer is operating as a 3-line-to-8-line decoder. Another design operates as a 4-line-to-16-line decoder.

Three-State Buffers

Another type of multiplexer employs three-state buffers. Three-state buffers are widely used in bus-organized microprocessor systems, as depicted in Fig. 9-6. A three-state buffer is more flexible than a conventional buffer, because it is effectively disconnected from the load when its control line is driven logic-low. When its control line is driven logic-high, the buffer feeds data through to the load in the same manner as a conventional buffer.

In the example of Fig. 9-6, the three-state buffers operate as enabling devices. In other words, the data at the output terminals of the digital transmitting section cannot enter the data bus while the control line is logic-low—the transmitting section is effectively disconnected from the bus. On the other hand, when the control line is driven logic-high, the transmitting section is enabled, or, its output terminals are connected to the data bus.

Three-state buffers greatly simplify bus-organized microprocessor systems because the data bus functions as a "party line," wherein any one of many transmitting sections may be switched into or switched

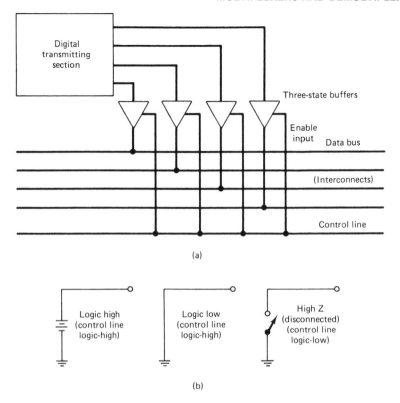

(a)

(b)

Fig. 9-6. Three-state buffers are used to switch transmitting sections into or out of the data bus. (a) Three-state buffer connections; (b) three-state buffer output may be logic-high, logic-low, or disconnected from the bus.

out of the bus by means of control lines. By way of comparison, a three-state buffer functions as an output gating device, much as an AND gate functions as an input gating device. (Refer back to the Inhibit line in Fig. 9-2.)

Virtual Multiplexer

Virtual multiplexers employ three-state buffers to process signals from multiple sources into a lesser number of outputs. As an illustration, three data sources are shown in a virtual-multiplex relation to a single data line in Fig. 9-7. Only one of the sources will be channeled into the output line (data line) at a particular time. Thus, the "binary addresses" are 001, or 010, or 100. In this example, the "binary address" 010 is applied, and Data Transmitting Section II outputs information into the data line.

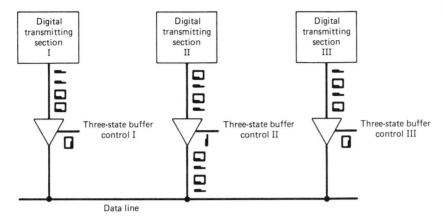

Note: Digital Transmitting Section I outputs the data word 1100; Digital Transmitting Section II outputs the data word 0101; Digital Transmitting Section III outputs the data word 1010. Since the "binary address" is 010, the data word 0101 is virtually multiplexed into the data line.

Fig. 9-7. Basic example of virtual multiplexing.

Multiplexed Seven-Segment Display

Seven-segment displays are often multiplexed as shown in Fig. 9-8 in order to minimize hardware requirements. The multiplexer scans the row of numerals and decimal points, with the result that each character is illuminated for only one-eighth of the total time. However, selected characters appear to glow steadily, due to persistence of vision. Note also that a selected LED is pulsed to a higher output than if it were being steadily energized; in turn, the pulsed LED appears to have normal brilliance.

Observe in Fig. 9-8 that operation of the seven-segment decoder is timed to coincide with the sequence of outputs from the multiplexer. All of the LED's in a single character are returned to a particular multiplexer output. Accordingly, this group of LED's can glow only while that particular output from the multiplexer is logic-high. Thus, when the LSD digit (9) is driven logic-high by the multiplexer, the seven-segment decoder is outputting a "9" signal. Note that this decoded "9" signal is also applied to the MSD device—but the MSD device does not glow at this time because its multiplexer line is logic-low.

Immediately after the LSD has been scanned, the MSD is scanned by the multiplexer. At this time, a "1" signal is outputted by the seven-segment decoder, and the MSD device displays the "1." Note that this

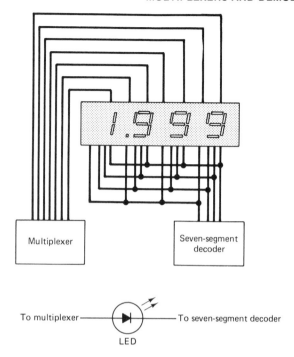

Note: The LED's in the display device are all driven in parallel (simultaneously) by the seven-segment decoder (only four lines are shown).
However, the LED's in each numeral are returned to the multiplexer.
Accordingly, only one numeral can be energized at a given time,
depending on the multiplexer output.

Fig. 9-8. Displays are often multiplexed to minimize hardware.

decoded "1" signal is being applied to all four display devices. However,
only the MSD device displays the "1," inasmuch as it is the only device
that is returned to a logic-high multiplexer output at this particular
time. Similar considerations apply to display of the decimal point.

This multiplexer/decoder display circuitry is further detailed in
Fig. 9-9. As previously noted, each segment in a seven-segment display
is illuminated by an LED, lettered a through g. The LED's are selected
by the seven-segment decoder, and, if the multiplexer is energizing
this numeral at this particular time, the selected segments will glow
and display the specified numeral. Although the decoder is also selecting
corresponding LED's in the other numerals at this time, those segments
do not glow because they are not being energized by the multiplexer.

Troubleshooting Notes

As previously noted, an LED in a multiplexed seven-segment
display is pulsed to a higher output level than if it were being steadily

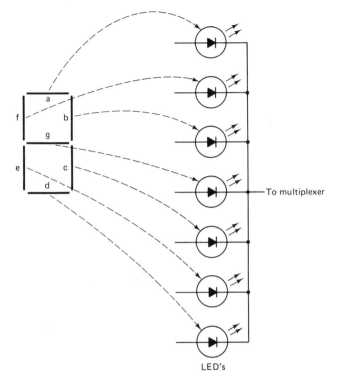

(Terminals a, b, c, d, e, f, and g
connect to the seven-segment
decoder)

Note: Seven LED's are shown, corresponding to the segments in a numeral. In practice, each numeral is accompanied by a decimal point, for which a separate LED is provided. The decimal-point LED is often denoted "h." It is also energized by the multiplexer, via the decoder.

Fig. 9-9. LED arrangement in a seven-segment display device.

energized. This overdrive does not damage the LED because it represents only one-eighth of the total elapsed time. On the other hand, if this overdrive level happens to be continuously maintained, the LED will become damaged. For this reason, static stimulus tests are not suitable in troubleshooting procedures for multiplexed seven-segment display networks. Instead, analysis of trouble symptoms must be made with normal clocking of the network.

Novel Scanning-Action Quick Test

Scanning of a multiplexed seven-segment display proceeds at a rate that exceeds the persistence of vision. For example, scanning might

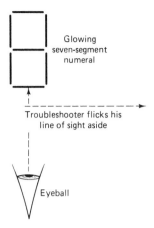

Glowing
seven-segment
numeral

Troubleshooter flicks his
line of sight aside

Eyeball

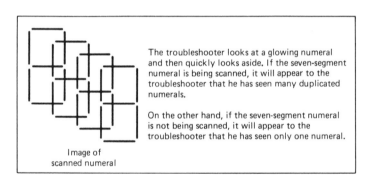

Image of
scanned numeral

The troubleshooter looks at a glowing numeral
and then quickly looks aside. If the seven-segment
numeral is being scanned, it will appear to the
troubleshooter that he has seen many duplicated
numerals.

On the other hand, if the seven-segment numeral
is not being scanned, it will appear to the
troubleshooter that he has seen only one numeral.

Fig. 9-10. To determine whether the display device is being
scanned, flick your line of sight aside from the glowing numeral.

occur at a 50-Hz rate. Although it might seem to be "impossible" to
"see" the 50-Hz scanning action, the troubleshooter can easily extend
his sense of sight in this situation by employing a new "trick of the
trade." This technique consists of optically scanning the scanned
display.

In other words, the troubleshooter looks at the glowing seven-
segment numeral, and then quickly looks aside—thereby optically
scanning the numeral. (See Fig. 9-10.) If the glowing numeral is being
scanned by a multiplexer, it will appear to the troubleshooter that
he has seen a long string of duplicated numerals. However, if the seven-

segment numeral is glowing steadily and is not being scanned, the troubleshooter's mind sees only one numeral. This new trick of the trade is helpful in preliminary troubleshooting procedures.

> Experiment: Try the foregoing trick of the trade with a pocket calculator that employs seven-segment LED readout, such as a Commodore SR4912. This experiment clearly demonstrates the image resulting from multiplexing of a seven-segment display. The string of duplicated numerals is perceived best when only one numeral is being displayed. However, the same basic (if confused) result is obtained when a complete row of numerals is being displayed.

IC's Plugged into Sockets

Most IC's are soldered into PC boards. However, an occasional IC will be found plugged into a socket. In such a case, it is good practice to check for proper seating of the IC—it could be "tilted" so that some pins do not make normal contact in the socket. Also, in the case of an IC with a large number of pins, check to make certain that a pin may not be bent under the IC, so that it is not inserted into the socket. In such a case, the pin should be carefully straightened— if the pin should break while being straightened, the IC must be replaced.

Disassembly Precautions

Disassembly of a microcomputer or other microprocessor-based unit may or may not be straightforward. If you are not familiar with the particular equipment, it is advisable to check the service manual for possible precautions. For example, some of the interconnects inside of a microcomputer may be fragile, and require close attention during disassembly of the unit. Again, the disassembly and reassembly procedure for a calculator keyboard may be unexpectedly involved.

Measure V_{CC} First—and Also Check for Ripple

Before digging into the "innards" of a microcomputer, it is good foresight to measure V_{CC} to make certain that its value may not be marginal. Then, if V_{CC} is within rated value, follow up with a check for excessive ripple—this can be accomplished to best advantage with an oscilloscope, although a good ac voltmeter will also serve the purpose. Experienced troubleshooters know that marginal V_{CC} and/or excessive ripple can cause misleading and puzzling trouble symptoms.

Voltage and ripple checks made while the microcomputer is idle are not completely meaningful. These tests should be made while a program is being run. The instruction manual will list the rated values (and often permissible tolerances) on supply voltages. However, the manual may not state the permissible ripple percentage for a given voltage. In such a case, a comparison test is most helpful; if a similar microcomputer in normal operating condition is available, the troubleshooter can "get a handle" on ripple voltage.

The microcomputer service manual typically shows a picture of the PC board, with the power-supply test points called out. For example, +12V and a +5V terminals may be indicated; a −5V terminal may also be indicated. Typically, all power-supply voltages have a permissible tolerance rating of ±5 percent. You may find potentiometer adjustments for some or all of the power-supply voltages. However, if an adjustment is not provided, and the voltage is out of tolerance, you must proceed to check out the power-supply circuit and correct the fault.

Fig. 9-11. Logic probe, logic pulser, current tracer, and logic clip (*Courtesy, Hewlett-Packard*).

Fig. 9-12. Appearance of a logic comparator (*Courtesy, Hewlett-Packard*).

Detailed illustrations of the microcomputer circuit board may or may not be provided; however, you can expect to find a comprehensive schematic diagram in the service manual. At least a few of the key system waveforms are usually included. Circuit tracing on the PC board requires identification of suitable "landmarks," such as filter capacitors, the microprocessor, and the memory IC's. Then, the conductors for particular circuits can be identified with respect to the IC pinout numbers noted on the schematic diagram.

Circuit-action tests for tracking down faults can generally be made with basic logic test equipment, such as a logic probe, pulser, current tracer, clip, and comparator. (See Figs. 9-11 and 9-12.) In addition to a DVM, an oscilloscope will occasionally be of assistance. For example, a scope can be used to check the operating frequencies through a divider chain. If you encounter an incorrect divider frequency, you know that you have entered a trouble area. Note that a frequency counter can be used instead of a scope to check out a divider chain.

10

Comparators and
Parity Generator/Checkers

Data Sources and Destinations * Comparator Circuitry and Operation * Wired-AND (Wired-OR) * Polarity Comparator * Phase Comparator * Parity Generator/Checkers * Parity Trees * Troubleshooting Notes * Control Read-Only Memory * Control Random Access Memory

Data Sources and Destinations

A microprocessor is both a data source and a data destination, as depicted in Fig. 10-1. It functions as a data destination when signals flow from the data bus into the microprocessor. It functions as a data source when signals flow out of the microprocessor into the data bus. A microprocessor also functions as a data source (in the general sense of the term) when it outputs memory control words. As previously noted, a microprocessor may perform arithmetical operations, or it may perform logical operations—whence the "processor" terminology.

Data is processed in accordance with a stored program. A program often stipulates logical operations such as: *If A is greater than B, transfer program control to line 19.* The microprocessor makes this logical decision (whether A is greater than B), by means of a comparator that has three outputs. For example, if the words $A_0A_1A_2A_3 = 1011$ and $B_0B_1B_2B_3 = 1001$ are entered into the comparator, its $A>B$ output will go logic-high, but its $A<B$ and $A = B$ outputs will remain logic-low.

Data processing does not always proceed without error—and reliability is paramount. Therefore, microprocessor systems are designed

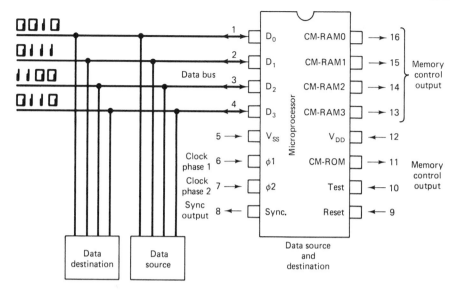

Note: The data bus is bidirectional; at one time it will be transmitting signals from the microprocessor to another device; at another time, the data bus will be transmitting signals from some device in the system to the microprocessor. Thus, a microprocessor is both a data source and a data destination. Memory control output signals are sourced by the microprocessor; in turn, data signals are sourced by the memory and are transmitted to the microprocessor.

Fig. 10-1. A microprocessor is both a source and a destination for data signals.

with built-in accuracy checking facilities. As previously noted, tape recorders are often used for external data storage. Although tape-recorder reliability is high, it is not perfect—once in a "blue moon," a bit might drop out because of a tape defect. Or, a spurious bit might be inserted due to a noise pulse. Built-in accuracy checking facilities commonly employ parity generator/checkers, as will be explained subsequently.

Comparator Circuitry and Operation

With reference to Fig. 10-2, a simple comparator functions as an equality (or inequality) checker for a pair of bits or a pair of words. It shows whether the inputs are equal or unequal; however, if the inputs are unequal, this configuration cannot indicate which of the inputs is the larger. Stated otherwise, it functions as a qualitative comparator on the basis of identity or nonidentity of the inputs.

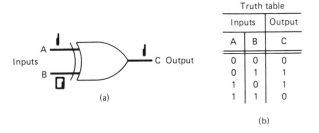

(a)

Truth table

Inputs		Output
A	B	C
0	0	0
0	1	1
1	0	1
1	1	0

(b)

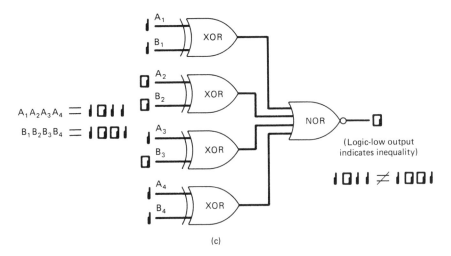

(c)

Note: The truth table shows that a single XOR gate operates as a comparator
(equality checker) for two bits. In other words, if the two bits are 1's, the
XOR output is 0; if the two bits are 0's, the XOR output is 0; but if one bit
is a 1 and the other bit is a 0, the XOR output is a 1. Thus, a logic-low
output indicates equality, and a logic-high output indicates inequality,
in example (a).

Fig. 10-2. A simple equality checker, or comparator. (a) XOR
gate; (b) truth table; (c) XOR gates and NOR gate provide equality
checking action for longer words.

A quantitative comparator that can indicate which of the inputs is
the larger (or the smaller) requires elaborated combinatorial logic, as
exemplified in Fig. 10-3. It directly generates A-greater-than-B and A-
less-then-B outputs. An A = B output is generated by decoding the A-
neither-less-than-nor-greater-than-B condition with a NOR gate. All
three outputs are activated by the active-low enable input $\overline{E}$. Observe that
the A_4 and B_4 inputs are the most significant inputs, and A_0 and B_0 are the
least significant inputs. Thus, if A_4 is logic-high and B_4 is logic-low, the
A>B output will go logic-high regardless of all other inputs except $\overline{E}$.

LOGIC DIAGRAM

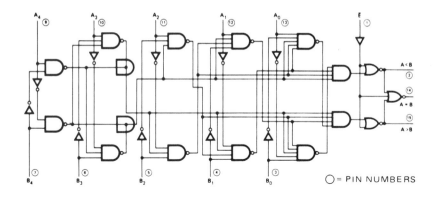

LOGIC SYMBOL

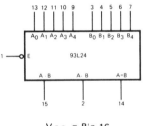

V_CC = Pin 16
GND = Pin 8

PIN NAMES

$\bar{E}$	Enable (Active LOW) Input
A_0, A_1, A_2, A_3, A_4	Word A Parallel Inputs
B_0, B_1, B_2, B_3, B_4	Word B Parallel Inputs
$A < B$	A Less than B Output
$A > B$	A Greater than B Output
$A = B$	A Equal to B Output

TRUTH TABLE

$\bar{E}$	A	B	$A < B$	$A > B$	$A = B$
H	X	X	L	L	L
L	Word A = Word B		L	L	H
L	Word A > Word B		L	H	L
L	Word A < Word B		H	L	L

L = LOW Voltage Level
H = HIGH Voltage Level
X = Either HIGH or LOW Voltage Level

—Fairchild

Fig. 10-3. A 5-bit comparator with A = B, A<B, and A>B outputs.

Wired-AND (Wired-OR)

The configuration in Fig. 10-3 includes wired-AND implementation. As shown in Fig. 10-4, the wired-AND circuit employs open-collector output transistors (Q3) with a pull-up resistor (R_L). Note that the "phantom-AND" symbol is not a physical gate—it is merely a connection point. This connection point is enclosed by the AND symbol to indicate that the circuit has wired-AND function.

This arrangement is also called a wired-OR circuit, although it is truly neither wired-AND nor wired-OR in the strict sense of the terms. In other words, as shown by the logic equations in Fig. 10-4, the circuit function is that of a negated-AND gate, which is the same as that of a NOR gate. Thus, in the strict technical sense, this circuit would be termed a wired-negated-AND or a wired-NOR configuration.

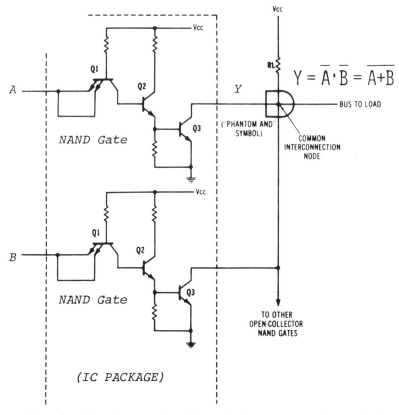

$$Y = \overline{A} \cdot \overline{B} = \overline{A+B}$$

(Y goes logic-low when inputs A and B are simultaneously pulsed logic-high. If input B is logic-low, Y will not go logic-low when A is pulsed logic-high, or vice versa)

Fig. 10-4. In wired-AND circuits, one gate constrains the other gate to a logic-low state (*Courtesy, Hewlett-Packard*).

Operation of the wired-AND circuit in Fig. 10-4 is based on the very low output resistance of Q3 when driven logic-low. In other words, if input A drives Q3 in the upper gate logic-low, then input B cannot drive Q3 in the lower gate logic-high. Stated otherwise, one gate will constrain the other gate logic-low. From the logical viewpoint, this is negated-AND action, or NOR action. Note that wired-AND implementation is used to minimize hardware requirements.

To clearly understand constraining action, note that if Q3 in the upper gate in Fig. 10-4 is driven logic-low (driven into saturation), the collector-to-ground resistance of Q3 can be regarded as a short circuit from a practical viewpoint. Then, if the lower gate attempts to drive the output logic-high, no output voltage change results inasmuch as the IR drop across a short-circuit is zero. However, if inputs A and B are simultaneously driven to cut off the Q3 transistors, the output will then go logic-high.

Polarity Comparator

Microprocessors may also be required to make logical decisions such as: *If V1 and V2 have opposite polarities, then transfer program control to*

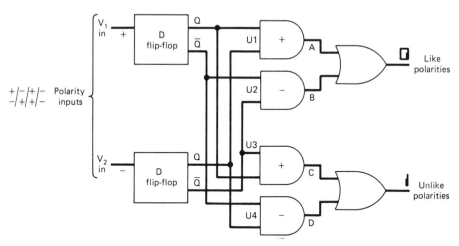

Note: In the above example, a positive voltage is inputted to the upper flip-flop, and a negative voltage is inputted to the lower flip-flop. In turn, the "Unlike Polarities" output goes logic-high, indicating that unlike polarities have been inputted to the polarity comparator.

Note: A D flip-flop transfers the input logic state to its Q output, and the complement of the input logic state simultaneously appears at its Q̄ output. Thus, the D flip-flops serve as true-complement processors for the input signals. Decoder operation requires availability of the input signals in both true and complement forms.

Fig. 10-5. Example of a polarity (sign) indicator configuration.

line 27. Logical operations of this type are performed by a polarity comparator, as exemplified in Fig. 10-5. Inputs V1 and V2 are applied to D flip-flops which are in turn connected to the decoder AND gates U1,U2,U3,U4. Observe that U1 goes logic-high if V1 and V2 are both positive; U2 goes logic-high if V1 and V2 are both negative. On the other hand, unlike input polarities cause either U3 or U4 to go logic-high.

Phase Comparator

Comparators are also used to indicate phase relations. With reference to Fig. 10-6, a single XOR gate functions as a phase comparator for square-wave inputs. Thus, if the two inputs are in phase with each other, the gate output is zero. On the other hand, if the two inputs are 180° out of phase with each other, the gate output is continuously logic-high. Intermediate phase relations produce pulse outputs with related widths, as shown in the diagram.

Note that a square wave has a 50 percent duty cycle with an average value that is equal to 50 percent of peak voltage. As shown in the diagram, if the comparator inputs are 45° out of phase with each other, the gate output has a 25 percent duty cycle. This duty cycle corresponds to an average value of 25 percent of peak voltage. Again, if the comparator inputs are 135° out of phase with each other, the gate output has 75 percent duty cycle with an average value of 75 percent of peak voltage.

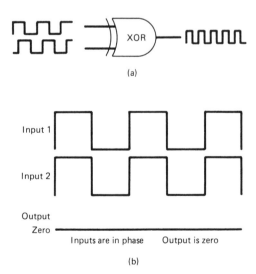

Fig. 10-6. XOR gate functions as a square-wave phase comparator.

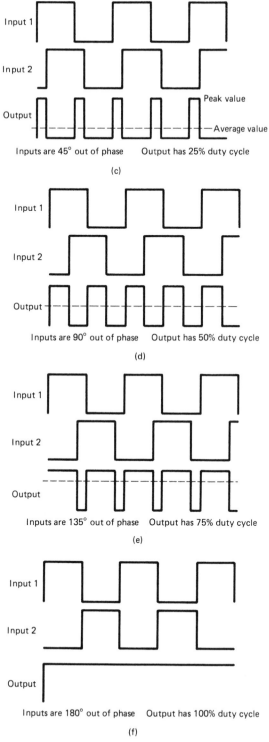

Input 1

Input 2

Output

Peak value

Average value

Inputs are 45° out of phase   Output has 25% duty cycle

(c)

Input 1

Input 2

Output

Inputs are 90° out of phase   Output has 50% duty cycle

(d)

Input 1

Input 2

Output

Inputs are 135° out of phase   Output has 75% duty cycle

(e)

Input 1

Input 2

Output

Inputs are 180° out of phase   Output has 100% duty cycle

(f)

Fig. 10-6 (*continued*)

Parity Generator/Checkers

As previously noted, errors can occur in data transmission. For example, when a magnetic tape with a recorded program is played back into the microprocessor, there is a possibility (although it may be quite small) that a bit could drop out, or that a false bit could be introduced as a result of a transient noise pulse. In turn, microprocessor system designers include error-detection circuitry in data transmission systems. Parity generator/checkers are the most common error-detection devices.

Parity error-detecting arrangements employ parity bits. For example, suppose that we are transmitting 3-bit data words which may be 000, 001, 010, 011, 100, 101, 110, or 111. If 010 "comes through" as 110, or 011, or 000, the CPU is clearly going to be "in big trouble." However, if we now add a special fourth bit (the parity bit) such that the number of 1's in a transmitted word is always even, the occurrence of an error can then be detected by an "even/odd comparator."

To continue the foregoing example, our transmitted 3-bit data words with an added even-parity bit will be 0000, 1001, 1010, 0011, 1100, 0101, 0110, and 1111. In other words, the MSB in the transmitted word is the parity bit, and the number of 1's in the transmitted word will always be even, at least in normal operation. Suppose next that a dropout occurs and that 0110 "comes through" as 0010; now, the number of 1's in the transmitted word is odd, and this condition will be immediately "caught" by an "even/odd comparator."

With reference to Fig. 10-7, a basic parity generator/checker configuration is shown. This arrangement provides four inputs, and indicates either even parity or odd parity. Consider the situation in which the 3-bit data word 110 is being transmitted with an even parity bit: 0110. When 0110 is inputted by the Fig. 10-7 configuration, the even-output line will go logic-high, and the odd-output line will go logic-low.

To continue the foregoing example, if a dropout occurs in transmission, and 0110 now "comes through" as 0010, the odd-output line goes logic-high and the even-output line goes logic-low in Fig. 10-7. Thereby, an error in data transmission is indicated—the error signal either stops data-processing action, or a warning signal is activated to alert the operator.

Next, consider the case in which we are using odd parity; the parity bit at the transmitter will be provided to make the number of 1's in the transmitted word odd. For example, 001 will be transmitted as 0001, 011 will be transmitted as 1011, and so on. Next, when 1011 is inputted by the Fig. 10-7 configuration, the odd-output line will go logic-high, and the even-output line will go logic-low. However, if a noise pulse should

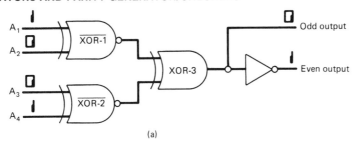

(a)

A₁	A₂	A₃	A₄	$\overline{XOR\text{-}1}$	$\overline{XOR\text{-}2}$	XOR-3	$\overline{XOR\text{-}3}$
0	0	0	0	1	1	0	1
0	0	0	1	1	0	1	0
0	0	1	0	1	0	1	0
0	0	1	1	1	1	0	1
0	1	0	0	0	1	1	0
0	1	0	1	0	0	0	1
0	1	1	0	0	0	0	1
0	1	1	1	0	1	1	0
1	0	0	0	0	1	1	0
1	0	0	1	0	0	0	1

(b)

Fig. 10-7. Basic parity generator/checker configuration. (a) logic diagram; (b) examples of output states with various nibble inputs.

change the transmitted data word 1011 into 1111, the odd-output line would go logic-low, and the even-output line would go logic-high, thereby indicating a data-transmission error.

It is evident that the same configuration can be operated as a parity generator or as a parity checker. At the transmitting location, input A4 of the Fig. 10-7 arrangement may be maintained logic-high. The data word to be transmitted is applied to inputs A1,A2,A3. Then, if the inputted data word is 001, the even-output line will go logic-high, and the odd-output line will go logic-low. If we are using even parity, the even-line output is the parity bit which we will include in transmission of data word 001.

Parity Trees

Similar circuitry is employed for error checking of longer data words. These networks are called parity trees, as exemplifed in Fig. 10-8. When a parity generator is employed at the transmitting location in a data-processing system, the output from the parity generator is added to

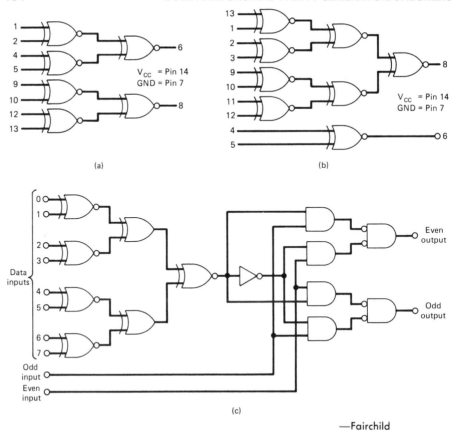

—Fairchild

Fig. 10-8. Examples of commercial parity trees. (a) A dual 4-bit parity tree; (b) an 8-bit parity tree; (c) an 8-bit parity generator/checker with odd-input and even-input control lines.

the data word by means of a register. In other words, the register might have four temporary storage positions; the output from the parity generator is fed into the register's MSB position, and the data word is fed into the three less significant positions. Then, the 4-bit word is unloaded into the data bus, and the circuit is ready to process the next data word.

Note in passing that the foregoing error-detection arrangements will detect any single-error transmission; however, they will not detect a double-error transmission. For example, if 1001 is transmitted with a single error, as 1101, it will be "caught" in an even-parity check. On the other hand, if 1001 is transmitted with a double error, as 1010, it will not be "caught" in an even-parity check. To guard against transmission of double errors, more elaborate parity-checking circuitry and special codes are employed.

Troubleshooting Notes

Experienced troubleshooters recognize various kinds of widely used microprocessors, and this is a key factor in "sizing up" trouble situations. It follows from previous discussion that a microprocessor is likely to employ two power supplies. For example, the comparatively simple 4004

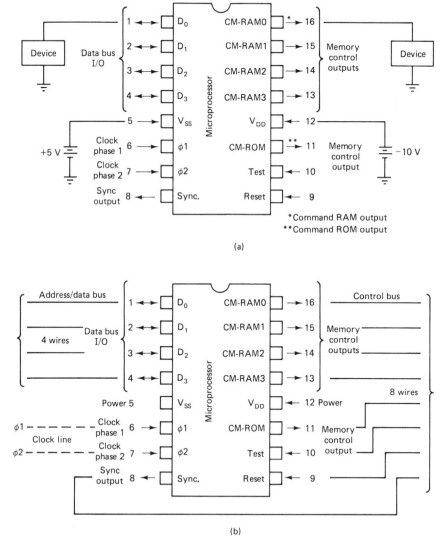

Fig. 10-9. Intel 4004 microprocessor. (a) +5V and −10V power supplies are used: (b) a four-wire address/data bus and an eight-wire control bus are utilized.

microprocessor, which is typically used in electronic cash registers, operates from +5V and −10V power supplies, as depicted in Fig. 10-9.

This microprocessor employs a 16-pin IC package; the power supplies and system devices are referenced to ground, as shown in Fig. 10-9(a). The input/output (I/O) address/data bus consists of four wires, and the control bus comprises eight wires. In general, we will find that microprocessor control buses have more wires than data buses. Two clock lines are utilized; the Ø1 clock waveform is 180° out of phase with the Ø2 clock waveform. The maximum rated clock frequency is 750 kHz. Pins are associated with the following circuit functions:

Pins 1-4: D_0-D_3

    Bidirectional data bus. All address and data communication between the microprocessor and the RAM and ROM chips is handled by way of these four lines.

    Bidirectional means that digital pulses can either flow into pins 1, 2, 3, or 4, or that digital pulses can flow out of pins 1, 2, 3, or 4. Data denotes information in the form of digital pulses.

    An address is a group of digital pulses that designates a specific location of data in a memory (a specific location of stored digital data).

    Data communication means the transfer of digital data from the "outside world" into the microprocessor, or, the transfer of digital data from the microprocessor to the "outside world."

    A RAM is a random-access memory (read-and-write memory). It is typically an integrated circuit that can store incoming digital pulses, retain them as long as may be required, and then output the stored pulses upon command. The stored contents of a RAM can also be erased upon command.

    A ROM is a read-only memory. It is typically an integrated circuit with permanently stored digital data. This data can be read out of the ROM at any time upon command.

    A data bus is a group of lines, such as printed-circuit conductors or associated circuitry which carries digital data in the form of digital pulses.

Pin 5: V_{SS}

    IC terminal connected to the most positive supply voltage. This will be +5 volts in most applications.

Pins 6-7: $Ø_1$-$Ø_2$

    Nonoverlapping clock signals (square waves) which determine processor timing. The clock signals synchronize microprocessor circuit actions; they are externally generated.

Pin 8: SYNC

    The SYNC output is a synchronizing signal generated internally by the microprocessor; it is applied to the RAM and ROM chips (integrated circuits).

The SYNC signal produced by the microprocessor indicates the beginning of the instruction cycle. An instruction is a set of digital pulses that defines a computer operation, such as to move data from a memory into a bus. An instruction cycle is the process of fetching (obtaining) a group of digital pulses (digital word) from a memory and executing the instruction. For example, an instruction might be executed by adding a digital word from a memory to another digital word that is temporarily stored in the arithmetic section of the microprocessor.

Pin 9: RESET

When the RESET input terminal is pulsed, the microprocessor circuitry is initialized for starting a new operation. Any "leftovers" that might be in temporary storage from the previous operation are erased when the RESET input is pulsed.

Pin 10: TEST

TEST input. In an automatic control application, this test input might be connected to a single switch which opens and closes at arbitrary times.

The course of the program can be changed by the logical state of the TEST input. In other words, if the state of the TEST input is logic-LOW (ground potential), the program execution will follow a prescribed course. On the other hand, if the state of the TEST input is logic-HIGH (supply-voltage potential), the program execution will then follow another prescribed course.

Pin 11: CM-ROM

Command-ROM output.

The CM-ROM pin enables (turns on) a ROM bank (a ROM with more than one section). A desired section is selected on command. The CM-ROM pin can also be used to enable input/output (I/O) devices which are connected to the ROM. Note that a ROM section is often called a bank.

Pin 12: V_{DD}

Main supply voltage to the microprocessor. Its value is equal to V_{SS} −15 volts. (V_{SS} is normally +5 volts.)

Pins 13-16: CM-RAM$_0$ to CM-RAM$_3$

Command-RAM outputs.

These outputs act as bank-select signals for the RAM chips. These outputs can also be used to select I/O devices such as keyboard-display devices.

Control Read-Only Memory

We will consider memory organization and operation in the next chapter. Here, let us briefly note the outward aspect of the control read-only memory (ROM) that is used with the 4004 microprocessor. With reference to Fig. 10-10, the CROM IC package has 24 pins (eight more

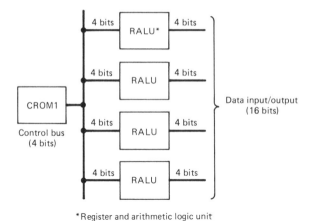

```
NJCND  →  1      CROM*    24  ←  V_GG (−12 V)
DI(7)  →  2               23  →  NFLEN
DI(6)  →  3               22  ←  HOCSH
DI(5)  →  4               21  →  LOCSH
DI(4)  →  5               20  →  NCB(0)
(GND)V_LL  6              19  →  NCB(2)
DI(3)  →  7               18  →  NCB(1)
DI(1)  →  8               17  →  NCR(3)
DI(0)  →  9               16  ←  φ1
DI(2)  → 10               15  ←  φ3
ENCTL  ← 11               14  ←  φ5
(+5 V)V_SS → 12           13  ←  φ7
```

*Control read only memory

```
          4 bits   ┌────────┐  4 bits
        ──────────┤ RALU*  ├──────────┐
          4 bits   └────────┘  4 bits │
        ──────────┤ RALU   ├──────────┤
┌───────┐4 bits   └────────┘  4 bits │  Data input/output
│CROM1  ├──────────┤ RALU   ├─────────┤     (16 bits)
└───────┘4 bits    └────────┘ 4 bits │
Control bus────────┤ RALU   ├─────────┘
(4 bits)           └────────┘
```

*Register and arithmetic logic unit

Fig. 10-10. CROM package and block diagram of basic system.

pins than the microprocessor). This is a specialized type of read-only memory that translates (changes) binary instructions into operational commands. Note that the program consists of instructions. Operational commands tell the CPU how data is to be processed.

Thus, when an instruction word enters the CROM, it triggers a series of commands to the register and arithmetic logic units (RALU's). As explained in greater detail subsequently, the chief types of CROM's are: a standard-instruction, 16-bit arrangement with 43 instructions, and an extended-instruction, 16-bit arrangement that has 17 additional instructions. These 17 instructions include multiplication, division, double-precision add/subtract (requiring two computer words to contain it), and other operations.

Control Random Access Memory

At this point, it is helpful to also briefly note the outward aspect of the control random access (read-and-write) memory (RAM) that is used with the 4004 microprocessor. A RAM is similar to a ROM, except that the contents of a RAM can be erased on command, and new data written into the memory. On the other hand, the contents of a ROM are permanent and cannot be erased. Both types of memory are employed in running a program.

11

Memory Organization and Operation

Microcomputer Organization * Semiconductor Memory Principles * Instruction Register * Memory Address Register * Read-and-Write Memory Operation * Recirculating (Serial) Memory * "Embryo" Computer Experiment * Troubleshooting Considerations * IC and Card "Swapping" * Some Ground Rules

Microcomputer Organization

As seen in Fig. 11-1, a microcomputer is bus-organized with bidirectional and one-way buses interconnecting a program memory and data memory with the central processing unit and the input/output section. As previously noted, a microcomputer is distinguished from a calculator by its program memory with stored instruction words and data words. Data processing is completely automatic in accordance with the instructions that have been entered into the program memory.

In the past, separate memories were used for the program and for the data; thus a program memory and a data memory were provided, with individual memory addressing units. As indicated in Fig. 11-1, microcomputers now utilize a single memory for the program and the data. In general, the program memory (often abbreviated P.M.) is a section contained within a larger memory. The program and data memory is a short-term, high-speed storage device. It is supplemented by medium-term, medium-speed storage devices and by long-term, low-speed storage devices.

The chief distinctions among these three types of memories are in their storage capacities. Thus, a program and data memory has a

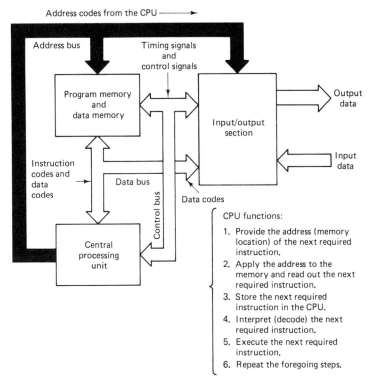

Fig. 11-1. Elementary organization of a microcomputer.

comparatively limited storage capacity; on the other hand, it operates at high speed. High-speed operation is essential in sequencing program instructions. Again, a medium-term memory (such as a floppy disk) has medium storage capacity; it can store much more data than a random-access memory such as used for program storage. However, a floppy disk operates at medium speed, compared with RAM operation.

Finally, a long-term memory (such as magnetic tape) has a high storage capacity; by way of comparison, it operates at low speed. Microcomputers can be regarded as processing data from working storage and from medium-term mass storage. However, we will also encounter microcomputers that operate from magnetic-tape software—this type of microcomputer processes data from long-term storage. Note that the high-speed program and data memory operates back-and-forth with the low-speed mass-storage memory.

Semiconductor Memory Principles

Semiconductor memories are used in microcomputers for program and data storage. With reference to Fig. 11-2, a semiconductor memory

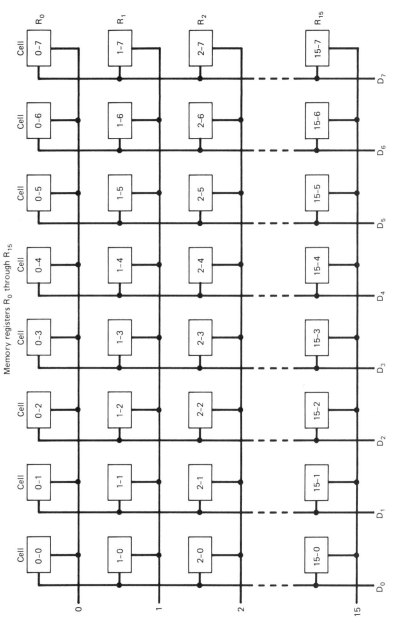

Memory registers R_0 through R_{15}

Note: If register (line) 1 is addressed, the logic states of data lines D_0 through D_7 reflect the logic states of cells 1-0 through 1-7.

Note: Each 8-bit byte occupies its own register in the memory (R_0 through R_{15}). A cell may employ a diode, or it may contain a flip-flop. Simple arrangements utilize diodes, and are in the ROM category.

Fig. 11-2. Logic diagram for a 16-byte memory.

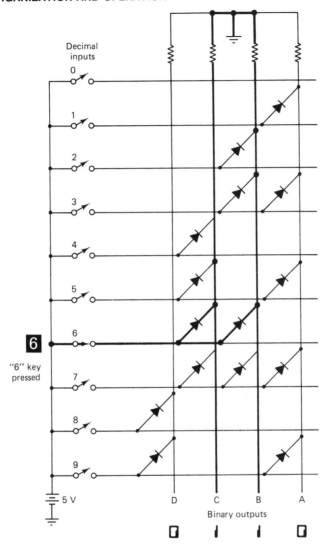

Fig. 11-3. Decimal-to-binary encoder implemented as a diode matrix (read-only memory).

contains rows and columns of devices. The rows are called registers; programmers often call a register a line—thus, line 3, or line 14. Each register consists of cells; typical microprocessor registers contain eight cells (one byte) in each register. A byte consists of eight bits. A memory may be "read out" by registers, or it may be "read out" by cells.

A read-only memory (ROM) has its cells permanently programmed. For example, consider the encoder diode matrix depicted in Fig. 11-3. This type of ROM was previously noted; it is addressed ("read out") register-by-register. Each register comprises a nibble (four bits) in this example. The memory is addressed via ten keyboard switches; in turn, corresponding BCD signals are outputted. Thus, when keyboard switch 6 is closed, the binary coded decimal number 0110 is outputted (ABCD = 0110).

Observe that the memory is directly addressed in the foregoing example. When a large memory is employed, the required number of input lines would be excessive. Accordingly, address decoders are provided between the address lines and the memory per se, as shown in Fig. 11-4. In this example, 16 registers can be addressed via the 1-out-of-16 decoder. The addresses are automatically supplied one after another from the program counter, as detailed subsequently.

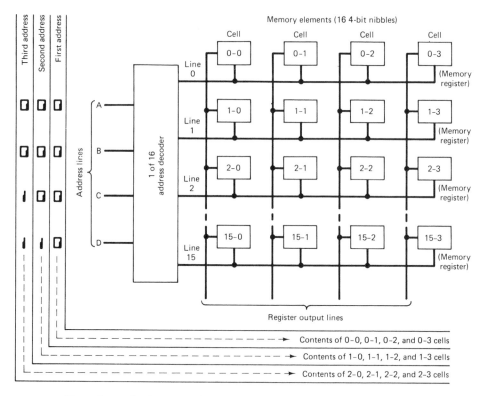

Note: Generally, the ROM will be addressed systematically. Thus, the address 0000 is applied first, with the result that the contents of the "zero" register appear on the output lines. Next, the address 0001 will be applied, with the result that the contents of the "1" register appear on the output lines, and so on.

Fig. 11-4. ROM address inputs and corresponding register outputs.

In the example of Fig. 11-4, the first address is 0000; in turn, the decoder outputs an enabling pulse to the first register and the contents of cells 0-0, 0-1, 0-2, and 0-3 are unloaded into the register output lines. The second address is 0001; the decoder now outputs an enabling pulse to the second register and the contents of cells 1-0, 1-1, 1-2, and 1-3 are unloaded into the register output lines. Note that this memory has a capacity of 16 nibbles, or 64 bits; the memory depicted in Fig. 11-2 has a capacity of 16 bytes, or 128 bits.

Instruction Register

Observe in Fig. 11-5 that when a register is addressed in the memory, its contents flow immediately into the instruction register. However, the contents of the instruction register will then be temporarily stored.

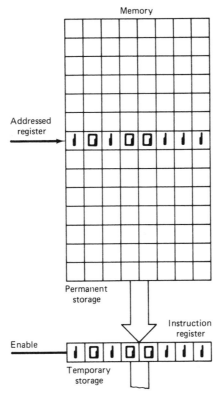

Fig. 11-5. The addressed register in the memory unloads immediately into the instruction register; the instruction register does not unload until its Enable line is driven logic-high.

When the data bus is ready to receive the word that was addressed in the memory, the control section in the CPU will drive the instruction register's enable input logic-high. In turn, the register contents are unloaded into the data bus, and the memory circuits await arrival of another address.

In the example of Fig. 11-5, the addressed register contains the word 10100111. When the decoder outputs a pulse to this register, each cell is connected to a corresponding location in the instruction register. Thus, the word 10100111 is loaded into the register—but the contents of the addressed register in the memory remain unchanged. When the instruction register is enabled (unloaded), it is also cleared, and awaits arrival of the next memory word for temporary storage.

Memory Address Register

At this point, we recognize that most of the activity on the microcomputer buses consists of information transfers from one register to another. This is one of the basic aspects of a bus-organized microprocessor system. With reference to Fig. 11-6, a memory address register (MAR) is located between the address bus and the ROM. (The ROM has on-chip decoding.) The MAR can be loaded (as from the program counter), provided that the MAR Load line is driven logic-high. Only then can an address word be entered into the MAR.

Observe that the MAR does not have an Enable line—only the ROM has an Enable line. Also, the ROM does not have a Load line. In turn, as previously noted, as soon as an address word enters the MAR, it proceeds immediately into the ROM where it is decoded and releases the contents of the addressed register into the instruction register. Then, when the Enable line is driven logic-high, the contents of the addressed register in the ROM are outputted to the bus. Note in this example that four of the bus wires comprise the address bus; whereas, all eight wires comprise the data bus.

Observe in Fig. 11-6 that the address word is designated $W_3W_2W_1W_0$, and that the ROM output word is designated $W_7W_6W_5W_4W_3W_2W_1W_0$. The MAR is clocked, as are all registers in the bus-organized configuration. Note that the ROM is not clocked—the ROM is an asynchronous network. This subsystem is an example of sequential logic—the ROM output word depends upon the previous states of the input and control lines. This characteristic must be kept in mind during troubleshooting procedures. In other words, successive input states must be recognized to evaluate the output states.

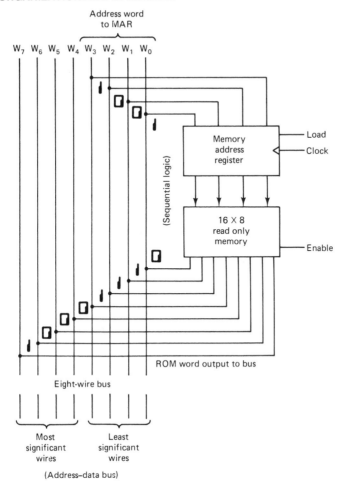

Fig. 11-6. Connections of a memory address register and an eight-bit memory into an eight-wire bus.

Note: Address word to MAR has its source from another register farther up the bus. ROM word output is entered into another register farther down the bus.

Note: This is an example of an address-data bus; address words and data words flow alternately in the least significant wires.

Read-and-Write Memory Operation

Program memories are necessarily read-and-write (random access) devices. Semiconductor RAM's commonly employ flip-flops in register cells, whereby a 1 or a 0 can be stored, retrieved (read out), or erased, as desired. In turn, a RAM requires more elaborate circuitry than a

ROM. With reference to Fig. 11-7, a basic RAM arrangement is depicted; it has a capacity of 16 nibbles, or 64 bits. Its data-in and data-out lines provide nibble input and nibble output.

A 1-out-of-16 address decoder is utilized to select any one register in the memory. Thus, if the decoder "2" output is activated, then the 2-0, 2-1, 2-2, and 2-3 cells become available for reading or for writing. If a nibble is to be written into this register, the write-enable line is

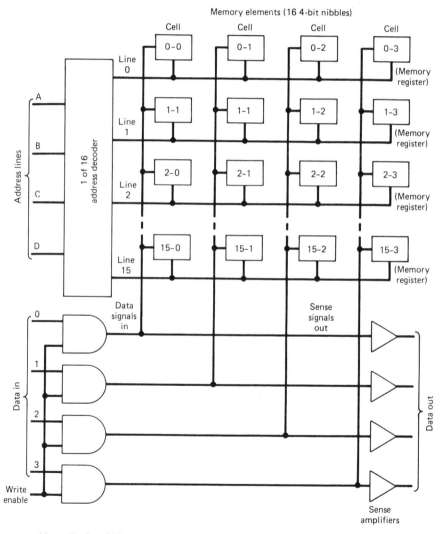

Note: Each nibble occupies its own register in the memory. Cells consist of flip-flops as depicted in Fig. 11-8.

Fig. 11-7. Logic diagram for a 16-nibble RAM.

driven logic-high; the four nibble bits are applied to the data-input lines, and this word sets or resets the 2-0, 2-1, 2-2, and 2-3 flip-flops accordingly. The decoder "2" output is then deactivated, and the word remains written into the memory.

Next to recall (read out) the nibble that has been written into the 2-0, 2-1, 2-2, and 2-3 flip-flops, the memory is addressed and the decoder "2" output is activated. In turn, the states of the voltage levels on the output lines proceed through sense amplifiers (buffers) and thence into the data output lines. With reference to Fig. 11-8, the memory-cell flip-flop in a RAM employs a pair of multi-emitter transistors. The cells is selected by the decoder output when its X select line and Y select line are driven logic-high.

When the X and Y select lines are driven logic-high, the associated emitters are reverse-biased, and virtually no current can flow from the transistors into the X and Y select lines. The sense lines are returned to ground through low-resistance sense amplifiers. If a 1 has been previously written into the cell, current will flow in the 1 sense line. On the other hand, if a 0 has been previously written into the cell, current will flow in the 0 sense line.

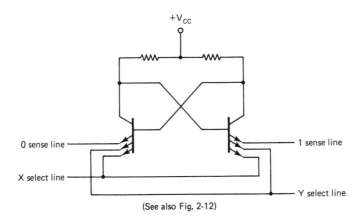

(See also Fig. 2-12)

Note: One transistor will rest in the cut-off state and the other transistor will rest in the saturated state. The cut-off transistor has a collector potential of approximately 3V, while the saturated transistor has a collector potential of virtually zero. The collector with a 3V potential can cause base-to-emitter current flow through the other transistor into its sense line. Note, however, that current can flow into a sense line only when the X and Y select lines are both driven logic-high. If the X and Y select lines are logic-low, their associated emitters provide a very low resistance to ground, and very little current can then flow into a sense line.

Fig. 11-8. Configuration of a memory-cell flip-flop in a RAM.

Next, to write a 1 or a 0 into the cell (and incidentally to erase the former data), the X and Y select lines are held logic-high; if the 0 sense line is then driven logic-high while the 1 sense line is grounded, a 1 will be written into the cell. On the other hand, if the 1 sense line is driven logic-high while the 0 sense line is grounded, a 0 will be written into the cell. Then, the sense line goes logic-low; both sense lines are now logic-low, and the written-in data is retained by the cell.

Recirculating (Serial) Memory

Microprocessor systems also use recirculating or serial-access memories, such as depicted in Fig. 11-9. These devices are basically clocked shift registers. When data is entered into the shift register, it is continually clocked through from left to right. The gates are arranged so that as long as the Mode line is held logic-low, the data cycles around from the output end to the input end of the register. This recirculating action will continue indefinitely.

Note in Fig. 11-9 that if the Mode line is driven logic-high, the stored data will clock out of the register to the right, but cannot

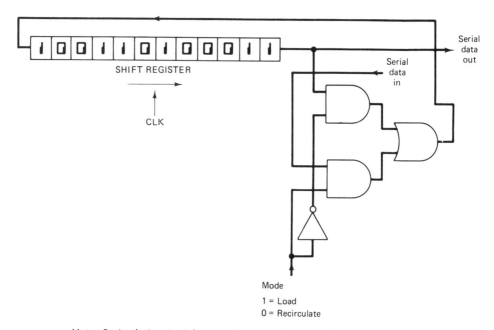

Note: Recirculating (serial) memories are well adapted to use in systems that employ serial addition, as depicted in Figs. 6-6, 6-7, and 6-8.

Fig. 11-9. Basic recirculating (serial) memory configuration.

recirculate. The register becomes cleared after the data clocks out (overflows). Now, new data can be entered into the serial memory, if desired. As soon as the new data entry is completed, the Mode line must be driven logic-low so that the data will recirculate. Some serial memories are large, and can store 1,000 bits, for example.

The chief disadvantage of a serial memory is its slowness in loading and unloading. In some microprocessor systems, high-speed data processing is not required. Serial memories employ less hardware than memories with parallel loading and unloading facilities. In turn, designers sometimes use serial memories because of their economy. Also, there are a few applications, such as in the display of alphanumeric characters on a CRT screen, wherein serial memories are functionally better suited than are other types of memories.

"Embryo" Computer Experiment

Historically, computers were originally programmed by operation of rows and columns of manual switches. These switches corresponded to the cells in a programmable read-only memory (PROM). In other words, the programmer did not have a keyboard available—he entered a program by throwing scores of SPDT switches arrayed on the front panel of the computer. This method of programming was very slow; on the other hand, it illustrates some fundamental facts of interest at this time. Accordingly, we will use this method of programming in the following experiment.

With reference to Fig. 11-10, a programmable read-only memory (PROM) is constructed from three SPDT switches. The Run switch is not a part of the PROM. Readout is provided by two LED's. This elementary configuration provides addition of three bits from a stored program. Thus, the arrangement processes data as follows:

$$0 + 0 + 0 = 0$$
$$1 + 0 + 0 = 1$$
$$0 + 1 + 0 = 1$$
$$0 + 0 + 1 = 1$$
$$1 + 1 + 0 = 10$$
$$0 + 1 + 1 = 10$$
$$1 + 0 + 1 = 10$$
$$1 + 1 + 1 = 11$$

To program the system, a chosen combination of 1's and 0's is entered into the PROM by setting the toggle switches correspondingly. If a switch is thrown to the left, a 0 is entered into the PROM; if

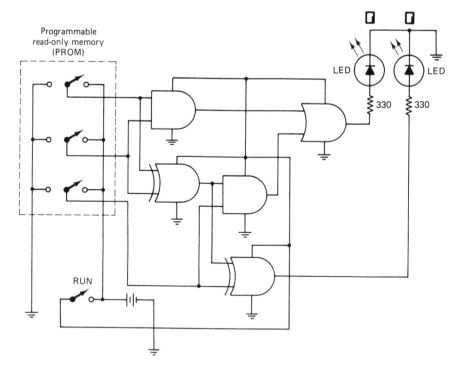

Note: This "embryo" microcomputer can be constructed from standard TTL
AND, OR, and XOR gate IC's. A 5V V_{cc} source is used; the V_{cc} and
ground gate connections are provided inside of the IC packages.
SPDT toggle switches may be used in the PROM. The RUN switch
is an SPST type.

Fig. 11-10. Experimental "embryo" microcomputer arrangement.

the switch is thrown to the right, a 1 is entered into the PROM. After
the desired program has been entered, the Run switch is closed. In
turn, the stored program is processed by the gates, and the sum of
the 1's that were programmed is displayed by the LED readout.

Note in Fig. 11-10 that the SPDT switches should be set to the
left, or set to the right, before a program is run. In other words, a
switch should not be left "open," inasmuch as an open circuit "looks
like" a logic-high source to a TTL gate. This is just another way
of saying that an incorrect answer will be obtained if the programmer
attempts to enter a 0 by leaving a switch open. A 0 can be programmed
only by grounding a gate input.

Observe that V_{cc} and ground connections are shown for each gate
in Fig. 11-10. These dc power-supply terminals are generally omitted

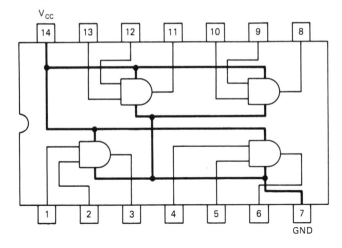

(Heavy lines denote V_{CC} and ground
interconnects inside of the IC package)

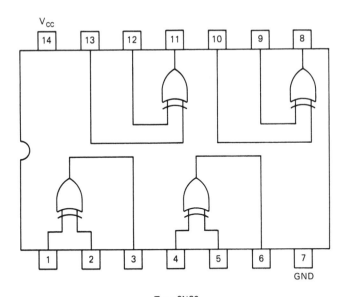

Type 9N86

Note: This is an example of a quad XOR gate package. Its V_{CC} and ground
interconnects are provided inside of the IC package, as for the AND-
gate IC package shown above. Interconnects inside of an IC package
are seldom shown, in order to avoid cluttering the diagram.

Fig. 11-11. Examples of commercial TTL gate IC packages.

in logic diagrams to avoid clutter. However, the V_{CC} and ground connections are detailed in this diagram because they are the operative consideration in the Run circuit. In commercial practice, an IC package has internal connections to the V_{CC} and ground terminals of each gate, and the package pinout provides only a common V_{CC} pin and a common Gnd pin, as shown in Fig. 11-11.

Troubleshooting Considerations

Diagnostic programs are often used in preliminary troubleshooting procedures for microcomputers. A diagnostic program is a user-inserted test program that often helps to isolate hardware malfunctions. For example, with reference to Fig. 11-10, the input combination 0,0,0 would serve as a diagnostic program, inasmuch as the readout would be 10 (instead of 00) in the event that the upper AND gate were "stuck high." On the other hand, the input combination 1,1,0 would not serve as a diagnostic program in this situation, because the readout would be 10 whether or not the upper AND gate were "stuck high."

Again, consider a trouble situation in which the upper AND gate in Fig. 11-10 is "stuck low." In such a case, the input combination 1,1,1 would serve as a diagnostic program, since the readout would be 01 (instead of 11). On the other hand, the input combination 1,0,0 would not serve as a diagnostic program—the readout would be 01 whether or not the upper AND gate were "stuck low." These elementary examples illustrate the fact that the troubleshooter needs to know what device is being tested by a particular diagnostic program.

Note also that if the troubleshooter does not know what device is being tested by a particular diagnostic program from the viewpoint of his understanding of circuit action, he may be able to find this information in the microcomputer service manual. Ideally, the troubleshooter would be completely familiar with all of the circuit actions in a microcomputer system. However, this may not even be possible in some situations. For example, some of the more elaborate microcomputer systems employ design "tricks of the trade" which baffle everyone but their inventor.

It might be supposed that when a design "trick of the trade" is employed in a microprocessor system, it would be noted in the service manual. Unfortunately, this is not necessarily the case, due to the highly competitive nature of the industry, wherein a novel design "trick of the trade" may be treated as a "trade secret." In such a case, the troubleshooter is thrown upon his own resources; if he cannot cope with the "tricky" system, the unit must then be returned to the factory for repair.

IC and Card "Swapping"

Microprocessor systems often have some IC's which are plugged into sockets, instead of being soldered into the PC board (card). In such a case, it may be possible to make preliminary quick checks of trouble symptoms by "swapping" similar IC packages back-and-forth. Also, a substitution test can easily be made by plugging a new IC into the socket in place of the suspected IC.

A large and complex microprocessor system may include numerous cards, of which two or more may have identical circuitry. In turn, preliminary quick checks of trouble symptoms can be made by "swapping" similar cards back-and-forth into the edge connectors. In turn, if the trouble symptoms change when a pair of similar cards are "swapped," the troubleshooter has useful clues from which to proceed. *Warning:* If dissimilar cards are accidentally "swapped," the result is likely to "make a bad card out of a good one."

Some Ground Rules

As previously noted, it is good practice to look for the obvious at the outset when tracking down trouble symptoms. For example, start by measuring V_{CC}; check all cables and connectors; make certain that operating controls are correctly set. It is a disconcerting experience to waste time looking for an interface device fault when it turns out that the volume control on the tape recorder was set too low. Similarly, it is disconcerting to waste time looking for a defect in the tape recorder when it turns out that the interconnect plugs have been reversed in the jacks.

The microprocessor system should be subdivided for trouble analysis. Sometimes a trouble symptom is being caused by a peripheral that is not in use. In case of doubt, it is advisable to disconnect peripherals and to check out the basic system. Then, if no trouble symptoms are noted, the peripherals may be reconnected one-by-one. Also, a known good peripheral may be substituted for a suspected unit— for example, if it is not clear whether the fault is in a printer or in the interface device, a known good printer may be substituted for a test.

Typical IC Complement

It is helpful to note the IC complement for a typical microcomputer: Quad 2-input NAND gate, hex inverter, dual D positive-edge-triggered flip-flop with preset and clear, dual 4-line to 1-line data selector/multiplexer, 8-bit parallel in/serial out shift register, divide-by-8 binary counter selector/multiplexer, dual 2-line to 4-line decoder/ multiplexer, tri-state hex buffer, quad 2-input OR gate, dual 4-input NAND gate, quad D flip-flop with clear, hex D flip-flop with clear, character generator, quad 2-input NOR gate, quad 2-line to 1-line data selector/multiplexer, divide-by-8 binary counter selector/multiplexer, $2K \times 8$ ROM, microprocessor, relay driver, 1K static RAM, divide-by-6 binary counter selector/multiplexer, triple 3-input AND gate.

Elements of
Microprocessor Architecture

Microprocessor Organizational Structure * Operation of a Simple Microprocessor System * Programming Topics * Programmed Addition of a Pair of Numbers * Programmed Instruction Words * Gating of Instruction Words * Recap of Operating Sequence * Hexadecimal Numbers

Microprocessor Organizational Structure

Architecture is a general term that applies to microcomputer systems; however, it usually denotes the organizational structure of the microprocessor or CPU. Recall that the central processing unit, or central processor, contains the main storage unit, the arithmetic unit, and special register groups. It performs arithmetic operations, provides control of instruction processing, supplies timing signals, and automatically performs incidental "housekeeping" operations.

A CPU has a basic architecture comprising storage devices (registers), computational circuitry (ALU), a control section, and various input/output ports. A port is associated with hardware; a data port (I/O port) is controlled by its data direction register hardware. Note that a port comprises a group of individual I/O lines; the number of lines is equal to the length of the basic microprocessor word (such as 8 bits). A port may be bidirectional or unidirectional. Ports are generally associated with interface circuitry to link one type of device to another, by provision of appropriate voltage and current levels, often supplemented by code converters and incidental data-processing circuitry.

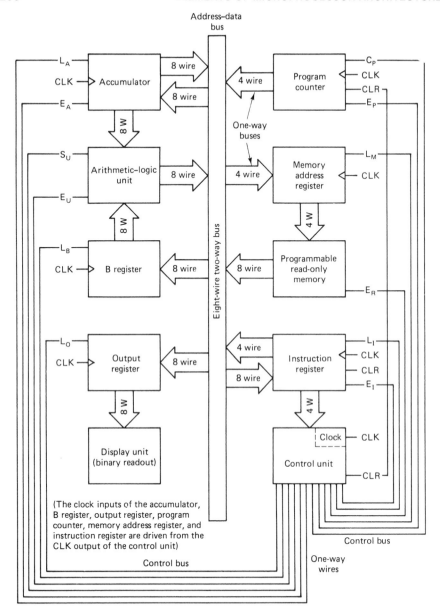

Note: The control bus is explicitly detailed with its individual wires. The
      address-data bus is shown in generalized form with implied wires.

Fig. 12-1. Inner architecture of a simple microprocessor system.

With reference to Fig. 12-1, the inner portion of an architectural plan for a simple microprocessor is exemplified. It comprises an 8-wire bidirectional address-data bus, and a 12-wire control bus; this control bus is depicted as two 6-wire buses in the diagram. Note the following points:

*ACCUMULATOR: Connects to the address-data bus via two 8-wire unidirectional buses, and to the ALU via a unidirectional 8-wire bus. The accumulator is controlled from a load-accumulator (L_A) line, an enable-accumulator (E_A) line, and a clock line.

*ARITHMETIC-LOGIC UNIT: Connects to the address-data bus via a unidirectional 8-wire bus, and to the B register via a unidirectional 8-wire bus. The ALU is controlled from a sum-input-unclocked (S_U) line and an enable-input-unclocked (E_U) line. Observe that this ALU operates asynchronously.

*B REGISTER: Connects to the address-data bus via an 8-wire unidirectional bus, and to the ALU via an 8-wire unidirectional bus. The B register is controlled from a load-B-register (L_B) line, and a clock line. In operation, the B register would temporarily store an addend; whereas, the accumulator would temporarily store an augend, for example.

*OUTPUT REGISTER: Temporarily stores data until it can be output to an external device (peripheral). Connects to the address-data bus via an 8-wire unidirectional bus, and to the peripheral via an 8-wire unidirectional bus. The output register is controlled from a load-output (L_O) line and a clock line.

*PROGRAM COUNTER: Connects to the address-data bus via a 4-wire unidirectional bus. The program counter is controlled by an increment-pulse (C_P) line, an enable-pulse (E_P) line, a clear (Clr) line, and a clock line.

*MEMORY ADDRESS REGISTER: Connects to the address-data bus via a 4-wire unidirectional bus, and to the programmable read-only memory via a 4-wire unidirectional bus. The memory address register (MAR) is controlled by a load-MAR (L_M) line and a clock line.

*PROGRAMMABLE READ-ONLY MEMORY: Connects to the address-data bus via an 8-wire unidirectional bus, and to the MAR via a 4-wire unidirectional bus. The programmable read-only memory (PROM) is controlled from an enable-PROM (E_R) line. Observe that this PROM operates asynchronously.

*INSTRUCTION REGISTER: Connects to the address-data bus via an 8-wire unidirectional bus and a 4-wire unidirectional bus, and to the control unit via a 4-wire unidirectional bus. The instruction register (IR) is controlled from a load-IR (L_I) line, an enable-IR (E_I) line, a clear (Clr) line, and a clock line.

*CONTROL UNIT: The control unit connects to the instruction register via a 4-wire unidirectional bus, and to the controlled inputs of the system devices via a 12-wire control bus. The control unit is itself controlled from a clear (Clr) line. The clock is contained in the control unit; the control unit per se operates asynchronously.

Operation of a Simple Microprocessor System

With reference to Fig. 12-2, a desired program is entered into the memory from the input, such as a keyboard. This program consists of control words and data words. Thus, 1011 might be a control word, and 0100 might be a data word. After all of the control words and data words have been entered into the program memory, the operator actuates the Run control, and the program is automatically executed. The final result, such as the sum of a pair of numbers, is displayed by a readout device.

In the example of Fig. 12-2, the programmer instructs the microcomputer to add 42 and 77. After the necessary control words and data words have been stored in the program memory, and the Run control has been actuated, the CPU decodes the first instruction—this is a so-called microinstruction that orders the memory to send the data words 42 and 77 to the memory registers in the CPU. In turn, the addend and augend are temporarily stored in the CPU memory registers.

The next instruction is then decoded—this is a microinstruction that orders the ALU to add the pair of numbers that are stored in the CPU memory registers, and to store the resulting sum in the accumulator. The following instruction is then decoded—in this example, it will be an order to the accumulator to unload its contents into the output section. Observe that the foregoing data processing involves a fetch cycle, in which instructions (and/or data) are fetched from the memory, followed by an execution cycle in which the data are processed according to the prevailing instruction.

Programming Topics

One programming-made-easy technique is exemplified in Fig. 12-2. As noted in the diagram, instead of programming a detailed addition program to find the sum of a pair of numbers, you can operate the microcomputer in its calculator mode. In turn, simple arithmetic

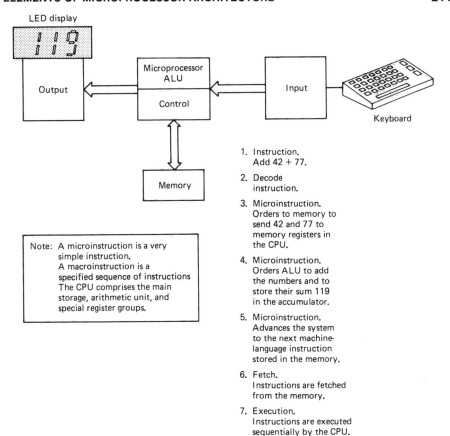

LED display

Output

Microprocessor
ALU

Control

Input

Keyboard

Memory

Note: A microinstruction is a very
simple instruction.
A macroinstruction is a
specified sequence of instructions
The CPU comprises the main
storage, arithmetic unit, and
special register groups.

1. Instruction.
   Add 42 + 77.

2. Decode
   instruction.

3. Microinstruction.
   Orders to memory to
   send 42 and 77 to
   memory registers in
   the CPU.

4. Microinstruction.
   Orders ALU to add
   the numbers and to
   store their sum 119
   in the accumulator.

5. Microinstruction.
   Advances the system
   to the next machine-
   language instruction
   stored in the memory.

6. Fetch.
   Instructions are fetched
   from the memory.

7. Execution.
   Instructions are executed
   sequentially by the CPU.

Note: Instead of employing a detailed program for addition of a pair
of numbers, the programmer usually operates the microcomputer in
its calculator mode. This mode of operation does not process the
data from a stored program; instead, it directly calculates a sum,
difference, product, or quotient, from the keyboard signals as in
a pocket calculator. In turn, simple arithmetic problems can be solved
rapidly without detailed programming. As an illustration, if you are
operating a TRS-80 Model 1 microcomputer, and wish to quickly add
42 + 77, you need only type: PRINT 42 + 77, and then when you
press the ENTER key, the sum—119—is immediately displayed on
the screen.

Comment: The foregoing operation of the microcomputer in its calculator
mode requires that the BASIC language be used, inasmuch as
PRINT is a BASIC statement. Also, the microprocessor is not "really"
in a calculator mode, since a calculator does not require the
word PRINT to be entered before an expression. In the strict sense,
this is an example of a single arithmetic statement that does not
require a stored program.

Fig. 12-2. Basic sequential operations in a microprocessor
system.

problems can be solved rapidly—almost as if you were using a pocket calculator. In the example cited, the programmer would type PRINT before he enters the addend and augend; this instruction word orders the microprocessor system to operate in its calculator mode. Then, after the programmer enters the augend and addend, he presses the Enter key, which is equivalent to the = key on a calculator keyboard. In turn, the sum is displayed on the microcomputer screen.

Programmed Addition of a Pair of Numbers

Consider next the programmed addition of a pair of numbers, as exemplified in Chart 12-1. With reference to the microprocessor architecture shown in the diagram, this addition program comprises the data words 101 and 001, and the instruction words 010, 001, 100, 011, and 000. The first instruction word forms the first line in the program, and is entered into the first register of the program memory, as indicated in the diagram.

The first data word forms the second line in the program, and is entered into the second register of the program memory, as indicated in the diagram. The first instruction word orders the memory to load the general register with the data word 101 (the augend). The second

Chart 12-1

Example of Instruction Words in Program
(Addition of 101 and 001)

Instruction word programmed into the memory	Definition of instruction word	Data processing activity
010	Load Register	Load the general register with the data word (101) from the next memory location
001	Load Accumulator	Load the accumulator with the data word (001) from the next memory location
100	Add	Add the data words (101 and 001) and temporarily store their sum in the accumulator
011	Output	Output the sum (110) from the accumulator into the video display unit
000	Halt	Stop data processing activity

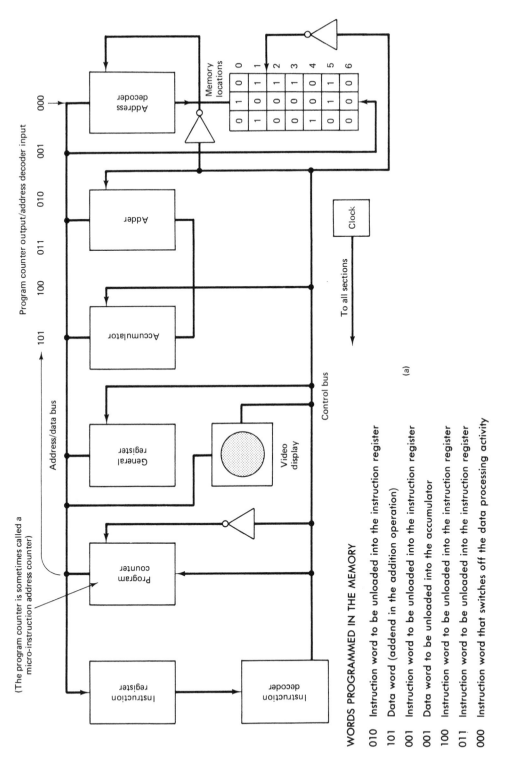

(The program counter is sometimes called a
micro-instruction address counter)

Memory
locations

0	1	0	0
1	0	1	1
0	1	1	2
0	0	1	3
1	0	1	4
0	1	1	5
0	0	0	6

Address
decoder

Adder

Accumulator

General
register

Video
display

Program
counter

Instruction
register

Instruction
decoder

Clock

To all sections

Control bus

Address/data bus

(a)

WORDS PROGRAMMED IN THE MEMORY

010 Instruction word to be unloaded into the instruction register

101 Data word (addend in the addition operation)

001 Instruction word to be unloaded into the instruction register

001 Data word to be unloaded into the accumulator

100 Instruction word to be unloaded into the instruction register

011 Instruction word to be unloaded into the instruction register

000 Instruction word that switches off the data processing activity

Chart 12-1 (*continued*)

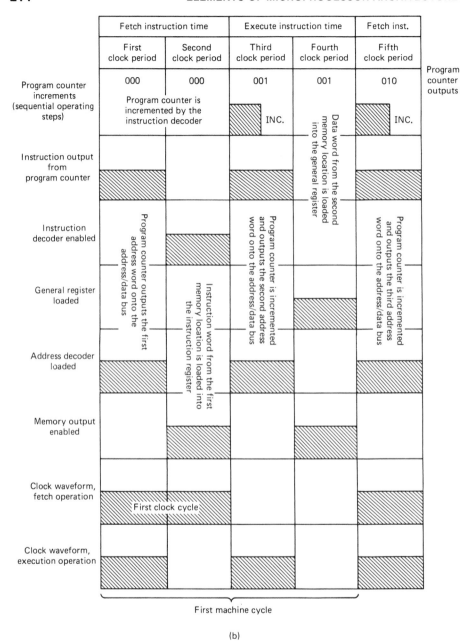

(b)

Chart 12-1 (*continued*)

instruction word, 001, forms the third line in the program, and is entered into the third register of the program memory, as indicated in the diagram.

This second instruction word, 001, orders the memory to load the accumulator with the data word, 001, from the next memory register. The third instruction word, 100, forms the fifth line in the program, and is entered into the fifth register of the program memory, as indicated in the diagram. This third instruction word, 100, orders the ALU (adder) to form the sum of the data words 101 and 001, and to temporarily store their sum in the accumulator.

The fourth instruction word, 011, forms the sixth line in the program, and is entered into the sixth register of the program memory, as indicated in the diagram. This fourth instruction word, 011, orders the accumulator to output the sum, 110, into the video display unit. The fifth instruction word, 000, forms the seventh line in the program, and is entered into the seventh register of the program memory, as indicated in the diagram. This fifth instruction word, 000, orders the microprocessor system to cease activity.

As previously noted, running a program entails a fetch cycle and an execution cycle, as shown in the sequential operating diagram in

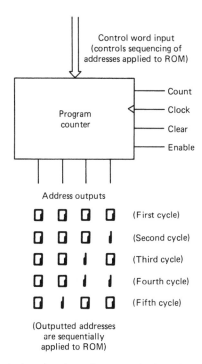

Note: After 16 clock pulses have been applied to the Program Counter,
a 16-register ROM will have been completely read out

Fig. 12-3. Typical program-counter operation.

Chart 12-1. It is evident that if the program memory is compared to an army general, the program counter is comparable to the sergeant who orders the privates to execute prearranged acts and maneuvers. Observe that the program usually reads out the memory systematically, as depicted in Fig. 12-3. Thus, the program counter (sometimes called the function sequencer) is automatically incremented by one count when the CPU is ready to process the contents of the next register in the program memory.

Programmed Instruction Words

With the foregoing process of programmed addition in mind, let us return briefly to Fig. 12-1 and consider how instruction words are programmed in "machine language." In this example, there are 12 control inputs to be activated, and the generalized instruction word is $L_A E_A S_U E_U L_B L_O C_P L_M E_R L_I E_I$. In the course of data processing, this instruction word might be 100000000100 at one time, and then be 000010000100 at another time. These are examples of machine language—binary numbers that the microprocessor can "understand."

By way of comparison, L_A is an element of programming language—not machine language. Thus, in Chart 12-1, L_A denotes Load Accumulator, and its corresponding machine-language word is 001. Next, observe in Chart 12-2 that when $L_A E_A S_U E_U L_B L_O C_P E_P L_M E_R L_I E_I$ = 100000000100, the memory is ordered to load the accumulator with the contents of the addressed register. Again, if $L_A E_A S_U E_U L_B L_O C_P E_P L_M E_R L_I E_I$ = 001000000000, the ALU is ordered to add the number that is in the B register to the number that is in the accumulator.

Recap of Operating Sequence

It is helpful at this point to briefly recap the operating sequence for a simple microprocessor, as tabulated in Chart 12-3. Here, each block in the system is numbered; each number indicates the order in which that block is activated while running a program. Thus, the program counter is activated first; and, as follows from prior discussion, the program counter will again be activated on the fifth step, and still again on the ninth step.

Similarly, the address decoder is the second block to be activated; and, as we will recognize, it will be again activated on the sixth, tenth, and fourteenth steps in running the program. As before, the program is for the addition of a pair of numbers. When Chart 12-3 is compared with Chart 12-1, it is evident that the same data-processing activity is described in both; however, the operating sequence is broken down into detailed steps in Chart 12-3.

Chart 12-2

*Gating of Instruction Words in a
Microprocessor System*

A simple microprocessor system is bus-oriented, as shown in the accompanying diagram. Both one-way and bidirectional buses are used; some of the buses in this example have eight wires, whereas others have four wires. An instruction word for this system has the format:

$$L_A E_A S_U E_U L_B L_O C_P E_P L_M E_R L_I E_I$$

Each bit in an instruction word is identified as follows:

L_A	Load Accumulator	C_P	Increment Program Counter
E_A	Enable Accumulator	E_P	Enable Program Counter
S_U	Add	L_M	Load Memory Address Register
E_U	Enable Adder	E_R	Enable Read-Only Memory
L_B	Load B Register	L_I	Load Instruction Register
L_O	Load Output Register	E_I	Enable Instruction Register

Inputs and outputs of the sections are gated; thus, the accumulator cannot be loaded from the bus until input L_A is driven logic-HIGH. Similarly, the digital word stored in the accumulator cannot be unloaded into the arithmetic-logic unit until input E_A is driven logic-HIGH. Examples of programmed instruction words are as follows:

$L_A E_A S_U E_U L_B L_O C_P E_P L_M E_R L_I E_I$
1 0 0 0 0 0 0 0 0 1 0 0　Load accumulator from the output of the memory

$L_A E_A S_U E_U L_B L_O C_P E_P L_M E_R L_I E_I$
0 0 0 0 1 0 0 0 0 1 0 0　Load B register from the output of the memory

$L_A E_A S_U E_U L_B L_O C_P E_P L_M E_R L_I E_I$
0 0 1 0 0 0 0 0 0 0 0 0　Add the binary number from the B register to the number from the accumulator

$L_A E_A S_U E_U L_B L_O C_P E_P L_M E_R L_I E_I$
0 0 0 1 0 1 0 0 0 0 0 0　Unload the sum from the arithmetic-logic unit into the output register
*(Sum is read out on the
display unit.)*

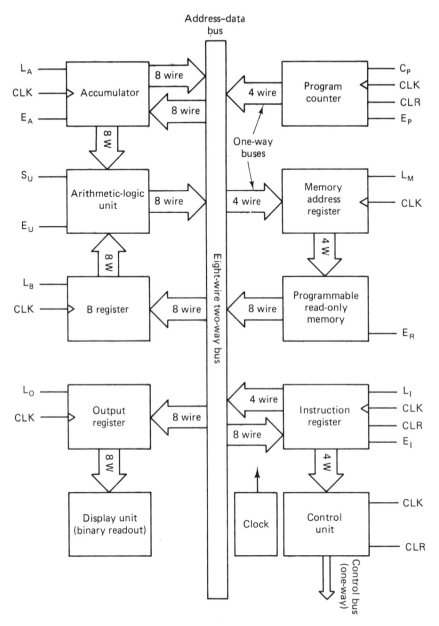

Example:

I⬜⬜⬜⬜⬜⬜⬜⬜⬜I⬜⬜ = $L_A E_A S_U E_U L_B L_O C_P L_M E_R L_I E_I$

means "load the accumulator from the output of the memory"

Chart 12-2 (*continued*)

Chart 12-3

Operating Sequence for a Simple Microprocessor

1. The program counter outputs a binary word which is inputted into the address decoder.

2. The accessed number in the memory is outputted into the instruction register.

3. In turn, the output from the instruction register is decoded by the instruction decoder.

4. The decoded instruction activates the control bus and increments the program counter.

5. In turn, the program counter outputs another binary word which is inputted into the address decoder.

6. The address decoder accesses another binary number in the memory.

7. Next, the accessed number in the memory is outputted into the general register.

8. This binary number is temporarily stored in the general register.

9. Next, the program counter is again incremented.

10. The program counter outputs a binary word which is inputted into the address decoder.

11. Then, the address decoder accesses another binary number in the memory.

12. Next, the accessed number in the memory is outputted into the accumulator.

13. The binary number that was stored in the general register is then added to the number in the accumulator.

14. In turn, the sum of the two numbers which is temporarily stored in the accumulator, will be stored in the memory at an address that is specified by the address decoder.

15. The sum that was held in the accumulator is outputted into the addressed location of the memory.

16. Storage of the sum completes the operating cycle.

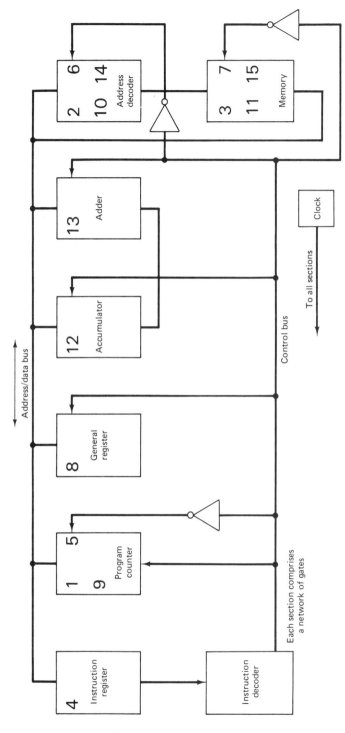

Chart 12-3 (*continued*)

Hexadecimal Numbers

As we proceed to delve deeper into the details of programming, we will have occasion to use hexadecimal numbers; octal numbers will also come into the programming picture. Accordingly, let us note the addition tables for octal numbers and for hexadecimal numbers shown

(cont'd. on page 224)

OCTAL ADDITION TABLE

(Decimal)		0	1	2	3	4	5	6	7	8	9	10	11	12	13	14	15	16	17	18
	+	0	1	2	3	4	5	6	7	10	11	12	13	14	15	16	17	20	21	22
0	0	0	1	2	3	4	5	6	7	10	11	12	13	14	15	16	17	20	21	22
1	1	1	2	3	4	5	6	7	10	11	12	13	14	15	16	17	20	21	22	23
2	2	2	3	4	5	6	7	10	11	12	13	14	15	16	17	20	21	22	23	24
3	3	3	4	5	6	7	10	11	12	13	14	15	16	17	20	21	22	23	24	25
4	4	4	5	6	7	10	11	12	13	14	15	16	17	20	21	22	23	24	25	26
5	5	5	6	7	10	11	12	13	14	15	16	17	20	21	22	23	24	25	26	27
6	6	6	7	10	11	12	13	14	15	16	17	20	21	22	23	24	25	26	27	30
7	7	7	10	11	12	13	14	15	16	17	20	21	22	23	24	25	26	27	30	31
8	10	10	11	12	13	14	15	16	17	20	21	22	23	24	25	26	27	30	31	32
9	11	11	12	13	14	15	16	17	20	21	22	23	24	25	26	27	30	31	32	33
10	12	12	13	14	15	16	17	20	21	22	23	24	25	26	27	30	31	32	33	34
11	13	13	14	15	16	17	20	21	22	23	24	25	26	27	30	31	32	33	34	35
12	14	14	15	16	17	20	21	22	23	24	25	26	27	30	31	32	33	34	35	36
13	15	15	16	17	20	21	22	23	24	25	26	27	30	31	32	33	34	35	36	37
14	16	16	17	20	21	22	23	24	25	26	27	30	31	32	33	34	35	36	37	40
15	17	17	20	21	22	23	24	25	26	27	30	31	32	33	34	35	36	37	40	41
16	20	20	21	22	23	24	25	26	27	30	31	32	33	34	35	36	37	40	41	42
17	21	21	22	23	24	25	26	27	30	31	32	33	34	35	36	37	40	41	42	43
18	22	22	23	24	25	26	27	30	31	32	33	34	35	36	37	40	41	42	43	44

Example: Decimal $5 + 4 =$ octal 11
Binary 1011010 = octal 562
BCD 0011 0110 = octal 44
Example: Addition of $736_8 + 315_8$

Note: $736_8 = 478_{10}$
$315_8 = 205_{10}$
$736_8 + 315_8 = 1253_8$
$478_{10} + 205_{10} = 683_{10}$

```
  1      1
      7   3   6
      3   1   5
  1  (10)  5  (11)
      8       8
  1   2   5   3
```

Note: $6 + 5 = 11$; subtract 8 from 11, leaving 3 and a carry of 1.

(a)

Fig. 12-4(a). Octal addition table.

CONVERSION OF OCTAL NUMBERS TO BINARY EQUIVALENT NUMBERS:

2	5	1	3	0	7	$\rightarrow$ Octal Number
010	101	001	011	000	111	$\rightarrow$ Conversion to Binary Number
0001		0101	0010	1100	0111	$\rightarrow$ Binary Number Regrouped
1		5	2	12	7	$\rightarrow$ Decimal Values of Groups

Decimal Equivalent of Octal 251307 = 86,727

The octal number is first converted into an equivalent binary number. This is done by expressing each octal digit in terms of three binary digits. For convenience in reading, the binary digits may be regrouped if desired. The decimal value of the binary number may be calculated in various ways. For example, we may write $7 \times 1 + 12 \times 16 + 2 \times 256 + 5 \times 4096 + 1 \times 65536$.

In turn, $7 + 192 + 512 + 20480 + 65536 = 86,727$.

Thus, the octal number 251307 is equivalent to the binary number 10101001011000111. In turn, the binary number 10101001011000111 is equivalent to the decimal number 86727.

This procedure is reversed to convert a binary number into an octal number.

To convert the binary number 10101001011000111 to an equivalent octal number, we regroup the binary number into groups of three digits.

Thus, we write: 010 101 001 011 000 111.

Finally, we express the value of each three-digit group as an octal digit.

In other words, the answer is 251307.

Fig. 12-4(b). Octal number conversion.

Hexadecimal Addition Table

(Decimal)		0	1	2	3	4	5	6	7	8	9	10	11	12	13	14	15	16
	+	0	1	2	3	4	5	6	7	8	9	A	B	C	D	E	F	10
0	0	0	1	2	3	4	5	6	7	8	9	A	B	C	D	E	F	10
1	1	1	2	3	4	5	6	7	8	9	A	B	C	D	E	F	10	11
2	2	2	3	4	5	6	7	8	9	A	B	C	D	E	F	10	11	12
3	3	3	4	5	6	7	8	9	A	B	C	D	E	F	10	11	12	13
4	4	4	5	6	7	8	9	A	B	C	D	E	F	10	11	12	13	14
5	5	5	6	7	8	9	A	B	C	D	E	F	10	11	12	13	14	15
6	6	6	7	8	9	A	B	C	D	E	F	10	11	12	13	14	15	16
7	7	7	8	9	A	B	C	D	E	F	10	11	12	13	14	15	16	17
8	8	8	9	A	B	C	D	E	F	10	11	12	13	14	15	16	17	18
9	9	9	A	B	C	D	E	F	10	11	12	13	14	15	16	17	18	19
10	A	A	B	C	D	E	F	10	11	12	13	14	15	16	17	18	19	1A
11	B	B	C	D	E	F	10	11	12	13	14	15	16	17	18	19	1A	1B
12	C	C	D	E	F	10	11	12	13	14	15	16	17	18	19	1A	1B	1C
13	D	D	E	F	10	11	12	13	14	15	16	17	18	19	1A	1B	1C	1D
14	E	E	F	10	11	12	13	14	15	16	17	18	19	1A	1B	1C	1D	1E
15	F	F	10	11	12	13	14	15	16	17	18	19	1A	1B	1C	1D	1E	1F
16	10	10	11	12	13	14	15	16	17	18	19	1A	1B	1C	1D	1E	1F	20

Example: Decimal $6 + 5 =$ Hexadecimal B
Binary $100000 =$ Hexadecimal 20
Decimal $114 =$ Binary $1110010 =$ Hexadecimal 72

Example: Addition of $5D3_{16} + 818_{16}$

Note: $5D3_{16} = 1491_{10}$
$818_{16} = 2072_{10}$
$5D3_{16} + 818_{16} = DEB_{16}$
$1491_{10} + 2072_{10} = 3563_{10}$

$$\begin{array}{ccc} 5 & D & 3 \\ 8 & 1 & 8 \\ \hline (13) & (14) & (11) \\ D & E & B \end{array} = DEB_{16}$$

Fig. 12-5(a). Hexadecimal addition table.

CONVERSION OF HEXADECIMAL NUMBERS INTO BINARY EQUIVA-
LENT NUMBERS:

8	6	0	B
1000	0110	0000	1011
8	6	0	7

Decimal Equivalent of Hexadecimal 860B = 8,583

The hexadecimal number is first converted into an equivalent binary number.

This is done by expressing each hexadecimal digit in terms of four binary digits.

The decimal value of the hexadecimal number may be calculated in various ways.

For example, we may write: $7\times1 + 0\times16 + 6\times64 + 8\times1024$.

In turn, $7 + 0 + 384 + 8192 = 8{,}583$.

Thus, the hexadecimal number 860B is equivalent to the binary number 1000011000001011.

In turn, the binary number 1000011000001011 is equivalent to the decimal number 8583.

This procedure is reversed to convert a binary number into a hexadecimal number.

To convert the binary number 1000011000001011 to an equivalent hexadecimal number, we regroup the binary number into groups of four digits.

Thus, we write: 1000 0110 0000 1011.

Finally, we express the value of each four-digit group as a hexadecimal digit.

In other words, the answer is 860B.

Example of Hexadecimal Addition:

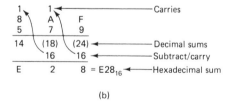

(b)

Fig. 12-5(b). Hexadecimal number conversion.

in Figs. 12-4 and 12-5. Octal numbers have a base 8, and hexadecimal numbers have a base 16 (decimal numbers have a base 10, and binary numbers have a base 2). Octal and hexadecimal numbers are helpful to programmers because large numbers can be more easily written in hexadecimal notation. For example, binary 1011 = decimal 11 = hexadecimal B.

13

Elaborated Microprocessor Architecture

Starting of a Program Run * Instruction Word Flow * Troubleshooting Notes * Operation of Instruction Decoder * Programming Pointers * Ring Counter in Control Section * Mnemonics and Assembly Language * High-Level Language * Shorthand Dialect * Simple Program Examples

Starting of a Program Run

Microprocessor architecture is bus-oriented with respect to data processing functions. In turn, it is helpful to observe the starting of a program run, as exemplified in Chart 13-1 for a very simple microprocessor system. The diagram depicts instruction-word flow into, through, and out of the instruction decoder. Data processing starts with closing of the "Start Run" switch on the program counter. The program memory has been previously loaded, as indicated.

Activation of the program counter results in outputting the memory address 000; this address is interpreted by the address decoder, and in turn the first register (R_0) in the program memory is unloaded into the instruction register. Note that this instruction word (010) corresponds to address word 000. From the instruction register, 010 flows into the instruction decoder where it is interpreted and is then outputted as a group of control signals.

Operation of the instruction decoder is shown in Chart 13-2. In this example, four inputs ($I_1 I_2 I_3 I_4$) are provided, and five outputs ($L_A L_B S_U L_O HLT$) are available to supply various combinations of control signals. As previously noted, an L_A output signal orders the data-

Chart 13-1

Instruction Word Flow into, Through, and Out of the Instruction Decoder

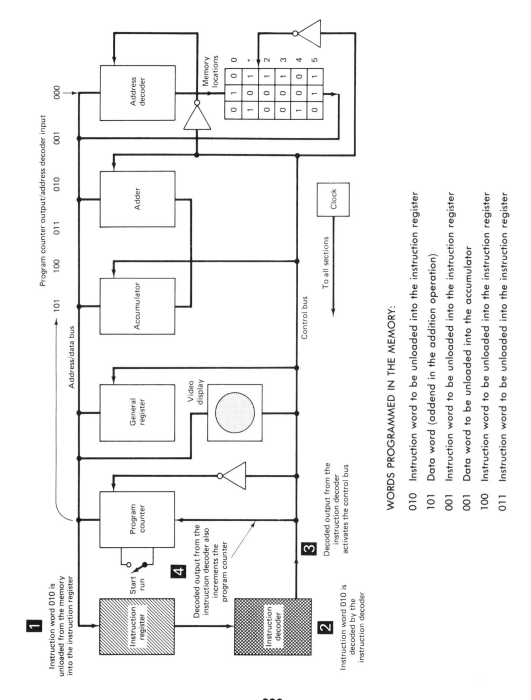

WORDS PROGRAMMED IN THE MEMORY:

010 Instruction word to be unloaded into the instruction register

101 Data word (addend in the addition operation)

001 Instruction word to be unloaded into the instruction register

001 Data word to be unloaded into the accumulator

100 Instruction word to be unloaded into the instruction register

011 Instruction word to be unloaded into the instruction register

Chart 13-2
Operation of Instruction Decoder

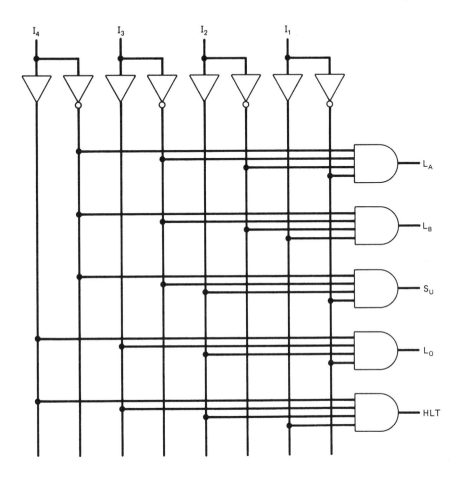

Configuration for a simple instruction decoder.

An instruction register outputs instruction words into an instruction decoder. An instruction word corresponds to a decoder output signal. For example, an instruction word in this example has four bits: $I_1 I_2 I_3 I_4$. The control words corresponding to various instruction words are: L_A, L_B, S_U, L_O, and HLT. If $I_1 I_2 I_3 I_4 = 0000$, the L_A output goes logic-HIGH and the other four outputs remain logic-LOW. Again, if $I_2 I_3 I_3 I_4 = 1111$, the HLT output goes logic-HIGH and the other four outputs remain logic-LOW. Or, if $I_1 I_2 I_3 I_4 = 0100$, the S_U output goes logic-HIGH and the other four outputs remain logic-LOW.

(a)

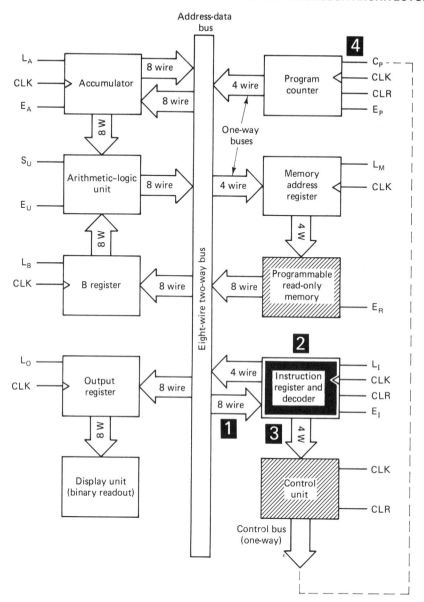

(1) Instruction word is unloaded from the PROM into the instruction register.

(2) Instruction word is decoded by the instruction decoder.

(3) Decoded output from the instruction decoder activates the control unit.

(4) Control unit increments the program counter in preparation for unloading the next data word or instruction word from the PROM.

(b)

Chart 13-2 *(continued)*

processing circuitry to load the accumulator with a data word from the program memory. An HLT output signal tells the data-processing circuitry that the program has been completed, and to cease processing activity.

The gates that form the combinational logic network in the instruction decoder may output any one of five possible control signals, or none at all, in response to an inputted 4-bit instruction word. As an illustration, if $I_4 I_3 I_2 I_1 = 1,000$, no control signals are outputted, inasmuch as none of the AND gates is driven logic-high. On the other hand, if $I_4 I_3 I_2 I_1 = 0001$, an L_B control signal is outputted. Again, if $I_4 I_3 I_2 I_1 = 0000$, an L_A control signal is outputted. Or, if $I_4 I_3 I_2 I_1 = 1111$, an HLT control signal is outputted.

Troubleshooting Notes

Microcomputers sometimes have limited program-memory capacity. For example, the TRS-80 PC-4 microcomputer has a built-in memory that accommodates 544 program steps. However, this program-memory capacity can be expanded to 1,568 steps by the addition of an expansion RAM pack. Since this memory employs MOS transistors, it is subject to damage from static electricity, if improperly handled. Thus, the troubleshooter should ground his hand or wrist before handling the expansion RAM pack. For example, he may use a flexible wire to connect his wrist to a water pipe.

A RAM expansion pack should be inserted or removed from a microcomputer only while the power switch is turned off. It is good practice to avoid touching the connector portion of the RAM, or its pad in the microcomputer; greasy fingerprints on contact surfaces can result in memory malfunction. By the same token, dust should not be allowed to settle in the RAM compartment, and it should not be left uncovered longer than necessary during troubleshooting procedures. An expansion RAM is packaged in a dust-proof case, and it should be returned to its case whenever it is removed from the microcomputer. Note that a RAM can become damaged from mechanical stress if it is accidentally dropped on the floor, for example.

Note in passing that a RAM program memory may appear to be defective if operation is attempted during extremely cold winter weather, or extremely hot summer weather. For example, a typical MOS type RAM is rated for normal operation over the temperature range from 32° to 104°F. Keep in mind also that liquid crystal displays in microcomputers may appear to be defective in extremely cold weather. Accordingly, preliminary troubleshooting tests should be made at normal room temperature.

When batteries are replaced in a microcomputer, it is good practice to wipe their surfaces with a clean, dry cloth before inserting the batteries into their compartment. This precaution avoids the possibility of poor contacts due to greasy fingerprints, dust, or perspiration. Note also, that microcomputers may appear to be defective if operated in an area with unusually high humidity. In case this cause of malfunction is suspected, the troubleshooter should first "dry out" the microcomputer, and then proceed with preliminary troubleshooting tests.

Microcomputers and pocket calculators normally radiate more or less radio-frequency interference (RFI). This characteristic can sometimes be used to advantage in preliminary troubleshooting procedures. For example, if a microcomputer is placed over an AM radio receiver, you will normally hear multiplexer RFI from the radio. In case the display section in the microcomputer is "dead," but the processing circuitry is operating, this fact becomes immediately evident in an RFI test.

Programming Pointers

It was previously noted that simple arithmetic problems need not be programmed in detail, and that most microcomputers can be operated in the calculator mode. However, it should not be supposed that there is an industry standard in this regard. Even different models of the same brand of microcomputer may have different keyboard facilities for operation in the calculator mode.

As an illustration, recall that the TRS-80 Model I operates in the calculator mode when the operator types, for example: PRINT 4*5 and then presses the ENTER key. In turn, the product 20 is displayed on the monitor screen. (Note that * symbolizes multiplication in this situation.) Then, the operator may make another calculation such as: PRINT 15/3. When he (or she) presses the ENTER key, the quotient 5 is displayed on the monitor screen.

On the other hand, if you are operating the TRS-80 PC-1 in the calculator mode, you must proceed as follows: Press the CL key to initialize the microprocessor circuitry for calculation. Then you may type 4*5, and when you press the ENTER key, the product 20 will be displayed in the readout. Before you can start another calculation, you must press the CL key. Otherwise, the 20 will be processed as the first number in any problem that you may type into the microcomputer. In other words, a TRS-80 Model I automatically clears itself and initializes the microprocessor circuitry for a new calculation. On the other hand, the TRS-80 PC-1 does not do so.

As another illustration, if you are operating the TRS-80 PC-4 in the calculator mode, the procedure is quite similar to operation of the PC-1, except for one important point: you do not have a CL key provided, and you must press the AC key instead, to display an answer in the readout. These examples are typical, and underscore the necessity for familiarizing yourself with the operating manual for a particular microcomputer before attempting to operate it—or to troubleshoot its "innards."

Ring Counter in Control Section

We have seen how an instruction decoder operates. Next, it is helpful to observe how a ring counter in the control section typically provides six phases of operation in each machine cycle. After a program has been entered, the program counter starts to run the program, as depicted in Fig. 13-1. Stored data is processed in a sequence of machine cycles. Each machine cycle consists of an address phase and an execution phase. In this example, there are three address phases and three execution phases in each machine cycle.

The address and execution phases are sometimes called cycles. A ring counter in the control section sequences the address phase and the execution phase. Machine cycles are repeated until the program has been completely run, and an HLT signal is outputted by the instruction decoder (see Chart 13-2). Thereupon, data processing ceases. Note in Fig. 13-1 that at the end of the first execution phase, the ALU outputs its processed data into the accumulator. At the end of the next machine cycle, the ALU might output its processed data into the output register and interface.

Operation of Control Matrix

The ring counter sequences the control matrix, as shown in Fig. 13-1. The control matrix inputs words from the instruction decoder and outputs control words, as seen in Fig. 13-2. In turn, the control words determine the execution sequence for instructions that have been programmed into the PROM. Thus, the control matrix is driven by both the instruction decoder and by the ring counter. In turn, the outputted control words from the control matrix correspond to the address and execution phases noted in Fig. 13-1.

Address phases are sometimes called a fetch routine, and execution phases are sometimes called an execution routine. With reference to the control matrix exemplified in Fig. 13-2, six AND gates and two OR gates are employed to generate control words. The control matrix connects to six lines from the ring counter, and to four lines from the instruction

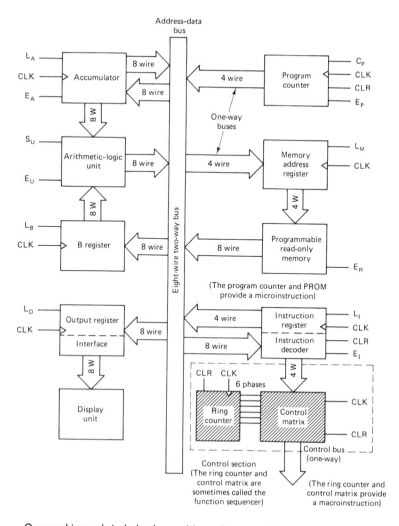

One machine cycle includes three address phases and three execution phases:

Address Phases:

1. Program counter unloads an address into the MAR

2. PROM unloads an instruction word into the instruction register

3. Program counter is incremented by one bit

Execution Phases:

4. Instruction register unloads an address word into the MAR

5. PROM unloads a data word into the B register

6. ALU outputs its processed data into the accumulator

Fig. 13-1. Ring counter in control section provides six phases in each machine cycle.

232

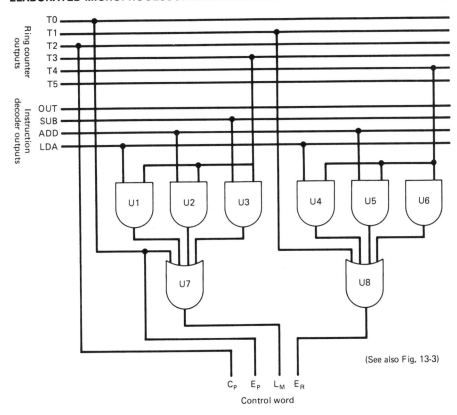

Fig. 13-2. Logic diagram for one section of a simple control matrix.

decoder. Only one of the lines from the instruction decoder is held logic-high at any particular time. During the time that an instruction decoder line is being held logic-high, the ring counter outputs $T_0 T_1 T_2 T_3 T_4 T_5$ signals sequentially.

As an illustration, suppose that the LDA line is being held logic-high (Fig. 13-2). In turn, the T_0 signal will first drive the E_P and L_M lines logic-high. Next, the T_1 signal will drive the E_R line logic-high, while L_M goes logic-low. Then the T_2 signal drives the C_P line logic-high, while E_R goes logic-low. The C_P line goes logic-low, and activity is then completed for the address phase. Note that the execution phase is implemented by another control-matrix section. An elementary microprocessor system may employ a total of three control-matrix sections.

Mnemonics and Assembly Language

Observe in Fig. 13-2 that the control-matrix output signals OUT, SUB, ADD, and LDA are called mnemonics, and are examples of assembly language for a microcomputer. As previously noted, the ALU employs machine language (binary numbers). With reference to Fig. 13-3, computer instructions are usually written in a form that the programmer can easily remember, but which must be later converted into machine language. A mnemonic in assembly language (a type of programming language), is based on easily remembered symbols. In turn, a program introduced in assembly language is assembled into machine language by the computer.

As an illustration, the mnemonic MPY typically represents "multiply" to the programmer in assembly language, and it will correspond to

INSTRUCTION SET AND OPERATION CODE

Mnemonic	Operation	Op-Code
LDA	Load accumulator with PROM word	0000
ADD	Add PROM word to the accumulator	0001
SUB	Subtract PROM word from the accumulator	0010
OUT	Load output register from accumulator	1110
HLT	Halt	1111

PROGRAM DESCRIPTION   CONVERSIONS

High-level Language: Program is written in a high-level language such as BASIC; the high-level language is formatted in a way that is related in a general manner to the way that people solve problems. In turn, the high-level language program is translated into a corresponding assembly language program by a compiler.

High-level language program is processed by a compiler

Assembly-Language Program: Program is written in assembly language which consists of abbreviated instructions called mnemomics. In turn, the assembly language program is translated into a corresponding machine-language program by an assembler.

Assembly language program is processed by an assembler

Machine-Language Program: Program is written in binary code words which can be directly processed by the CPU. No interpretation is required.

Machine-language program directly operates the CPU.

(Compilers and assemblers are essentially conversion programs, or software which is generally built into the microcomputer.)

Fig. 13-3. Typical mnemonics in assembly language, with designated operations and representative op-codes in machine language.

a particular binary number in machine language. An assembly language is a programming language that has one-to-one correspondence with an assembly program. An assembly program directs the computer to interpret a symbolic-language program into a machine-language program. (Symbolic language denotes any computer language other than machine language.)

With reference to Fig. 13-4, a source program is written by the programmer; the object program is a corresponding machine-language program. Although a microprocessor can be programmed in machine language, this is almost never done. It may be programmed in assembly language, or it may be programmed in a high-level language such as BASIC. In either case, interpretation is required before machine language is available to operate the CPU. Interpretation is accomplished by means of assemblers and compilers inside the microcomputer.

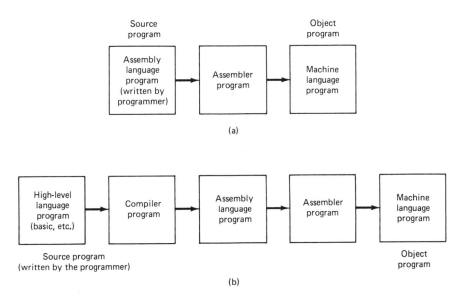

Note: We will find that assembly language with its mnemonics is architecture-oriented; on the other hand, high-level languages are task-oriented. Thus, assembly language format is more closely related to microprocessor design, whereas BASIC is more closely related to English. Programmers do not necessarily need to know anything about digital electronics.

Fig. 13-4. Assembler arrangements. (a) Assembler inputs assembly language program and outputs a machine-language program; (b) compiler inputs high-level language program and outputs an assembly language program.

With reference to Fig. 13-4, an assembler is a program that processes a symbolic-language program and outputs a machine-language program. Otherwise stated, an assembler translates symbolic operation codes into absolute operation codes, and substitutes absolute or relocatable addresses for symbolic addresses. An absolute operation code is a machine-language code. A compiler is similar to an assembler, except that a compiler processes a high-level language program and interprets it into an assembly program. Accordingly, a compiler must be followed by an assembler.

High-Level Language

High-level languages such as BASIC are characterized by traditional English words, such as RUN, PRINT, READ, and STOP. Note, however, that BASIC words have specific meanings that are defined by the microprocessor designer. For example, PRINT might mean to print the answer to a problem on a paper tape; again, PRINT might mean to recall an entry from memory and to display it on the video-monitor screen; or, PRINT might mean to calculate and display the sum of a pair of numbers.

Programmers employ different varieties of BASIC, depending on the particular microcomputer that is in use. For example, when operating one model of microcomputer in its calculator mode, ENTER means EQUALS, or ANSWER. On the other hand, when operating another model of microcomputer, EXE means EQUALS, or ANSWER. Again, CL for one microcomputer means CLEAR THE DISPLAY, whereas AC means CLEAR THE DISPLAY for another microcomputer. The translation of a program written in one variety of BASIC to a corresponding program in another variety of BASIC is termed conversion. We will find that there is a large amount of commonality between the BASICs of different manufacturers; the variance occurs primarily in the different manufacturer's *extensions* to the language.

Shorthand Dialect

Microcomputer architecture may also provide for use of a shorthand dialect by the programmer. For example, with reference to Fig. 13-5, Level-I BASIC shorthand dialect for the TRS-80 Model I microcomputer is shown. Thus, the programmer may enter the command PRINT,* or, he may enter its shorthand dialect equivalent, P. The end result will be the same in either case. Note that P. is not the same as P—unless the period is included in the command, the compiler will process the

---

*Commands and statements are detailed subsequently.

Command/Statement	Abbreviation	Command/Statement	Abbreviation
PRINT	P.	TAB (after PRINT)	T.
NEW	N.	INT	I.
RUN	R.	GOSUB	GOS.
LIST	L.	RETURN	RET.
END	E.	READ	REA.
THEN	T.	DATA	D.
GOTO	G.	RESTORE	REST.
INPUT	IN.	ABS	A.
MEM	M.	RND	R.
FOR	F.	SET	S.
NEXT	N.	RESET	R.
STEP (after FOR)	S.	POINT	P.
STOP	ST.	PRINT AT	P.A.
CONT	C.		

Note: The term "dialect" is also applied to variations in a high-level language such as BASIC, for use with particular designs of microcomputers.

Fig. 13-5. Level-I BASIC shorthand dialect utilized by the classical TRS—80 Model I microcomputer.

shorthand entry as a PRINT entry. For example, if the programmer enters P.4+5, the sum 9 will be displayed. On the other hand if he (or she) enters P4+5, the error message WHAT? will be displayed. Note that omission of the period in the foregoing entry is an elementary example of a program "bug."

Other typical error messages are HOW? and SORRY. (The latter means that the programmer has run out of memory locations.) When a bug is encountered, the program must be debugged. The first step is to try to answer the questions: Could it be an operator problem? Is it probably a hardware problem? Is it probably a software problem? Is everything plugged in properly? Are recorder batteries okay (if you are using batteries)? Is recorder volume control properly set? Is recorder tone control on "high"? Are you using "legal" commands?

If it appears that the trouble is in the program, load in a known good program and run it. This provides a definitive hardware and operator checkout. A microcomputer such as the TRS-80 Model I will usually point to the "illegal" program line by inserting a question mark just before the "illegality" starts in the display following WHAT? In the case of HOW? a question mark will be inserted just after the "illegality." Program debugging procedures will be explained in greater detail subsequently.

Simple Program Examples

At this point, it is helpful to observe the examples of simple programs for addition and subtraction shown in Fig. 13-6. A program memory is depicted with seven registers and their absolute addresses. Two assembly-language programs and two machine-language programs are exemplified. Five mnemonics with their definitions and operation codes (op codes) are stipulated. Each program comprises four lines. First, the accumulator is loaded with a data word from the addressed register. Next, an arithmetic operation is performed on this data word and another data word from the following addressed register. Then, the result of the arithmetic operation is outputted. Lastly, a Halt command is issued to terminate data processing.

OPERATION CODE

LDA	1000
SUB	1001
ADD	1010
OUT	1011
HLT	1100

Mnemonic definition

LDA	Load accumulator
SUB	Subtract addressed word
ADD	Add addressed word
OUT	Output contents of accumulator
HLT	Halt data processing

Program memory

Absolute addresses					Register numbers
0000					R_0
0001					R_1
0011					R_2
0100					R_3
0101					R_4
0110					R_5
0111					R_6

Program No. 1

LDA 4
ADD 1
OUT
HLT

Program No. 1 (machine language)

1000	0101
1010	0001
1011	
1100	

Program No. 2

LDA 5
SUB 4
OUT
HLT

Program No. 2 (machine language)

1000	0110
1001	0101
1011	
1100	

Note: These programs are not detailed; it follows from Fig. 13-1 that various fetch and execution routines with associated phases are involved in running the programs.

Fig. 13-6. Examples of simple programs for addition and for subtraction.

Note that the details of data processing depend in part on the organization of the program memory. A command specifies an operation to be performed; it is necessarily accompanied by data on which the operation is to be performed. With reference to Fig. 13-7, the control word and its associated data word generally occupy the same register in the program memory. However, this organization is not invariable—the control word might occupy one memory location and the associated data word might occupy some other memory location.

In the example of Fig. 13-7, we say that the register contents have an instruction field and an address field. The instruction field is the control word (command); the address field is the data word (memory location of the associated data). We term 1011 the op-code which specifies the operation to be performed. We term 0100 the operand—the address of the associated data. In other words, the operand tells the CPU where to find the pertinent data. Thus, if you are programming in machine language, your program lines will be entered in this (or basically similar) form.

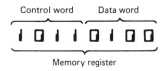

Control word   Data word

Memory register

Note: Microcomputer instruction may be grouped into data-movement instructions such as "load," arithmetic instructions such as "add," comparison instructions such as "find whether A is equal to, greater than, or less than B," logical instructions such as "find A XOR B," and branch instructions such as "jump program control to line 19." Every microcomputer has its own instruction set, as explained subsequently.

Fig. 13-7. A control word and a data word may occupy the same register in a memory.

Troubleshooting Note

Troubleshooting of microprocessor systems in the design phase is usually accomplished with logic state analyzers, in addition to basic testers such as logic probes, pulsers, current tracers, clips, and comparators (and oscilloscopes). Another sophisticated technique employs digital logic simulation, wherein the response of a physical circuit to sets of stimuli is determined by the use of comparatively simple, but nevertheless informative, models. For an introduction to design-phase troubleshooting of microprocessor systems, see *Digital Equipment Troubleshooting*, M. Namgostar, Reston Publishing Company.

14

Stored-Program
Processing

Microprocessor Characteristics * Instruction Set *
Microprocessor System * Program Counter * Inter-
rupts * Instruction Cycle * Accumulator Group
Instruction Set * I/O and RAM Instruction Set *
Programming Trick of the Trade * Language Selec-
tion * Historical Note

Microprocessor Characteristics

Microprocessor architecture is reflected in its instruction set. With reference to Fig. 14-1, the architecture for a simple microprocessor exemplifies a bus-organized system with a data bus, a control bus, clock lines, and power-supply lines. It operates with a program counter supplemented by a scratch-pad register, an ALU, accumulator, instruction decoder, and control section. These sections are interconnected with external RAM and ROM memories and to an external clock.

This microprocessor employs a 4-bit CPU. As detailed subsequently, its instruction set contains 46 entries. Note that the microprocessor can directly address 4,000 (4K) 8-bit instruction words in its program memory and 5,120 bits of data words stored in its random-access memory. It can also directly address up to 16 4-bit input ports and 16 4-bit output ports. Observe that 16 index registers (scratch-pad) are provided for temporary data storage.

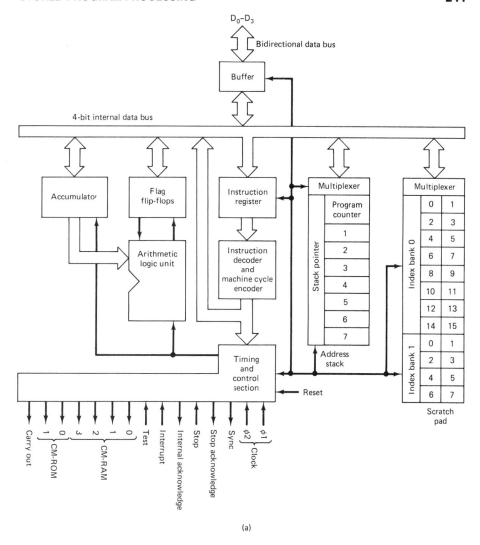

(a)

Note: This is a simplified block diagram of the classical 4/40 microprocessor.
Large numbers of these microprocessors have been built into electronic
cash registers, process controllers, and other industrial applications.
Although the 4/40 is not used in new equipment, it is the "grandfather"
of all microprocessors, and it is helpful to observe how it operates
and how it is programmed.

Fig. 14-1(a). General block diagram for a type 4/40
microprocessor.

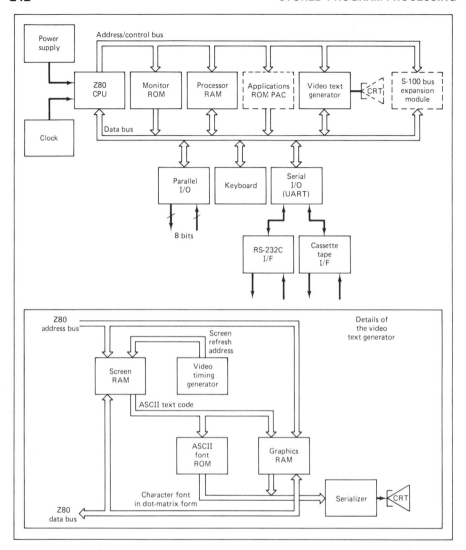

Fig. 14-1(b). Block diagram for a typical personal computer
with a Z80 microprocessor. *Courtesy, Hewlett-Packard.*

Data and control lines for the microprocessor depicted in Fig. 14-
1 function as follows:

D0-D3: Bidirectional data bus for provision of all address and data
communication between the microprocessor and the external RAM
and ROM.

01-02: Nonoverlapping clock signals that determine the timing of the
microprocessor.

Sync: Synchronizing signal that indicates the beginning of the instruction cycle to the ROM and RAM.

Reset: When a "1" is applied to the Reset terminal, the program counter is forced to return to 0, and all status and flag flip-flops are cleared.

Test: An input line that responds to the closing or opening of an external switch.

CM-ROM: Command control line that enables a ROM bank and I/O devices connected to the CM-ROM line.

CM-RAM0 through CM-RAM3: Command control lines that provide bank select signals for the RAM chips.

Instruction Set

An instruction set lists all of the instructions that a microcomputer can execute. As previously noted, an instruction usually specifies a data-processing operation such as "add," and includes the location of the data on which the operation is to be performed. From the programmer's viewpoint, instructions are concerned with data movement, or data manipulation, or decision and control, or with input/output operations. (See. Fig. 14-2.)

In this example, the instruction set is subdivided into machine instructions, accumulator group instructions, and I/O or RAM instructions. There are 16 machine instructions in this example, as follows: NOP, JCN, FIM, SRC, FIN, JIN, JUN, JMS, INC, ISZ, ADD, SUB, LD, XCH, BBL, and DDM. These are the assembly-language mnemonics for the machine instructions; the mnemonics are used in assembly-language programming. The foregoing mnemonics have the following meanings:

NOP means *No Operation* (microprocessor "marks time").

JCN means *Jump* (to a stipulated address, on the condition that a specified relation is true).

FIM means *Fetch Immediately* (the addressed data direct from ROM).

SCR means *Send Register Control* (contents of index register).

FIN means *Fetch Indirect* (from ROM via index register).

JIN means *Jump Indirect* (send register contents out as an address at specified times).

JUN means *Jump Unconditionally* (to specified ROM address).

JMS means *Jump to Subroutine* (at specified ROM address).

INC means *Increment* (contents of specified register).

ISZ means *Increment* (contents of specified register, on the condition that a specified relation is not equal to zero).

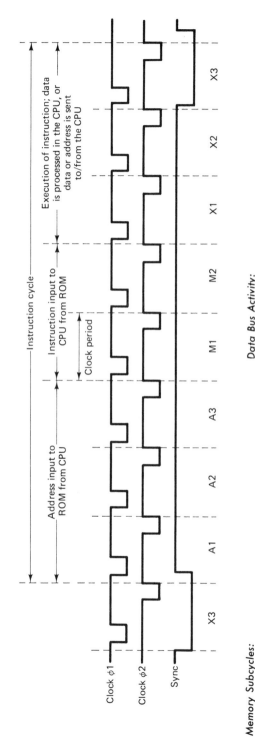

Memory Subcycles:

CPU is enabled over memory subcycles X3, A1, A2, A3.

Selected ROM is enabled over memory subcycles M1, M2.

CPU is enabled over memory subcycle X1.

Selected ROM is enabled; or CPU is enabled over memory subcycle X2.

CPU is enabled over memory subcycle X3.

Data Bus Activity:

Lower 4-bit address to ROM's over memory subcycle A1.

Middle 4-bit address to ROM's over memory subcycle A2.

Higher 4-bit address to ROM's (chip-select code) over memory subcycle A3.

Instruction to CPU over memory subcycles M1, M2. (X1 subcycle not used.)

Data or address to RAM's and ROM's, or data to CPU, over memory subcycle X2.

Address to ROM's (if SRC instruction) over memory subcycle X3.

Fig. 14-2. Subdivision of the microprocessor instruction cycle.

ADD means to *Add* (contents of specified register to contents of accumulator).

SUB means to *Subtract* (contents of specified register from contents of accumulator).

LD means to *Load* (contents of specified register into accumulator).

XCH means *Exchange* (contents of specified index register with contents of the accumulator).

BBL means *Branch Back* (down one level in the stack, and to load the data into the accumulator).

LDM means *Load* (specified data into the accumulator).

Microprocessor System

At this point, it is helpful to briefly review a basic microprocessor system. (See Fig. 14-3.) As previously noted, a typical system includes a CPU, memory facilities, and I/O ports. We have seen that the program memory serves primarily as a storage device for instructions—those coded items of data which direct CPU activity. We have also seen that a group of logically related instructions which have been stored in the memory is called a program. The CPU "reads" each instruction fetched from memory in a sequence determined by the program counter. These instructions initiate data-processing activity. Provided that the program contains no "bugs," data processing results in intelligible and useful conclusions.

We recognize that the data memory stores the data words that are to be processed. Although the CPU can access any data stored in the data memory, it may not always be large enough to store all of the data required for a particular problem. This limitation can be overcome by use of the input ports. In other words, the CPU can address the input ports and read the data that may be available. Thus, the CPU might address an input port for access from a tape reader.

Most microcomputers require one or more output ports whereby the CPU can communicate the results of its data processing activity to the "outside world." As previously noted, these results may be fed to a video monitor; again, they may be fed to a line printer, or to a magnetic tape, or even to another system for controlling its operations. Recall that output ports, like input ports, are addressable by the programmer. (Keyboard and tape peripherals are seen in Fig. 14-4.)

It is evident that the CPU unifies a microprocessor system. Stated otherwise, it controls the functions performed by the other devices within the architectural system. To briefly recap, the CPU fetches instructions from memory, decodes the instruction words, and executes their

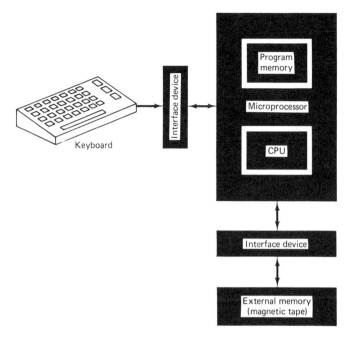

Note: In addition to a CPU, memory facilities, and I/O ports, a basic microprocessor system requires input and output interface devices. Interrupt facilities were indicated in Fig. 14-1; these facilities are associated with interfacing action to improve operating efficiency. An interface is essentially a code converter that provides communication between the microprocessor and a peripheral. An interrupt function permits the CPU to operate continuously, and to "pay attention" to the interface only when it is ready to receive or transmit data.

Fig. 14-3. An interface device permits two-way communication between a microcomputer and an external device.

commands. The CPU accesses memory locations and I/O ports as stipulated in the program during execution of commands. These activities are provided by various registers, the ALU, and the control section.

The accumulator has been noted previously; observe that it usually stores one of the operands that are to be processed by the ALU. Thus, a typical instruction might command the ALU to add the contents from some other register to the contents of the accumulator, and to store the sum in the accumulator itself. This is just another way of saying that the accumulator is both a data source (operand) and a data destination (result) register. Note in passing that a CPU often

Radio Shack TRS-80 Microcomputer System

Fig. 14-4. View of keyboard and external memory (tape cassette) interconnected with the classical TRS-80 Model I microcomputer (*Courtesy, Radio Shack, a Division of Tandy Corporation*).

includes a number of additional general-purpose registers which can be used to store operands or intermediate "scratch-pad" data (Fig. 14-1). A widely used accumulator arrangement is depicted in Fig. 14-5.

Program Counter

As we have seen, the program counter orchestrates microcomputer activity. We are now in a good position to consider jumps, subroutines, and the register memory area termed the stack. The instructions that constitute a program are stored in the program memory, and the CPU examines its contents to determine what action to take. Thus, the processor must "know" where the next instruction is located. Or, the processor must know the address for the next instruction.

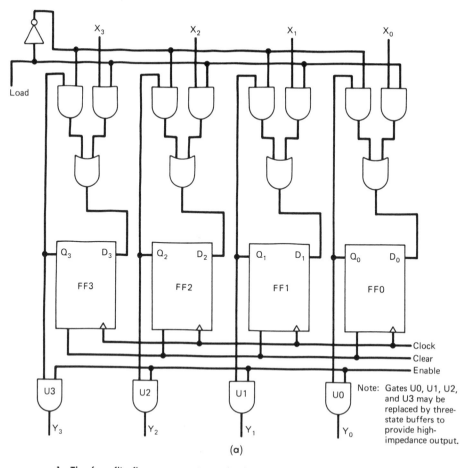

(a)

1. The four flip-flops are continuously clocked.

2. When the clear input is driven logic-high, the flip-flops are reset to 0000.

3. If the load input is logic-low, the X bits cannot enter the accumulator.

4. When the load input is logic-high, the X bits are loaded into the accumulator.

5. Then, when the load input goes logic-low, the inverted load signal goes logic-high, and each flip-flop feeds back its output to the input; the data is thereby recirculated, or held until it needs to be outputted.

6. If the enable input is driven logic-high, the contents of the accumulator are unloaded.

7. After the accumulator is unloaded, it still holds its contents until the clear input is driven logic-high, or until the load input is driven logic-high.

(b)

Fig. 14-5. A widely used accumulator arrangement. (a) Logic diagram; (b) circuit actions; (c) data recirculating logic action.

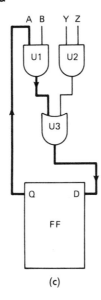

(c)

DATA RECIRCULATING LOGIC ACTION:

When the Load input goes logic-low, it maintains input Z logic-low. In turn, the U2 output is held logic-low, regardless of any change in state of input Y.

Also, when the Load input goes logic-low, input B is maintained logic-high. Consequently, the FF Q output feeds back to its D input.

Since the FF Q output must follow its D input, the FF is held in its prevailing state, regardless of any change in state of input Y.

The 0 or the 1 data bit being recirculated by U1 and U3 will be unloaded when the FF Enable input is driven logic-high.

Fig. 14-5 (*continued*)

We will recall that this address is sequenced by the program counter. However, this automatic sequencing may be violated by the programmer by introducing a jump instruction. This jump instruction contains the address of the instruction which is to follow next. This following instruction may be stored in any memory location; the programmer, of course, must specify the appropriate address. In turn, during execution of a jump instruction, the processor replaces the (usually) sequenced contents of the program counter with the jump address. Conventional sequence is violated, but the logical continuity of the program is nevertheless maintained.

We will recognize that a special kind of program jump occurs when the program "branches" to a subroutine. Recall that a subroutine is a "side function" in which the microcomputer performs an arithmetic or logical operation within a complete routine. As an illustration, a short program "sandwiched" into a main program is a subroutine. When the program branches to a subroutine, the processor must "remember" the contents of the program counter at the point where the jump occurred. In turn, the processor can resume execution of the main program when the last instruction in the subroutine is completed.

A subroutine is sometimes characterized as a program within a program. Note that the processor has a particular way of handling subroutines to ensure logical continuity in return to the main program. Thus, when the processor jumps to a subroutine instruction, the program counter is incremented, and the counter's contents are stored in a register memory area called the stack. In turn, the stack "saves" the address of the instruction which is to be executed after the subroutine is completed. This "saved" address is returned to the program counter so that execution of the main program will resume.

Note that the last instruction in a subroutine is called a branch back. When a branch back instruction is fetched by the processor, it then replaces the current contents of the program counter with the address on the top of the stack. In turn, the processor resumes execution of the main program at the point immediately following the prior branch. Programming of subroutines requires careful attention to the addresses that are involved; in other words, memory "labels" are required at the beginning and end of a subroutine.

Interrupts

Interrupt facilities are provided on various CPU's to improve operating efficiency. As an illustration, a microcomputer may be processing a large sequence of data, more or less of which is outputted to a printer. As we have seen, the CPU can output a byte of data over one instruction cycle; however, it may require a period of several instruction cycles for the printer to strike the character specified by the data byte. To avoid "tying up" the CPU, an interrupt facility can be employed; it returns the CPU to data processing while the printer is striking a character.

When the printer is ready to input the next data byte, it requests an interrupt. In turn, the CPU acknowledges the interrupt, suspends main program execution, and automatically branches to a subroutine that outputs the next data byte. Then, after the byte is outputted, the CPU continues again with main program execution. We will recognize that interrupt activity is similar to a subroutine call, except that the jump is automatically initiated, instead of being programmed by the operator.

Instruction Cycle

With reference to Fig. 14-1, data transfers take place on a 4-bit data bus (D_0-D_3), with D_3 being the MSB. The data bus transfers information such as instruction addresses, operand addresses, and I/O data from the memory (RAM or ROM) and the I/O units. Also, the processor receives instructions, operands, and I/O data back from these other units. Note that all traffic on the bus is contained within a single instruction cycle for one-cycle instructions.

As previously noted, an instruction cycle is subdivided into segments. Each segment, in this example, is equivalent to one period of the system clock. We have seen that information on the data bus will change from one segment to another. The first three time segments provide a 12-bit (three groups of four bits) instruction address to the memory, with the least significant nibble first. Next, the fourth and fifth segments supply the 8-bit instruction sequentially inputted to the data bus by the program memory. Then, the sixth segment is utilized for instruction decoding. Finally, the remaining two segments are utilized for program execution. Operands and I/O data are transmitted to the bus during this time; the words depend upon the instruction being executed.

Some of the instructions in this example require two cycles; however, the procedure is similar to the foregoing description. The complete execution requires 16 clock periods which are subdivided into eight segment cycles. The instruction is fetched during the first cycle. Note that information fetched during this first cycle may also include a portion of the operand, or an indirect address register. The second cycle always fetches the operand and performs the execution. Distinction between one- and two-cycle instructions is made by all units on the data bus by decoding of the unique instructions (See Figs. 14-6 and 14-7.)

Accumulator Group Instruction Set

Consider next the accumulator group instruction set for the microprocessor in Fig. 14-1. There are 13 instructions in this example, as follows: CLB, CLC, IAC, CMC, RAL, RAR, TCC, DAC, TCS, STC, DAA, KBP, and DCL. As before, these are assembly-language mne-

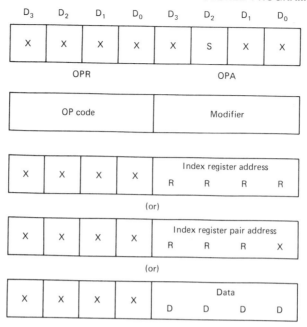

Note: This is a machine instruction format wherein a one-word instruction comprises eight bits and is processed over an instruction cycle of eight clock periods. Observe that each instruction consists of two 4-bit fields; the OPR field contains the operation code, and the OPA field contains the modifier (a modifier alters the address of an operand). Observe that X denotes either 1 or 0.

Fig. 14-6. One-word machine instructions.

monics for the machine instructions; the mnemonics are used in assembly-language programming. The foregoing mnemonics have the following meanings:

CLB means *Clear Both* (accumulator and carry)

CLC means *Clear Carry*

IAC means *Increment Accumulator*

CMC means *Complement Carry*

CMA means *Complement Accumulator*

RAL means *Rotate Left*

RAR means *Rotate Right*

TCC means *Transmit Carry*

DAC means *Decrement Accumulator*

TCS means *Transfer Carry Subtract*

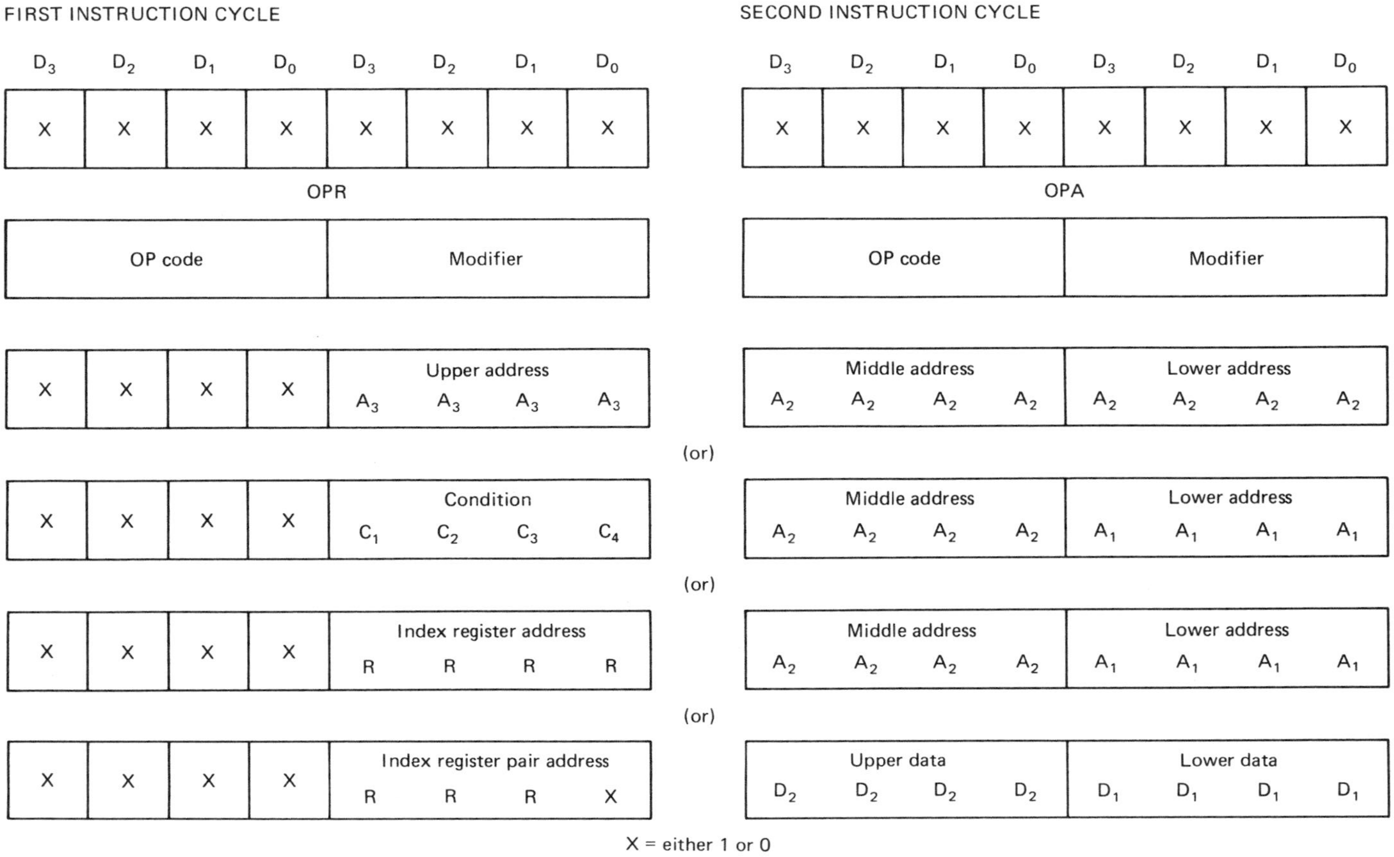

FIRST INSTRUCTION CYCLE

SECOND INSTRUCTION CYCLE

OPR

OPA

D_3	D_2	D_1	D_0	D_3	D_2	D_1	D_0
X	X	X	X	X	X	X	X

OP code

Modifier

OP code

Modifier

Upper address: A_3 A_3 A_3
Middle address: A_2 A_2 A_2 A_2
Lower address: A_2 A_2 A_2 A_2

(or)

Condition: C_1 C_2 C_3 C_4
Middle address: A_2 A_2 A_2 A_2
Lower address: A_1 A_1 A_1 A_1

(or)

Index register address: R R R R
Middle address: A_2 A_2 A_2 A_2
Lower address: A_1 A_1 A_1 A_1

(or)

Index register pair address: R R R X
Upper data: D_2 D_2 D_2 D_2
Lower data: D_1 D_1 D_1 D_1

X = either 1 or 0

Fig. 14-7. Two-word machine instructions.

253

STC means *Set Carry*

DAA means *Decimal Adjust Accumulator*

KBP means *Keyboard Process*

DCL means *Designate Command Line*

Note that rotate means to recirculate, shifting either in a left hand or right hand direction. When data is rotated, the bit that leaves one end of the register simultaneously enters the other end of the register. Accumulator group instruction formats are depicted in Fig. 14-8. (Input/output and RAM instruction formats are included.)

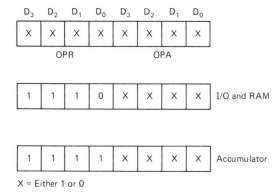

Note: These groups of instructions are all single-word instructions. The OPᴋ field comprises a 4-bit code which serves to identify either an I/O instruction or an accumulator group instruction. The OPA field comprises a 4-bit code which serves to identify the operation that is to be performed. As before, each machine instruction consists of two 4-bit fields.

Fig. 14-8. Accumulator group instruction formats (with I/O and RAM instruction formats).

I/O and RAM Instruction Set

Finally, let us consider the I/O and RAM instruction set for the microprocessor. There are 16 instructions in this example, as follows: WRM, WMP, WRR, WPM, WR0, WR1, WR2, WR3, SBM, RDM, RDR, ADM, RD0, RD1, RD2, and RD3. As before, these are assembly-language mnemonics for the machine instructions; the mnemonics are used in assembly language programming. The foregoing mnemonics have the following meanings:

WRM means *Write into RAM Memory*

WMP means *Write into RAM Port*

WRR means *Write into ROM Port*

WPM means *Write into Program Memory*

WR0 means *Write into RAM the Status Character 0*

WR1 means *Write into RAM the Status Character 1*

WR2 means *Write into RAM the Status Character 2*

WR3 means *Write into RAM the Status Character 3*

SBM means *Subtract RAM Character with Borrow*

RDM means *Read RAM Character into Accumulator*

RDR means *Read ROM Input Port into Accumulator*

ADM means *Add RAM Character to Accumulator*

RD0 means *Read RAM Status Character 0 into Accumulator*

RD1 means *Read RAM Status Character 1 into Accumulator*

RD2 means *Read RAM Status Character 2 into Accumulator*

RD3 means *Read RAM Status Character 3 into Accumulator*

Programming Trick of the Trade

Until the operator has become quite familiar with a particular microcomputer, the keyboard may seem confusing—particularly when employing different modes. As an illustration, when the TRS-80 Model I is operated in its calculator mode, the operator must remember that the numbers cannot be "typed" (such as the augend and addend) until after PRINT has been "typed." With reference to Fig. 14-9, the word PRINT means SOLVE when the microcomputer is operated in its calculator mode. (See also Fig. 14-10.)

In order to ease the operator's task, gummed labels can be marked as shown in the illustration, and attached to the front surface of the keys. Thus, an S label is attached on the front surface of the keys. Thus, an S label is attached on the front surface of the P key, and so on. These labels do not interfere with microcomputer operation in other modes—however, they serve as a ready reminder that PRINT means SOLVE in the calculator mode. Similarly, inasmuch as ENTER means ANSWER in the calculator mode, an ANSWER label may be attached on the front surface of the ENTER key.

Also, multiplication, or times, employs the asterisk (*) symbol on the TRS-80 Model I. In turn, it may be helpful to attach an $\times$ label on the front surface of the * key. These calculator-mode keyboard labels are particularly helpful for the beginner who has no previous experience with microcomputers, but who is familiar with the operation of pocket calculators. Note that pocket calculators provide an equals (=) key;

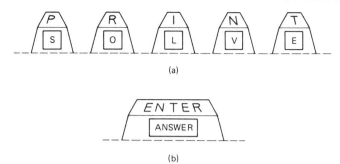

(a)

(b)

Note: The keys are tapered on the Model I, but not on the Color Computer. Therefore, it is preferable to attach labels beside the keys on the Color Computer.

Note: The space bar is unmarked in the Model I and the Color Computer. Beginning programmers may find it helpful to attach a SPACE label on the space bar.

Note: The operator may also find it helpful to attach an ✕ (multiplication) symbol on the front surface of the * key. Similarly, it may be helpful to attach a ÷ (division) symbol on the front surface of the / key, when operating the TRS-80 Model I in its calculator mode.

Note: Although the TRS-80 Model I is no longer manufactured, a large number of these microcomputers are in current use. An understanding of Model-I operation is helpful in approaching more elaborate types and models of microcomputers.

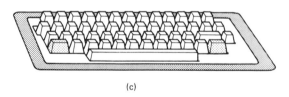

(c)

Fig. 14-9. Auxiliary labels facilitate key identification. (a) SOLVE labels attached to PRINT keys; (b) ANSWER label attached to ENTER key; (c) perspective view of keyboard.

although microcomputers have an (=) key, it is not used in the calculator mode. Therefore, it is advisable to supplement the ENTER key with an ANSWER label (not an = label), to avoid confusion.

Next, let us consider operation of the TRS-80 PC-1 in its calculator mode. The procedure is simpler than in the case of the Model I, inasmuch as we are not concerned with a PRINT (SOLVE) command. After the

```
READY
> PRINT 13 + 19
  32
READY
> ____
```

Note: More detailed explanation of microcomputer operation is provided in the next chapter. However, the above diagram gives you a "bird's eye view" of operation in the calculator mode. At this point, note that the ENTER key must be pressed at the end of each line (after you have "typed in" the line). This procedure is like pressing the carriage-return key on a typewriter. In other words, after you press the ENTER key on the microcomputer, you can then start to "type in" another line. Note also that just as the carriage-return key on a typewriter does not print anything on the paper, neither does the ENTER key on a microcomputer display anything on the screen.

Note: The TRS-80 color computer can be operated as a calculator in this same general manner. Observe, however, that OK will be displayed on the screen, instead of READY.

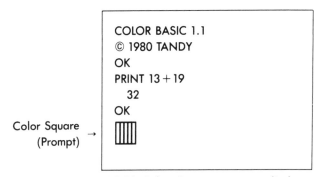

Color Square (Prompt) →

```
COLOR BASIC 1.1
© 1980 TANDY
OK
PRINT 13 + 19
  32
OK
▯▯▯▯▯
```

TRS-80 Color Computer screen display when operated in its calculator mode.

Note: The Color Computer displays a color panel bordered by a blank screen, whereas the Model I employs the entire area of the video-monitor screen. Observe that Color Basic 1.1 is a Dartmouth Basic dialect which is quite similar to Level I Basic utilized in the Model I computer. However, there are some differences between Color Basic 1.1 and Level I Basic.

Fig. 14-10. Examples of screen displays when the TRS-80 Model I and the Color Computer are operated in their calculator modes.

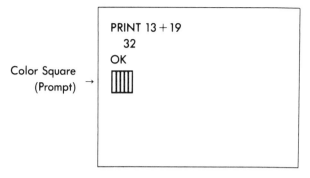

Color Square
(Prompt) →

Note: Most microcomputers have different keyboard layouts, with various numbers of keys. All keyboards include the standard alphabetic and numerical characters used on typewriters, plus various special keys such as CLR, ENTER, BREAK, and so on. Many microcomputers also provide a keypad to the right of the main keyboard. This keypad concentrates the numerals 0 through 9, along with a few special symbols, as on a digital calculator.

TRS-80 Color Computer screen display when operated in its calculator mode and the CLEAR key is pressed before the data is "typed in."

Figure 14-10 (*continued*)

arithmetic problem is "typed in," we press the ENTER key (not the = key) to display the answer. Accordingly, it is helpful to attach a small ANSWER label to the front panel behind the ENTER key. Note that it is impractical to attach a label to the front surface of the ENTER key. An X label may also be attached to the front panel behind the * key (see Fig. 14-11).

In the case of the TRS-80 PC-4, operation in its calculator mode is much the same as described above. We are not concerned with a PRINT (SOLVE) command. However, after the arithmetic problem is "typed in," we press the EXE key to display the answer (not the ENTER key). Accordingly, we may attach a small label to the front panel behind the EXE key. An X label may also be attached to the front panel behind the * key, as before. These examples illustrate the fact that there are no microcomputer industry standards, and that keyboards must be considered individually.

Language Selection

It follows from previous discussion that machine-language programming is the most difficult, assembly-language programming is less difficult, and high-level language programming is the least difficult. Machine language is circuit-action oriented; a program written in machine language specifies the progressive circuit actions that are required. It specifies these circuit actions in complete detail. In turn, a machine-language program requires a comprehensive knowledge of

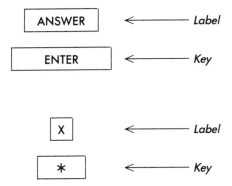

Note: This same principle of key identification can be employed with any type of microcomputer. In a particular case, the keys that are involved when the microcomputer is operated in its calculator mode are labeled in English, instead of BASIC.

Fig. 14-11. Auxiliary label placement for operation of the PC-1 in its calculator mode.

digital electronics and the logic circuitry that is employed by the particular microcomputer.

Assembly language is less difficult because it is architecture-oriented. In other words, mnemonics are employed which activate various circuit functions, rather than the detailed circuit actions. Thus, LDA 4 in assembly language typically corresponds to 1000 0101 in machine language. It is much easier for the programmer to specify the loading of the accumulator with the mnemonic LDA 4 than with the binary number 1000 0101 because LDA relates to a processing function, rather than to the logic-highs and logic-lows that are involved in carrying out the function.

Although BASIC is more closely related to English and to problem formulation than is assembly language, we will find that it is a highly disciplined language format from which the slightest deviation is forbidden. There are also various specially defined "grammatical rules" which must be memorized and strictly observed by the programmer. Microcomputer "grammar" is distantly related (and occasionally unrelated) to English grammar. Also, various types of microcomputers employ different "grammars."

High-level language is less difficult than assembly language because it is task-oriented. This is just another way of saying that English words (and some semi-English words) are employed which relate, at least in a general way, with the programmer's task in hand. Stated otherwise, a BASIC programmer does not need to know anything about accumulators and memories. Instead, he concerns himself with variables such as A and B, to which chosen values are assigned. For example, he may write (type) LET A = 3.1416, which is then ENTERed into the program memory.

Historical Note

The original BASIC language is called Dartmouth BASIC, and was developed by Dartmouth College. Original BASIC is the "mother" programming language from which many BASIC dialects have been derived. A BASIC "vocabulary" includes specified statements. It is instructive to note that Dartmouth BASIC contains 17 statements; on the other hand, the Level-I BASIC dialect employs 20 statements.

Dartmouth BASIC Statements

DATA	Defines a block of data
DEF	Defines a function
DIM	Allocates space for an array
END	Terminates source input
FOR	Establishes a loop
GOSUB	Transfers program control to a subroutine
GOTO	Transfers program control to a specified line
IF-THEN	Conditionally transfers program control
INPUT	Enables input of variables
LET	Assigns a numerical value to a variable
NEXT	Defines the end of a loop
PRINT	Enables printing of variables and/or text
READ	Reads from a block of data
REM	Defines a remark or comment
RESTORE	Resets data block pointer
RETURN	Returns control to the calling program
STOP	Stops program execution

As previously noted, personal computers employ various dialects of the Dartmouth BASIC programming language. In turn, some programs will run on several types of personal computers, whereas other programs must be converted (translated) to run on a type of computer other than that for which it was written. This is generally "no big deal" insofar as professional skills are concerned.

It is evident from the foregoing list of Dartmouth BASIC statements that although the BASIC language is task-oriented, it is not closely related to Basic English. BASIC "grammar" and "syntax" are different from Basic English grammar and syntax. All BASIC dialects are quite limited, compared to an English vocabulary—and the lines in a program must be written in accordance with rigid rules. Program lines must also follow one another in a certain order—an order that is not always obvious to the beginner.

Dartmouth BASIC, like all BASIC dialects, includes groups of words other than statements. Thus, Dartmouth BASIC employs six relational operators such as EQUAL TO, NOT EQUAL TO, LESS THAN, and so on. It also employs math operators, such as signs for addition, subtraction, multiplication, division, equality, and an "up arrow" for exponential notation. Level I BASIC, for example, uses the Dartmouth relational operators; however, it does not use the "up arrow" sign.

Again, a particular microcomputer BASIC language such as Level-I BASIC, includes various groups of words which are extensions of Dartmouth BASIC. Thus, Level-I BASIC employs the PRINT modifiers AT and TAB which are not present in Dartmouth BASIC. Similarly, Level-I BASIC employs the logical operators AND and OR which are not present in Dartmouth BASIC. Although these words may look like "Greek" at this time, if you are unfamiliar with computer programming, do not be concerned—they are merely mentioned here to illustrate typical extensions of Dartmouth BASIC that you are likely to encounter in programming various types of personal computers.

Although a microcomputer troubleshooter does not have to be a programmer, much time and effort can often be saved if the trouble-shooter understands how to write programs—particularly diagnostic programs. The professional troubleshooter will find it well worthwhile to learn as much as possible about programming. Note, however, that commercial software may be utilized to check out microcomputer operation in the event that the troubleshooter does not understand how to write programs.

15

New Microcomputer Test Equipment You Can Build

Charge-Storage, Logic-High Beeper * Differential Temperature Checker * Adjustable Single-Shot Pulser * Digital System Noise * Short-Circuit Localization * Troubleshooting Short-Circuited PC Conductors * Circuit Internal Resistance * RFI Checkout

Charge-Storage Logic-High Beeper

The charge-storage logic-high beeper shown in Fig. 15-1 is a new type of logic-level sound indicator that provides high input impedance and which is economical and easy to build. This logic-level beeper comprises a microswitch, piezo buzzer such as the Mallory Sonalert®, a 22 μF electrolytic capacitor, and a 100-kilohm resistor. In operation, the test tip is touched to a node in the digital circuit, and the capacitor charges through the 100-kilohm resistor. As the troubleshooter increases pressure on the test tip, the microswitch closes and the charged capacitor discharges through the piezo buzzer, giving a sharp beep (provided that the point under test is logic-high).

This logic-level beeper is suitable for use in TTL circuitry—it may or may not be suitable for use in CMOS circuitry. CMOS devices normally operate from supply voltages in the +3- to +15-volt range.

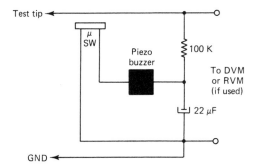

Note: The test tip is mechanically linked to the microswitch actuator, so that appreciable pressure on the test tip closes the microswitch. Observe that the beeper arrangement may also be connected to a dc voltmeter, if desired.

Note: Intermittent operation is the "troubleshooter's curse." This malfunction can often be tracked down to better advantage by using a recording voltmeter (RVM) instead of a digital voltmeter (DVM). Thereby, voltages can be monitored over a period of time and under various conditions of operation. Observe that some RVMs have a slow response time, such as 1 sec. Others have comparatively fast response time, although they are more expensive. It is desirable to use an RVM that has a reasonably fast response time.

Fig. 15-1. Arrangement of a charge-storage, logic-high beeper.

From a practical viewpoint, CMOS logic-high and logic-low levels are defined as follows:

1. If the supply voltage is in the range from 30 to 10 volts, the normal logic-high level is a voltage greater than 0.7 of the supply voltage ±0.5 volt. The normal logic-low level is a voltage less than 0.3 of the supply voltage ±0.5 volt.

2. If the supply voltage is in the range from 10 to 18 volts, the normal logic-high level is a voltage greater than 0.7 of the supply voltage ±1 volt. The normal logic-low level is a voltage less than 0.3 of the supply voltage ±1 volt.

Differential Temperature Checker

It was previously noted that a great deal of preliminary information concerning trouble areas can be accomplished by means of comparative temperature tests. In other words, if you have a duplicate microcomputer available in normal operating condition, you can make comparative temperature tests of corresponding ICs and quickly "spot" IC packages that are running too hot or too cold.

Although the differential temperature quick checker depicted in Fig. 15-2 is not really "new," it is of sufficient practical importance that it should be mentioned here. This quick checker shows whether

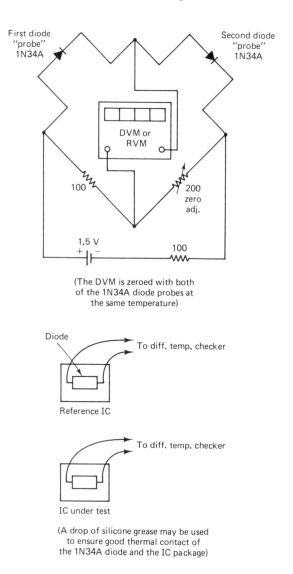

(The DVM is zeroed with both of the 1N34A diode probes at the same temperature)

(A drop of silicone grease may be used to ensure good thermal contact of the 1N34A diode and the IC package)

Note: More informative differential temperature tests can be made if you use a recording voltmeter instead of a DVM, and monitor the equipment over a period of time under various conditions of operation.

Fig. 15-2. A differential temperature quick checker.

a pair of corresponding devices are operating at the same temperature, or at different temperatures. For example, one diode of the first "probe" may be placed on a reference IC, and the other diode of the second "probe" may be placed on a corresponding suspected IC. If both ICs are operating at the same temperature, the DVM remains zeroed. On the other hand, if the ICs are operating at different temperatures, the DVM will indicate a positive voltage or a negative voltage.

The advantage of the differential temperature probe quick checker is its speed in application. That is, the troubleshooter does not take the time to measure individual temperatures, but merely notes whether the two temperatures are the same, or not. (Whether the DVM indicates zero, or a positive or negative reading.)

Adjustable Single-Shot Pulser

TTL and CMOS circuitry often operate at different logic-high and logic-low levels. In turn, if you do not have a commercial pulser with an adjustable output, the simple arrangement shown in Fig. 15-3 can save time in practical test procedures. This is not an entirely "new" type of tester, but it does not appear to be widely known, and merits note here. This pulser is often helpful in tracking down a marginal device. In other words, the troubleshooter may wish to determine the minimum voltage at which the device under test will trigger. (Ordinary logic pulsers do not provide this facility.)

In application, the pulser shown in Fig. 15-3 is connected to the V_{CC} source, and the capacitor charges up to a voltage which is determined by the setting of the 200-kilohm potentiometer. This voltage is indicated

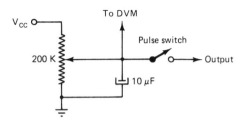

Note: This pulser arrangement permits the troubleshooter to determine the threshold at which a device will trigger. It may be used on a comparison test basis if a similar microcomputer in normal operating condition is available.

Fig. 15-3. An adjustable single-shot pulser arrangement.

by a DVM. When the pulse switch is closed, the pulser outputs a surge with an amplitude equal to the DVM reading. Although the width of the pulse will vary considerably, depending upon the circuit resistance at the point under test, the troubleshooter is generally concerned only with the pulse amplitude.

Digital System Noise

There is always a slight trace of noise (AC noise) in a digital system, and there may be a large amount of noise in a malfunctioning system. Excessive noise can cause various obscure trouble symptoms. The most practical approach to a suspected noise problem is to make comparison tests with an oscilloscope—the noise levels are compared in the malfunctioning microcomputer and in a similar comparison unit that is in normal operating condition.

Any AC noise waveform has a rate of change that exceeds the response capability of the device under test. The noise immunity of a device denotes its capability of maintaining a given logic state with AC noise present. In technical terms, the noise immunity of a device is measured with respect to noise-pulse width and the noise-pulse amplitude to which the device under test is unresponsive. Noise immunity is one of the basic measures of digital system reliability. If a device responds to a noise pulse, a data error is introduced. The meaning of noise versus bandwidth is depicted in Fig. 15-4.

In A, The digital system has a bandwidth of 2 units (such as 2 kHz, or 2 MHz). In this example, the noise has a value of 1 unit, and the signal has a value of 1 unit, or, the signal-to-noise ratio is 1. Next, in B and C, the bandwidth is twice as great. In turn, the noise increases to twice its value in A. The signal has the same value in B as in A (1 unit); accordingly, the signal-to-noise ratio decreases to 0.7.

Observe that the remaining bandwidth capacity in B is not used. However, this remaining bandwidth capacity is used in C for data enhancement. That is, the remaining bandwidth capacity is used to increase reliability by means of some form of redundant transmission. Data enhancement may employ actual redundant transmission (message repetition), special codes, multiple parity bits, or complement parity.

Short-Circuit Localization

Troubleshooters employ various methods to track down short circuits. A fault may occur inside of an IC, or it may occur in the

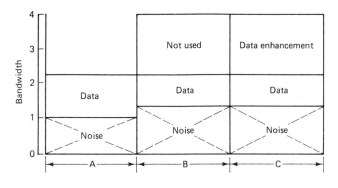

	BW	n	s	s/n
A	2	1.0	1.0	1.0
B	4	1.4	1.0	0.7
C	4	1.4	2.6	1.8

N is in average noise-power units
S is in average signal-power units
BW is the bandwidth in hertz
C is the channel capacity in bits per
  second (all of the yes-no decisions —
  not just the 1 bits)

$C = BW \log_2 (1 + s/n)$

BW = bandwidth
n = noise
s = signal (data)
s/n = signal-to-noise ratio

Note: Practical noise tests can be made on a comparison basis with a similar microcomputer in normal operating condition, using a high-performance oscilloscope.

Fig. 15-4. Noise vs. bandwidth in a digital system.

external node circuitry. In either case, the voltage to ground falls to practically zero in the case of a short circuit to ground. A special type of test, illustrated in Fig. 15-5, can be quite helpful.

First, consider a short circuit that occurs somewhere along a PC conductor, as depicted in Fig. 15-5. The troubleshooter's question is whether the short circuit is located at one end of the PC conductor, or whether it is located somewhere between the ends of the conductor. A DVM is connected at each end of the conductor, as shown in the diagram. The V_{CC} supply voltage is turned off.

To localize the short circuit, a test current considerably greater than the normal circuit operating current is injected, as shown in the diagram. A test current in the range from 150 to 200 mA is adequate to provide useful IR drop indications with most service-type DVM's.

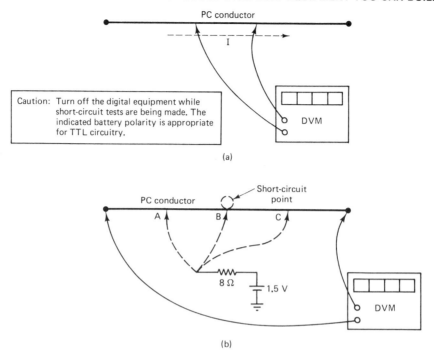

Fig. 15-5. Short-circuit localization with service-type DVM.

Note: The DVM indicates the IR drop along the PC conductor. A 1.5V battery in series with an 8-ohm resistor injects approximately 180 mA into the PC conductor, which produces measurable IR drops.

Short-circuit localization is made by injecting the test current at various points along the PC conductor. When the test current is injected at A, the DVM indicates a positive IR drop. When the test current is injected at C, the DVM indicates a negative IR drop. When the test current is injected at B, the DVM indicates zero voltage drop. This is the short-circuit point.

Comment: Although this is not an entirely new test technique, it does not appear to be widely known, and merits explanation here.

The test current is experimentally injected at various points along the PC conductor, and DVM indications are evaluated as follows:

1. If the DVM indicates a positive IR drop when current is injected at A, but indicates a negative IR drop when current is injected at B, the troubleshooter concludes that the short circuit is located between A and B.

2. When the test current is injected at B, the DVM will indicate zero.

3. On the other hand, if the DVM indicates a positive IR drop when current is injected at A, or B, or C, the troubleshooter concludes that the short circuit is located between C and the righthand end of the PC conductor.

4. In case there is a short circuit inside the IC package at the righthand end of the conductor, the DVM will indicate zero when the test current is injected at the righthand end.

5. Again, if the DVM indicates a negative IR drop when current is injected at A, or B, or C, the troubleshooter concludes that the short circuit is located between A and the lefthand end of the PC conductor.

6. In the event that there is a short circuit inside the IC package at the lefthand end of the conductor, the DVM will indicate zero when the test current is injected at the lefthand end.

As a practical note, any dc voltmeter can be used for short-circuit localization, if you inject a sufficiently high value of test current. However, it is good practice to use only enough test current to obtain clearly readable indications on your meter.

Troubleshooters can be guided by the rough rule-of-thumb that a printed-circuit conductor has 0.01 ohm of resistance per inch. Accordingly, a current flow of 100 mA will produce a voltage drop of 1 mV per inch along the PC conductor. If the PC conductor is comparatively short, you may need to use a current flow of several hundred mA to localize a short circuit with a service-type DVM.

Troubleshooting Short-Circuited PC Conductors

A common troubleshooting problem involves a suspected short circuit between PC conductors, as depicted in Fig. 15-6. In this situation, neither of the conductors is at ground or V_{CC} potential. A practical approach to this fault condition is to switch off V_{CC}, inject a comparatively large test current at the end of one conductor, and ground the corresponding end of the other conductor. A positive voltage is applied from the battery, inasmuch as the IC's associated with the conductors will usually "look like" open circuits to the positive voltage.

A service-type DVM may be used to check IR voltage drops along the PC conductors. For example, if there is a short circuit along the path of the conductors, as exemplified in Fig. 15-6, a positive voltage drop will be measured between points A and B. A larger voltage drop will be measured between points A and C. On the other hand, no change in voltage will occur when a check is made between points A and D.

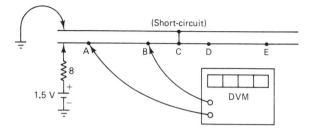

Troubleshooting Note: When a short-circuit is suspected between two PC
conductors, neither of which is at ground or V$_{CC}$ potential, a positive
test voltage may be applied as shown to produce a comparatively
large current flow in the PC conductors. Because the applied
voltage is positive, devices will ordinarily not conduct. A DVM is
used to trace the current flow to the short-circuit point.

Comment: The digital system under test should be turned off while
short-circuit tests are being made.

Fig. 15-6. Localizing a short circuit between two PC
conductors.

Observe that if the meter leads are applied at points C and D,
or points C and E, zero volts will be indicated. In turn, the troubleshooter
can approximate the short-circuit point. As previously noted, a higher
current can be injected if needed to obtain useful meter indications—
this depends upon the sensitivity of your DVM.

Next suppose that the short circuit is not along the path of the
PC conductors. For example, the short circuit might be inside of an
IC package at the lefthand end of the conductors. In such a case, the
troubleshooter will find zero voltage drop at any pair of test points
along the conductors. His procedure, in turn, is to inject the test current
at the righthand ends of the conductors. Now, if the short circuit is
actually in the lefthand IC package, voltage drops will be measured
at any pair of test points along the conductors.

Similarly, if the short circuit were in the IC package at the righthand
end of the conductors in Fig. 15-6, the troubleshooter would measure
voltage drops at any pair of test points. The same troubleshooting
principles apply also to branched nodes, wherein a short circuit occurs
in one of the branches. Each branch is regarded as an independent
pair of conductors. Localization of a short circuit is accomplished in
the same manner as in a simple circuit. Test current may be injected
at the ends of any pair of branched conductors.

Circuit Internal Resistance

We have seen that when a short-circuit occurs to ground, to V_{CC}, or to another conductor which is at neither ground nor V_{CC} potential, that localization of the short-circuit point involves current-oriented test procedures. The reason for this orientation is that a short-circuit condition is associated with very low internal resistance. In turn, voltage measurements to ground, or to V_{CC}, do not provide useful test data.

This is just another way of saying that voltage is a current-resistance product—and that, conversely, current is a voltage-resistance ratio. In turn, when the resistance value is very small, the current-resistance ratio is very large. Although the existing circuit current is often too small to provide useful IR test data, comparatively large test currents may be injected into the fault path to obtain easily measurable IR test data.

RFI Checkout

Preliminary troubleshooting clues can occasionally be obtained by making an RFI checkout of a malfunctioning microcomputer. In other words, every microcomputer has its characteristic RFI pattern in normal operation. The RFI pattern can be checked with an AM radio receiver. You will note that the "buzz" output from the microcomputer has various peaks and dips as you tune the radio through the AM broadcast band. (Check RFI patterns in a screen room, if broadcast stations confuse the test.)

Comparison tests are the most informative, if you have a similar microcomputer in normal operating condition. It is good foresight to make notes of abnormal RFI patterns versus the fault conditions that cause the RFI abnormalities. Then, when another troubleshooting job comes along, you can make a preliminary quick check with a radio receiver and possibly localize the fault immediately.

Glossary

A

Absolute Value. Numerical value of a number or of a symbol without regard to its algebraic sign.

Access Time. Time required in a computer to move information from the memory to the computing subsystem.

Accumulator. The register (row of flip-flops) that displays an answer such as in an adder or subtracter configuration; a register in an arithmetic unit for performance of arithmetic and logic functions such as addition and shifting.

Active Elements. Those components in a circuit that provide gain, or control DC flow; diodes, transistors, SCRs, and so on.

Add Control. The "halt" command used to control (or stop) the addition process in an adder subsystem.

Addend. The number to be added to another number in the process of addition.

Addend Register. The register (row of flip-flops) in which the number to be added is entered in an adder subsystem.

Adder. Switching circuits that combine binary bits to generate the sum and carry of these bits. An adder takes the bits from the two binary numbers to be added (addend and augend) plus the carry from the preceding less significant bit and generates the sum and carry.

Adder, BCD. An adder configuration that generates the sum of two binary coded decimal numbers.

Adder, Full. The complete logic circuitry that generates both a sum and a carry output.

Adder, Half. The logic circuitry that generates only a sum output and not a carry output; also called a *sum gate*.

Adder, Logic. A wired configuration of logic gates and/or flip-flops that will perform binary addition.

Adder, Nongated Binary. A wired configuration of flip-flops only, that will perform addition; that is, which will allow a binary number to be added in one register and the answer to be displayed in a second register.

Adder, Shift. A wired configuration of flip-flops and logic gates that consist of one full adder and three shift registers. Two shift registers shift the two numbers to be added through the full adder, and the answer is shifted out in the third shift register.

Addition Identity. A logic expression that defines a sum, a carry, or both for two or more binary numbers.

Address. A location, either a name or number, where information is stored in a computer. To select or pick out the location of a stored information, set for access.

Alphanumeric. Combination of alphabetic characters and digital numbers.

Analog. Representing something else. Thus, a meter movement that indicates a voltage value on a scale. A continuous variation from one value to another; thus, nondigital.

AND Gate. An electronic circuit that forms a logic gate whose output is a 1 only when all its inputs are 1. The gate output is 0 for all other combinations of inputs.

AND Logic Operation. The logic operation denoted by a dot (.), which answers the question "Are all the facts TRUE?" or, "Are all the inputs 1?"

ANDing. The process of applying signals to an AND function.

Anode. The lead on a diode or other device that receives positive voltage, as opposed to the other lead, the cathode, that receives negative voltage.

Architecture. The construction or making of a system.

Astable Multivibrator. A free-running pulse generator.

Asynchronous Inputs. Those terminals of a flip-flop that can affect the output state of the flip-op independently of the clock. Also called *set, preset, reset, DC set,* and *clear,* or *clear inputs.*

Asynchronous Operation. Usually, an operation started by a completion signal from a previous operation. It then proceeds at maximum speed until finished and then generates its own completion signal.

Augend. The number to which another number will be added.

B

Bar. Denotes the inverse, or complement, of a function. Example: The inversion of A is written $\overline{A}$ and is read A Bar, or A Not.

BCD. An abbreviation for Binary Coded Decimal.

Binary. Two-valued. Thus, the value may be True and False, 1 and 0, On and Off, and so on; one and only one of the two values is always present. Also, a number system to the base 2, which represents any number by combinations of the binary digits 1 and 0.

Binary Addition. A process of obtaining the binary sum of two binary numbers.

Binary Coded Decimal. Employs binary numbers in decimal positions. Thus, $35 = 11\ 101$.

Binary Complement. That binary number that has the 1's and 0's of its digits interchanged with those of the original binary number. The sum of a binary number and its complement is a third binary number whose digits are all 1's.

Binary Division. A process of dividing a binary number by another binary number to obtain a binary quotient.

Binary Fractional. All binary digits to the right of the binary point.

Binary Input. A binary 1 or 0 that is fed to a logic gate input of a flip-flop input in order to perform a logic function or flip-flop triggering operation; any pin on a flip-flop or logic gate that can receive a binary signal.

Binary Logic. Digital logic elements that operate with two distinct states. The two states are represented in calculators and computers by two different voltage levels.

Binary Multiplication. A process of multiplying two binary numbers together to obtain a binary product.

Binary Number. A digit that represents a power of 2 and can only be a 1 or 0; a number of two or more digits that represents powers of 2, and each digit is a 1 or a 0.

Binary Output. Any terminal of a flip-flop or logic gate that generates a binary 1 or 0 logic-level signal resulting from one or more input signals. Any terminal on a pulse generator that generates a pulse-voltage signal.

Binary Point. Similar to a decimal point (.), except that it is used to denote a binary fractional.

Binary Subtraction. A process of subtracting a binary number from another binary number to obtain the binary difference.

Binary System. The number system to the base 2.

Bistable Multivibrator. A flip-flop.

Bit. A bit is one character of a digital word. It can be either a 1 or 0. The position of the bit in the word usually determines its significance. The first bit may be a sign bit, with 0 representing a + sign and 1 representing a − sign.

Blanking Input. A control input for decoding circuits.

Block. A specified number of digital characters. The block may be of any size, but block size is usually uniform within a system or subsystem.

Boolean Approach. To impose the condition that all logic statements, reasons, conclusions, facts, and so on, are either true or false.

Boolean Expression. Mathematic expression of logic relationships in terms of true or false.

Borrow. The binary 1 that is removed from the adjacent column to the left by the subtraction of binary 1 from binary 0, leaving 1 in the column that was subtracted.

Braces. Symbols { } that denote logic grouping, along with parentheses and brackets.

Brackets. Symbols [ ] that denote logic grouping, along with parentheses and braces.

Buffer. An amplifier that processes digital information. A temporary storage location for a four-bit binary number.

Byte. A group of bits (usually eight bits).

C

Cancel. To remove a binary 1 from a flip-flop; to turn a flip-flop read-out light off; the process of removing a binary number from a register.

Carry. The binary 1 that is generated in the next column to the left by the addition of a pair of binary 1's, leaving 0 in the column that was added.

Carry Feedbàck. A carry, or binary 1, that is generated in a column other than the next column to the left; the carry of the last binary number at the extreme left of a register that is fed back into the first binary number (extreme right) of the same register.

Cathode. The lead on a diode or other device that receives negative voltage, as opposed to the other lead, the anode, which receives positive voltage.

Character. A combination of bits having a specified assigned meaning; one element of a code. Characters are usually composed of four, five, six, seven, or eight bits each.

Clear. A circuit is said to be cleared when it is set to all 0's.

Clear Input. A clear input generates a clear function.

Clock. A pulse train of known frequency and waveform, used to synchronize the operation of circuits within a specific device or system. A device may have several different clocks, but each clock bears a defined relationship to all other clocks.

Code. A means of representing information in digital form by assigning a specific pattern of bits to each item of information. Each information-item/bit-pattern pair is known as a character. An example is binary-coded-decimal assignment of four-bit binary representations to the decimal digits.

Coder. A device for converting data from one notation system to another.

Command Generator. A binary counter used in conjunction with AND gates to generate a repetitive series of command pulses.

An *n-bit* counter can generate up to 2^n repetitive command pulses.

Complement, Binary. That binary number that has the 1's and 0's of its digits interchanged from those of the original binary number.

Core. A particle of magnetic material used to store digital data, usually but not always in the shape of a toroid. By extension, an array of cores comprising a memory.

Counter. A device capable of changing state in a specified sequence upon receiving appropriate input signals. The output of the counter indicates the number of pulses that have been applied.

Counter, Binary. An interconnection of flip-flops having a single input so arranged to enable binary counting.

Counter, Binary-Coded-Decimal (BCD). A binary counter with logic gating that will count up to binary nine (1001), and then reset itself to 0000.

Counter, Down. A counter that starts from any specified number and decreases its value by 1 with each pulse signal input; it counts backward.

Counter, Gates Up-Down. A single-register binary counter that can be controlled by logic gating so as to count up or count down at the proper command.

Counter, Ring. A special form of counter with simple wiring. It forms a loop, or circuits of interconnected flip-flops so arranged that only one is 0 and that as input signals are received, the position of the 0 state moves in sequence from one flip-flop to another around the loop until they are all 0, after which the first one goes to 1, and this moves in sequence from one flip-flop to another until all are 1. It has $2 \times n$ possible counts where n is the number of flip-flops.

Counter, Up-Down. A binary counter wired with extra logic gates so that the free-running counter will count alternately up and then switch automatically to count down after resetting from the up count.

D

Data. Denotes facts, numbers, letters, symbols, in binary bits presented as voltage levels in a computer. Binary data can consist only of 0 and 1.

Data Domain. Tabulated patterns of 1's and 0's that represent flow of machine-language information.

Data Processor. Any digital device; usually associated with devices not used for mathematical computation.

Decimal System. Our conventional number system, which employs the digits 1, 2, 3, 4, 5, 6, 7, 8, 9, and 0.

Decoder, Binary-to-Decimal. A configuration of logic gating that will convert any binary number to a decimal number; usually employed with a binary-coded-decimal counter.

Decouple. To block out any electronic noise or interference generated by nearby circuits, by the power source (power supply), or by external noise sources.

Delay. The slowing up of the propagation of a pulse either intentionally to prevent inputs from changing while clock pulses are present, or unintentionally as caused by transistor rise-and-fall time, pulse-response characteristics.

DeMorgan's Theorem. This theorem states that the inversion of a series of AND implications is equal to the same series of inverted OR implications or the inversion of a series of OR implications is equal to the same series of inverted AND implications. $\overline{A \cdot B \cdot C} = \overline{A} + \overline{B} + \overline{C} \quad \overline{A} + \overline{B} + \overline{C} = \overline{A \cdot B \cdot C}$

Diagrams, Logic. Drawings that illustrate how flip-flops and logic gates must be connected to perform specific computer functions; the use of symbols to represent flip-flop, logic-gate, and pulse-generator electronic circuits without drawing out the full electrical schematic each time.

Difference. The answer that results from the subtraction of a number from another number; the binary digit that represents the subtraction of one binary digit from another binary digit, exclusive of the borrow.

Digit. A single number.

Digit, Binary. A single binary number; a 1 or a 0.

Digit, Least Significant. The digit at the extreme right of any number.

Digit, Most Significant. The digit at the extreme left of any number.

Digit, Sense. The use of an OR gate to determine whether or not a number is present in a register.

Digit Sense Logic. A gated logic circuit (usually a multi-input OR gate) that determines whether any numbers (or digits) are present in a register.

Digital. Representation of a number in discrete terms of On or Off. The flip-flop register is a digital representation of a binary number.

Digital Circuit (Binary Circuit). A semiconductor configuration that operates as a switch.

DIP. Abbreviation of dual-in-line package.

Direct Output Display. Use of a flip-flop to read the output from a logic gate by wiring that output of the logic gate directly into the flip-flop.

Discrete Circuits. Electronic circuits comprising separate, individually manufactured, and assembled diodes, resistors, transistors, capacitors, and other specific electronic components.

Dividend. A number to be divided (in the arithmetic process of division).

Divider, Logic. A configuration of gated logic circuits and registers that will divide one number by another.

Divisor. A number by which a second number is divided (in the arithmetic process of division).

Double Precision. Also called Double Length; data that requires two computer words for containment.

Doubling, Binary. The process of adding an extra 0 to the right of a given binary number. This added 0 results in doubling the number.

Down Counter. A counter that starts from a specified number and decreases its value by 1 with each pulse signal input; thus, the circuit counts backward.

Down-Swing, Voltage. A change in output voltage from a positive value to zero; or, a change from a negative value to zero (in positive logic).

Driver. An element coupled to the output stage of a circuit to increase its power capability or fanout.

DTL. Diode-transistor logic; employs diodes as switches with transistors as inverting amplifiers.

Duty Cycle. The ratio of on-time to total cycle time of a pulse waveform.

E

Enable. To permit an action by application of appropriate signals (generally a logic 1 in positive logic) to the appropriate input.

End-Around. Transfer of a pulse command from the last flip-flop in a register to the first flip-flop.

Enter. To place a binary 1 in a flip-flop or flip-flops.

Equality, Logic. Defines two or more logic expressions, equations, or facts to be identical.

F

Fact, Logic. A statement (which may be true or false) that is used in a reasoning process to arrive at a true or false conclusion.

Fall Time. The decay time of the trailing edge in a pulse waveform.

False. Statement for a 0 in Boolean algebra.

Fan-In. Total number of inputs to a particular gate or function.

Fan-Out. Total number of loads connected to a particular gate or function.

File. One or more records of information arranged in a sequence and stored for future use.

Flip-Flop. A circuit with two and only two stable states.

   D Flip-Flop: Delay binary; the output shows the input signal at the next clock pulse (one clock pulse delayed).

   JK Flip-Flop: Binary with synchronous set and reset inputs.

R-S Flip-Flop: (Latch) binary with set and reset inputs, and the restriction that both inputs shall not be energized simultaneously.

RST Flip-Flop: Binary with the features of an R-S and a T flip-flop.

RS/T Flip-Flop: An R-S flip-flop that may be connected to operate in the toggling mode.

T Flip-Flop: (Toggle) binary with a synchronous T input; if the T input is high, the flip-flop will toggle (change state) synchronously.

Full Adder. The complete logic circuitry that generates both a sum and a carry output.

Full Subtracter. The complete logic circuitry that generates both a difference and a borrow output.

Function, Logic. An expression that contains one or more logic operators, indicating logic operation(s) to be performed; a specific logic operation such as AND or OR.

G

Garbage. Computer jargon for unwanted and/or meaningless information; also called Hash.

Gate. The simplest logic circuit; its ouput voltage will be high or low depending on the states of the inputs and the type of gate that is employed.

General Register. A register employed for binary addition, subtraction, multiplication, and division.

GIGO. Abbreviation for Garbage In/Garbage Out (if garbage is inputted, garbage will be outputted).

Glitch. A false digital pulse.

Graphics. Pictorial display of data.

H

Half–Adder. A switching circuit that combines binary bits to generate the sum and carry; it can only take in the two binary bits to be added and generate the sum and carry.

Hang–Up. The inability of a flip-flop to be triggered from a pulse command.

High. *See* **Binary Logic.**

Holding Time. The period of time that the input states must remain after activation of the clock input.

I

Inhibit. To prevent an action (opposite of enable).

Integrated Circuit (IC). The physical realization of a number of electrical elements inseparably associated on or within a continuous body of semiconductor material to perform the functions of a circuit.

Inverter. A device or element to complement a Boolean function.

J

JK Flip-Flop. *See* **Flip-Flop.**

Joystick. A handle that can be tilted in various directions to control a characteristic of a graphics display.

K

Keyboard. A device for encoding information by depression of various key switches.

Kilobit. One thousand binary bits.

Kludge. Computer jargon for a jury-rigged repair.

L

Labels. Identifying statements or numbers used to describe flip-flop or logic-gate relative positions.

Latch. Usually, a feedback loop in a symmetrical digital circuit, such as a flip-flop, for retaining a state; synonym for a set-reset flip-flop.

Law, Logic. A relation that is proved or assumed to hold between other logic expressions (expressed as a logic equality).

Leaky. A poor front-to-back ratio in a semi-conductor junction.

Least Significant Bit. The bit in a number that is least important (has the least weight).

Linear Circuit. A circuit whose output is an amplified version of its input, or whose output is a continuous predetermined variation of its input.

Logic. The science of reasoning; making use of known facts to reason out a conclusion; the arrangement of electrical circuits that applies the defined rules or functions in input signals to produce output information.

Logic Diagrams. Drawings that show how flip-flops and gates must be connected to perform specific computer functions.

Logic Gate. An electronic circuit that performs a logic operation, such as AND or OR.

Logic Levels. One of two possible states; 0 or 1.

Logic Swing. The voltage difference between logic-high and logic-low levels.

Low. *See* **Binary Logic.**

LSB. Least significant bit; the lowest weighted digit in a binary number.

LSI. Abbreviation for large-scale integration; a chip containing more than 100 gates.

M

Master-Slave. A binary element containing two independent storage states, with a definite separation of the clock function to enter information in the master and to transfer it to the slave.

Matrix. A group of elements such as circuit components or information items arranged in a defined relationship in such a manner that the intersection of two or more inputs produces a unique output.

Memory. Any device used to store information; frequently a matrix of magnetic cores, or magnetic tapes, drums, or disks.

Microcomputer. A complete computing system in miniaturized form, with a comparatively low price (typically under $500).

Microprocessor. The central processing unit in a microcomputer.

MSI. Abbreviation for medium-scale integration; a chip having from 10 to 100 gates.

Multiplex. Commutate; to sequentially connect a central unit or system to one of several channels.

Multiplexing. The process of combining the data from a number of sources into one flow of data. The reverse process of sorting out multiplexed data is called *demultiplexing.*

N

NAND. Logic function that produces the inverted AND function.

Negation. Employs an overhead bar to denote not A when placed over logic fact A.

Negation, Double. A process of inverting twice or inverting the negative of a logic fact to revert it to the original fact.

Negative-Edge Gating. Circuit response as the control signal goes from high to low.

Negative Logic. Logic in which the more negative voltage represents the 1 state; the less negative voltage represents the 0 state.

NOR Gate. An electronic circuit that forms a logic gate and whose output is a 1 only when all its inputs are 0.

NOT. A Boolean logic operation denoting negation; an inverter.

Numeral, Double Length. A numeral that comprises twice as many digits as a conventional numeral; it requires two storage locations.

Numeric Keypad. A numeral key grouping similar to the keyboard on an adding machine.

O

Open-Collector Output. A TTL gate with only one output transistor, instead of a two-transistor totem-pole configuration.

OR. Logic operation that produces a 1 at the output if at least one input is a 1.

Output, Binary. Any pin of a flip-flop or logic gate that generates a binary 1 or 0 voltage resulting from one or more input signals.

Overflow. The carry or borrow output generated by the last flip-flop at the end of a register.

P

Parallel. A technique for processing a binary data word that has more than one bit; all bits are acted upon simultaneously.

Parallel Adder. A technique for addition in which the two multibit numbers are presented and added together simultaneously.

Passive Elements. Resistors, inductors, or capacitors; elements without gain.

Positive-Edge Gating. A circuit that responds as the control signal goes from low to high.

Positive Logic. Logic operations in which the more positive voltage represents the 1 state.

Preset. An input like the set input, which operates in parallel with the set.

Pull-Down Resistor. Usually, a resistor connected to ground or to a negative voltage, as from the base of a transistor to a negative voltage point.

Pull-Up (Active). A transistor that replaces the pull-up resistor to obtain low output impedance and low power consumption.

Pull-Up Resistor. Usually a resistor connected to the positive supply, as from V_{CC} to the output collector terminal.

Q

Q Output. The reference output of a flip-flop. If the Q output is in the 1 state, the flip-flop is said to be in its 1 state.

$\overline{Q}$ Output. The second output of a flip-flop; its logic level is always opposite to that of the Q output.

Qualifier. Analogous to an adjective in English grammar; a computer-language name that details another computer-language name.

R

Race. A condition that exists whenever a signal propagates through two or more memory elements during one clock period.

Register. A storage device for binary data generally used to store numbers for arithmetical operations or their result.

Reset. Setting a flip-flop to the $Q = 0$ state; also applies to any circuit when driven to its normal starting condition.

Rise Time. The time required for the leading edge of a waveform to proceed from its 10 percent to its 90 percent of maximum amplitude points.

S

Screen. Face of a cathode-ray tube.

Serial Data. The data are available as a series of bits occurring one after the other in a single file.

Set. Placing a flip-flop in its $Q = 1$ state.

Shift. The process of moving data from one place to another.

Shift Register. A wired configuration of flip-flops that will shift all 1's in a binary number either one position to the left or one position to the right with each pulse command.

Signature. The particular reference signal of a given circuit.

Sink Load. A load with current flow out of its input; a current load must be driven by a current sink.

Software. Programs, procedures, and languages employed in a computer system.

Source Load. A load with current flow out of its input; a current load must be driven by a current sink.

State. Refers to the condition of an input or output of a circuit concerning whether it is a logic 1 or a logic 0.

Strobe. An input to a counter or register that permits the entry of parallel data asynchronously.

Synchronous. Operation of a switching network by a clock-pulse generator. All circuits in the network switch simultaneously. All actions take place synchronously with the clock.

T

Test Card. A troubleshooting aid for comprehensive checkout of all I/O functions.

Toggle. To change a binary storage element to its opposite state.

Trigger. The input pin on a flip-flop; a pulse command signal will cause the flip-flop to change state; a timing pulse used to initiate the transmission of logic signals through the appropriate signal paths.

Troubleshoot. To search for errors or malfunctions in order to correct them.

True. A true condition is the statement for a logic 1 in Boolean algebra.

Truth Table. A tabular list with all possible input logic combinations and the resulting logic output for all these combinations.

U

Unload. To remove information in massive quantities.

Up Counter. A binary counter that starts from 0 and increases its value by 1 with each pulse signal input.

Up-Swing, Voltage. A waveform change in level from a lower value to a higher value.

V

VLSI. Abbreviation for very-large-scale integration; a chip containing more than 1,000 gates.

Index

287